WHISPERS OF THE HALLOW NIGHT

EDITINGLE INDIE HOUSE

Mumbai, India

www.editingleindiehouse.com

WHISPERS OF THE HALLOW NIGHT

ISBN: 978-93-94346-00-0

Published by Editingle Indie House
www.editigleindiehouse.com

Sign up for newsletter at
www.editingleindiehouse.com

Editor: In-House
Cover Design : Portia Pearls Designs
First Edition : October 2022

Whispers of the Hallow Night

(Volume IV)

Editingle Halloween Anthology

Contents

About the Authors.

Foreword

Dear reader,

It is to our great pleasure to showcase the following authors on our fourth of Halloween Anthology: Phil Hore, J. D. Edwards, M.M. Ward, Brandon Ebinger, Draven M., Asa Swift, Sayali D., Ashe Woodward.

We appreciate the authors for believing in us and submitted their stories for publication, their trust in us is our strength.

As a publication indie house, we strive to deliver best stories and bring out the potential in authors. Our company values are driven by authenticity, originality, and leaving reader's with unforgettable tales.

From bottom of our hearts we are thanking all of our authors for believing and keeping faith. Most importantly thank you to the readers for giving our stories chance. No words will be enough to express our gratitude.

Now we will stop here and let you enjoy the amazing stories from our amazing authors.

Happy Reading!

A Samhain Night's Scream

Chapter 1: The Wages of Sin

Hatred burned in the old crone's eyes beneath her hooded cowl. She watched from a shadowed alley as boisterous teens traipsed through the town, disregarding others and their property.

Vermin... filth! she hissed, glaring at them in disgust. *Each generation is worse than the next. They come here each year on my birthday and defile my home with their lude and vulgar antics.*

Dipping her head, the crone reached within her cloak and clutched a ruby pendant connected to a golden necklace. Within seconds, her aged infirmities faded, revealing a tall, attractive woman with smooth olive skin and flowing auburn hair. She flipped open a compact mirror, surveying her new body and dark, sultry eyes.

Yes... very nice. Time to get to work. I'm not getting any younger... yet.

Stepping from the shadows of the vacant alley, the crone scanned the bustling village of Pluckley for her first victim. Her dress swayed in the cool night breeze. A waiter and his twin caught her eye at Pisano's Kitchen. She sensed their duplicity, which she confirmed when one of them swiped another server's tip from the table.

A sly grin played at the corners of her mouth.

Oh yes... this should be fun.

Crossing the street, the crone reached for the door when it flew open, and a hulking young man plowed into her, knocking her to the ground. "Oi! Watch out, young man!"

He glanced down at the crone, his lust-filled eyes lingering on her chest. "Oh, pardon me!" He extended his hand to the crone, his gaze tracing the woman's voluptuous contours as he helped her to her feet.

Gripping his hand with strength belying her slender frame, she exhaled a fine golden mist.

I claim you for my own... The mist hung in the air before dissipating into his chest. *Forget me for now...*

The young man blinked several times, knitting his brows in confusion. "What just happened? Who are you? Why are we holding hands?"

Before she could respond, a petite blonde teen joined them and locked arms with the young man, breaking the ephemeral spell. Her cold eyes scanned the crone's sculpted body, and a sneer formed on her lips. "Pfft! Who is this, Tim, and why are you holding her hand?"

The young man blushed and dropped the crone's hand. "I have no idea, Bonnie! I remember leaving the restaurant to have a smoke and... I couldn't remember anything more until you arrived."

"Perhaps I can help clear things up." The crone extended her hand to the young woman with a cunning smirk. "Your friend bowled into me and knocked me to the ground. He was kind enough to help me to my feet." The moment their hands connected, a faint shimmering glow enveloped their grip, disappearing an instant later.

Tossing her dark auburn hair back, Bonnie pushed out her chest, revealing the low-cut neckline of her form-fitting top. "Whatever, lady... come on, Tim. Let's go already! You promised to take me on the haunted ghost tour." She rolled her eyes, tugging on her boyfriend's arm.

"Alright. Calm down... geez! We've got hours before the tour starts." Shrugging his shoulders, Tim grimaced at the crone, cocking his head toward Bonnie. "I doubt we'll see you again, ma'am, but have a good night, all the same."

The crone stood gobsmacked by the girl's rudeness and disrespect. Rage roiled within her, and she spoke under her breath as they turned down the sidewalk, "Oh, don't worry, my young friends." Her lips twisted in a distasteful sneer as her smoldering gaze followed the couple. "We'll meet again... I can promise you that."

Brushing the remaining dirt and debris from her silky black dress, the crone entered the restaurant to find a short, stocky woman texting on her iPhone at the reservation desk. The crone waited for half a minute before clearing her throat.

The hostess glanced up from her phone in surprise. "Oh. Hello! How may I help you?"

"I'd like a table for one on the veranda, please." The crone directed the woman's attention to a vacant spot overlooking the bustling community.

"Do you have a reservation?"

The crone tilted her head to the side in confusion. "No, I don't. Is that a problem? There are plenty of available tables on the veranda."

The hostess leaned forward and tapped the sign in front of her podium. "It says right here, **Reservations Are Required**. Sorry, lady... you'll have to come back another time when you have a reservation." Pulling up her phone, the waitress resumed her texting.

Fuming at the woman's insolence, the crone narrowed her eyes and glared at the hostess. She glanced down at the woman's nametag and cleared her throat again. "I'm sorry to bother you again, Tanika, but I have another question."

The hostess sighed and shoved the phone into her back pocket. She gripped the podium and leaned forward, hostility filling her voice. "Listen, lady, I told you... you can't get a table without a reservation. That's just the way it is."

"Oh, really? That's the way it is, eh?"

The hostess rolled her eyes, fixing the crone with a derisive sneer. "Yep! Sometimes, 'that's the way it is' is just the way it is."

Covering Tanika's hand with her own, the crone's cold eyes bore into the woman as a golden light spread from her hands until it covered the wide-eyed hostess. A satisfied smirk played at the corner of her mouth.

I claim your soul.

As the light diminished, Tanika shrank in size until she became a miniature statue resting in the crone's hand. No one saw a thing. Everyone was too busy in their own world.

She dropped the hostess's figurine into her purse and pressed a forefinger against the reservation book, causing her name to appear within its pages; **Eva Dering**.

The crone's eyes twinkled with satisfaction. "Yes, that will do nicely. It appears I had a reservation after all." Choosing a table along the railing, the crone scanned the bustling community. Time has changed this quaint English village over the last 400 years, but not for the better. Eva draped her purse over the back of the chair and drummed her fingers on the table, waiting for a server to arrive. She beamed as one of the cute twins arrived to take her order.

"Good evening, ma'am. May I start you off with a beverage, or are you ready to order?"

The crone glanced at the server's nametag and grinned. "Yes, thank you, Jonathan. I'd like white wine to go with my fish and chips. Which wine would you recommend?"

Jonathan beamed as he scribbled down her order. "That would be our New Zealand white wine, Marlborough Sauvignon Blanc. I'll be right back with your order."

As she waited, the crone noticed Jonathan's twin enter the veranda and clear away the dishes from the surrounding tables. Each time he found a tip, he pocketed the larger bill and placed the smaller bill in his shirt pocket. It was a smooth routine, but Eva was not fooled.

When Jonathan's twin cleared the table behind her, she sensed him reaching into her purse. Instantly, spinning in her seat, Eva clutched the server's wrist, digging her fingernails into his skin. "We mustn't take what isn't ours, now, should we... David?"

The server gasped, struggling to free himself from the crone's iron grip. Tears rolled down his cheeks as blood dripped to the stone tiles from his wrist. "Don't... s-st-stop... you're hurting me! I'm sorry, okay?"

Utilizing the same tact she used on Tanika, golden light consumed his body.

Your soul is mine.

As she spoke these words, a golden light diminished, and a miniature figurine of David rested in her hand. She dropped him in her purse and gave a satisfied smirk. "You wanted to see the inside of my purse. Now you get a closer look."

As Jonathan returned with Eva's food and wine, he gaped at his brother's abandoned bussing tray. "Where's my brother? Where did he go? He was just here. He passed me a minute ago." Jonathan frowned as he scanned the area for David.

The crone eyed the server with mock disdain. "He's learning a lesson, Jonathan. Did your parents never teach you about thievery?"

Jonathan paled, jerked backward, and stammered a hasty reply. "I-I'm sorry, ma'am... your meal is on the house tonight." Grabbing his brother's tray, Jonathan rushed from the room, speaking to a man in a suit as he departed.

Eva gave a contented sigh and tucked into her meal. A few minutes later, the man in a suit stopped at her table. Taking a deep breath to calm her growing frustration, she set down her fork and turned her attention to the newcomer.

"Good evening, Ms. Dering. My name is Robert Carillo, and I'm the manager of this fine establishment."

The crone sensed the manager held a hidden agenda, which increased her annoyance.

Why can't I simply enjoy my meal without these constant interruptions?

"Yes, Mr. Carillo. What can I do for you?"

Glancing at Eva's half-eaten meal, the manager blushed with embarrassment. "I apologize for interrupting your dinner. It'll only be a moment. My server informed me of your free meal, which will come from his paycheck tonight, but I'm curious about what caused this to happen. Would you be so kind as to fill me in?"

Eva shrugged and pointed to the empty tables. "There's not much to explain. I caught David stealing tips from the other servers but ignored his petty theft until he tried to steal from my purse. I confronted him, and he did a bunk. Jonathan attempted to hide his brother's thievery by bribing me with a free meal. There's not much more to tell. Now, may I please return to my dinner while it's still warm?"

The manager gave an emphatic nod and backed away with a small bow. "Of course, Ms. Dering. Please let me know if I can assist you in any other way."

The crone watched him leave with narrowed eyes. The confrontation was resolved with too much ease, but she couldn't ignore the niggling sensation in her chest. She tapped her manicured fingers on the table thoughtfully.

He's up to something. I just wish I knew what it was.

However, pushing the matter from her mind for the time being, Eva finished her dinner and drained her glass of wine. Then dabbing the ends of her mouth with a napkin, she dropped the cloth to the table and stood, making her way to the exit.

As she rounded the corner, the crone discovered the manager engaged in a heated discussion with Jonathan and slipped into the shadows to listen to their conversation.

"I'm telling you, sir, I don't know anything else. One minute, he was clearing the tables, and the next, that woman was boasting about teaching him a lesson. I haven't seen him anywhere since. She must've done something to him."

The manager stroked his chin in contemplation. "She accused your brother of thievery and you of bribery, but I believe she's a con artist trying to score a free meal by disparaging my employees. She must've threatened David to make him vanish without even a note. I think I'll call the police and let them investigate her. I don't believe she's being honest with us."

Eva clenched her fists, fuming at Jonathan's lies and the manager's incompetence. She waited for Robert to pass by her hiding spot before reaching out and clamping a hand over his mouth.

Your soul is mine.

Golden light gleamed from beneath her hands and expanded until it enveloped Robert.

The manager's body shrank as the light diminished, leaving a tiny figure resting in the palm of her hand.

"Oh yes... that's better. You'll be quite useful to me, Robert."

Opening her purse, the crone slipped the figurine inside and waited for Jonathan. She performed the same process on him as he passed, slipping his figurine into her purse next to the others.

CHAPTER 2: RESPECT YOUR ELDERS

Leaving the safety of her shadowed alcove, the crone crossed to the women's restroom and slid inside. She studied herself in the mirror, deciding on her new form.

I've interacted with too many people and brought too much attention to myself. It's time to go with a fresh, new look. Maybe something French...

Clutching her ruby pendant, the crone lowered her head and concentrated on her new appearance. When she lifted her head again, she examined her slender form with satisfaction. Her flowing auburn hair was now shoulder-length brunette with blonde highlights, and her short black dress was now a knee-length, red rollas wrap dress. Turning her head to the side, the crone admired her new face, tracing the sharp contours of her high cheekbones.

After four hundred years, Eva no longer remembered her original face. At first, it bothered her, but after so many centuries, she found it necessary to complete her noble work. Satisfied with her new appearance, the crone strode from the bathroom and left the restaurant without incident. The setting sun cast long shadows along the village street as she scanned the area for suitable victims. Spotting a dozen people along the sidewalk, Eva strolled along the curb, gazing at the crowd with interest.

Her eyes grew wide in amazement as she recognized some of the individuals.

Well, well, well... what do we have here? It's my young friends from the restaurant.

She paused for a moment before approaching them.

Of course, they won't recognize me in my new form. This should be pretty interesting.

Crossing the street, the crone joined the small group and waited to learn the reason for their gathering. Then, near the front of the crowd, she spotted a sandwich board displaying the words: **HAUNTED PLUCKLEY GHOST TOURS**.

A moment later, a stocky gentleman sporting a cap and ginger mustache clapped his hands to quiet the crowd. "Welcome to the Haunted Pluckley Ghost Tours! Thank you all for coming out tonight. My name is Adam Willis, and I'll be your guide for the evening. For those of you who don't know, Pluckley has the distinction of being named 'The Most Haunted Village in England' by the Guinness Book of World Records. I hope tonight will live up to its reputation! Please follow me. We'll start our tour at Dicky Buss's Lane."

As they walked, the crone scanned the crowd for her next victim. Aside from her two friends from the restaurant, the others appeared respectful. Appearances were always deceiving. Nobody was respectful in this century.

We shall see.

They traveled a short distance down the road before turning onto a dirt path leading into the darkened woods. Eva chuckled at those flicking on their torches. Her fairy eyes allowed her to navigate well in both darkness and light. Moments later, they arrived at the site of an old stone schoolhouse.

Adam stopped and directed the group's attention to the building. "This is the historic site of the Pluckley School. In 1920, the WWI veteran and schoolmaster Henry Turff took his own life by hanging himself from this massive laurel tree on a Sunday afternoon. When the children arrived for school the next morning, they found their teacher swaying from the tree branch. No one ever discovered the reason for his suicide, but on calm nights when there is a light breeze and a full moon, his ghostly body can be seen, swaying from the branch where he took his final breath."

The group stood in silent expectation, gazing at the tree in hopes of glimpsing the schoolmaster's phantom, but none appeared. Hanging their heads, the entire group followed their guide further down the path toward Park Wood, except for Eva and two teenage boys. Concealing herself in the mist, the crone stepped into the shadows to observe the teens.

"Come on, Bryan… help me reach that branch."

The other teen grimaced and shook his head. "I don't know, Ryan… this is a spooky place. Let's just catch up to the others before they get too far ahead."

Ryan sneered at the other teen. "What? Are you scared?"

"No, I just don't think we should be messing about with this stuff. You know what dad always says—the spirit world is nothing to mess about with."

Rolling his eyes, Ryan blew a raspberry at his brother. "Pfft... what does dad know about ghosts anyway? The guide said the schoolmaster's ghost only appears during a full moon, but that was three days ago, so we're fine. Come on, give me a leg up, will you?"

Shaking his head, Bryan trudged forward and lifted his brother in the air until the teen's hands gripped the rough bark.

"One... two... three..." Ryan counted his repetitions as he performed pull-ups from the branch where Henry Turff committed suicide. "... nineteen... twenty." He dropped to the ground with ease, beaming at his brother. "See? There's no barmy ghost around here. The story's just a load of tosh to scare tourists."

Bryan folded his arms over his chest, unimpressed with his brother's antics. "Great. You're still alive. Can we get going now?"

Before Ryan could answer, the crone dropped her misty disguise and stepped from the shadows. "What's your hurry, boys?"

The teens stopped in their tracks, gobsmacked by the crone's sudden appearance. "We were... we were just..." Ryan pointed over his shoulder but could not complete his sentence.

"We were with the ghost tour and got separated from the group, but we're on our way to catch up to them now." Bryan's explanation brought a sigh of relief from his brother.

The crone gave them a broad grin. "Well, what a coincidence! That's where I'm headed too. Give me your hands, and we'll navigate the darkened road together." She stepped into their torchlight and sensed their relief to find a gorgeous French woman offering them her hand. Eva read the lust filling their minds, and their thoughts disgusted her.

As they each gripped her hand, she interlaced her fingers with theirs, causing golden light to spread from her hands until it surrounded the teens' bodies. They each gave a shriek of terror as the light consumed them, and they shrank into miniature figures.

Your souls are mine now, boys.

Eva dropped the two figurines into her purse and returned to the road, searching for the paranormal tour group.

She arrived at Park Wood in time to catch their guide's final words. "As you can see, the woods were cleared to make room for the Elvey Farm. Perhaps that's why the Colonel roams the land today, unable to find peace. Our next stop is St. Nicholas Cathedral and the grave of the

Red Lady."

The crone fell in step behind the young couple from the restaurant. Tim laughed and joked with two young men on either side of him. Behind him, Bonnie crossed her arms and ground her teeth, glaring at her boyfriend.

Oh my... this is just too easy.

Resting a forefinger within Bonnie's flowing blonde hair, golden light drifted from the crone's fingertip, infusing itself into the teen. When Eva completed the spell, she withdrew her finger to watch the result of her work unfold.

Clenching her fists, Bonnie pushed her way forward to take Tim's arm, knocking one of the teens aside. "Oi! Watch it, you daft slag."

Rage flaring within her, Bonnie spun and slapped the teen, leaving an imprint of her hand on his cheek. "Tim, why are you allowing these tossers to interrupt our date?" She gazed up into his face and batted her sparkling eyes.

Tim's cheeks reddened as the group proceeded forward without them, and he stammered his reply, "Yes... yes, of course, this is our date. I'm sorry for being rude and ignoring you."

The first teen stood rubbing his throbbing cheek but did not make a retort. The other teen, however, stood his ground. "Blimey, Tim! You're gonna let some bleeding slapper control you like this?"

Bonnie fixed the teen with a baleful glare, causing him to flinch. "Come on, Tim. You don't need to hang around these muppets anyway. You're better than them."

Turning their backs on the gobsmacked teens, Tim and Bonnie slid to the front of the group. "Come on, Josh. Leave it alone, mate."

Josh rubbed his stinging cheek and spat on the ground. "Not on your life, Caleb! I'm gonna get that uppity tart if it's the last thing I do."

Eva pulled her hooded cowl over her head to hide her mischievous grin and followed the group to a medieval church surrounded by ancient tombstones.

Their guide, Adam, halted the group, pointing toward the ancient cathedral. "Early in the 17th century, the Dering family owned the entire Pluckley area. Lady Rose Dering was the youngest daughter of Sir Edward Dering. She was seduced by a dark and mysterious stranger, causing her to become pregnant out of wedlock. When confronted, the stranger sheds his mortal disguise to reveal a demonic form, killing the priest and Lady Dering's eldest sister, Lilly. Then the demon disappeared back into the pits of Hell itself, leaving poor Rose to bury her sister and face the condemnation of her family and community. Stricken with guilt, she crushed hemlock seeds and infused them into her tea, killing herself and her child."

Adam directed the group's attention toward the towering cathedral. "Rose's family buried her in an elegant red gown and placed a red rose beneath her hands. To ensure her demon spawn never escaped the womb, they secured her body within seven lead coffins, one within the other, and sealed the seventh coffin within an oak casket. She and her child were buried in a vault beneath the church, and no record was ever made of its exact location. The Red Lady roams the church cemetery, searching for her grave to this day. Her sister, Lilly, is known as the White Lady. She roams the church halls, ensuring the Red Lady never sets foot upon that holy ground and finds her grave."

Several members of the group gasped, covering their mouths in horror.

Unfazed by the horrific tale, Adam waved the group forward. "Now, if you'll follow me, we'll take a quick stop at Surrenden Dering, the ancestral home of Sir Edward Dering's family. This ancient estate is haunted by the specter of the White Lady."

Shaking their heads and casting furtive glances toward the church of St. Nicholas, most of the group followed their guide down the path to a magnificent manor house looming in the distance.

Josh and Caleb remained behind, causing the crone to melt into the shadows to observe their actions. Josh burst into laughter, giving Caleb's shoulder a light punch. "What a load of tosh! Can you imagine a demon seducing some doe-eyed lady in waiting only to disappear without claiming its whelp? The twat probably got knocked up by the priest and claimed 'the devil did it' to keep father pickle poker from being defrocked."

Dispelling the mist, the crone dropped her protective spell and emerged from the shadows, her face twisted into a mask of rage. "I don't care for your choice of words, young man."

Caleb swung his torch around to illuminate Eva's red rollas wrap dress before drifting upward to find her teeth bared. "Jo- Josh? I-It's the... it's... it's the Red Lady!" A dark wet stain formed on the front of his pants as his face drained of color.

A mocking smile formed on Eva's lips as she surveyed Josh's haughty bearing. "No... I'm not the Red Lady, but she is my ancestor on my mother's side. In a way, I'm the last of the Dering family. But... enough about me. Let's talk about you and your future." The crone closed the distance between the teens in a single stride, running a long finger down Josh's cheek.

For all his bravado, Josh whimpered as the crone's cold, bony finger brushed against his skin. "I was just joking, lady... geez! Lighten up. Bloody Hell, you're freaking us out!"

Eva's smile faded, and she advanced on Josh with her lips curled up into a sneer. "Oh, sonny... I haven't even begun to freak you out yet."

The crone latched onto Josh and Caleb's wrist with iron fortitude.

Your souls are mine now. Her dire portents drifted out through the English countryside into the eerie darkness.

In an instant, golden light consumed their bodies, causing them to shrink until two more miniature figures sat in the palm of her hands. "That's much better. Time to rejoin the main group, I suppose."

Dropping her new creations into her purse, Eva continued down the path toward Surrenden Dering and her ancestral home.

CHAPTER 3: UNTIL DEATH PARTS US

Rounding the corner of the lane, Bonnie's obnoxious laughter filled the air. Eva gritted her teeth and followed the grating noise until she reached the group standing in the lane between two massive mansions. One was composed of smooth, gray stones, while the other was comprised of chiseled river stones.

Turning his back to the homes, Adam spread his arms wide. "Welcome to one of the most tragic tales among tonight's tour. To my right is The Greystones and to my left is the Rose Court. The legend goes that The Greystones is haunted by a reclusive cleric, fondly referred to as 'The Monk.' Originally owned by Sir Edward Dering until he died in 1644, the home later became known as Rectory Cottage and served as the home for St. Nicholas Church's clergy. The neighbouring manor, Rose Court, is haunted by a ghost known only as 'The Tudor Lady' because she lived and died during the Tudor period. All we know for certain is she and the monk loved each other. Bound by a vow of celibacy, the monk could not return the Lady's affection. Unable to bear her grief, the Lady drank a poisonous concoction of ivy and nightshade. She died sitting by the upstairs window facing The Greystones. Overcome with heartache, the monk committed suicide and has roamed the property ever since."

Striding forward, the guide waved his arm in the air. "Now, if you'll follow me, we'll head to our last stop, The Pinnock and Fright Corner." As the group followed Adam down the lane, Tim and Bonnie remained behind, gazing at the abandoned manors.

Eva melted into the shadows as Bonnie wrapped her arm around Tim's waist and rested her head on his shoulder. "Isn't it sad? They'd rather have died than live life apart from each other. Would you do that for me if we were in their positions?"

Tim grimaced and shrugged, gazing at the dilapidated stone homes. "Blimey, Bonnie... I don't know. How can anyone know how they'd act in a situation like that?"

Bonnie's eyes narrowed, and she took a step back, glaring at her boyfriend. "It's her, isn't it? You love her more than you do me?"

He lowered his voice and hissed under his breath. "What are you going on about now? Who am I supposed to love more than you? You're the only woman in my life, and you know it!"

"Oh, don't give me that!" Bonnie spat on the ground at Tim's feet. "I saw how you looked at that whore this afternoon outside the restaurant! You couldn't wait to rip her dress off, could you?"

"Are you barking? Come on, let's catch up to the group." Tim's laughter infuriated Bonnie to her boiling point.

Stomping her foot on the ground, she punched his shoulder. "Don't turn your back on me! If you loved me, you'd be willing to die for me the same way the Monk did for the Lady."

Tim stood gobsmacked by Bonnie's hysterics and scanned the area for witnesses. Grabbing her wrists, Tim gave her a violent shake, snapping her head back and forth. "I was always taught to never hit a lady, but if you're going to be such a jealous tart, maybe Josh was right."

Bonnie broke into tears as Tim released her wrists, flinging her arms away from him. "Get away from me. I'm done with you."

At those words, Eva materialized from the shadows and grasped Bonnie's hand in hers. "I was hoping you'd say that..."

Your soul is mine.

She threw her head back and gave a moan of ecstasy as the magic flowed through her. An instant later, golden light consumed Bonnie, transforming her into a figurine.

Tim blanched, backing away from the crone with his hands raised in a defensive position. "Please... don't hurt me."

Eva chuckled, dropping Bonnie's figurine into her purse. "I wouldn't dream of it, Tim. I've chosen you to be mine, but not the same way as Bonnie or the others. I want you to be my eternal mate." She approached him with slow, careful movements sensing the fear and paranoia racing through him. "We could have a wonderful life together, you and I. You'd like to live forever, wouldn't you?"

Halting beyond the crone's reach, Tim narrowed his skeptical eyes. "Live forever? Nobody can live forever! Where's Bonnie? Where are my cousins? Did you capture them too?"

Eva edged closer to Tim, her voice even and dispassionate. "They're nearby, and you'll see them again, I'm sure. The question is, will you see them again as my prisoner or as my lover?"

The color drained from Tim's face and sweat beaded on his brow. "You… you want me to be your lover? No offense, lady, but you've got to be twice my age!"

The crone threw her head back, her raucous laughter filling the night air. "Age is merely a number, my young friend, but I guarantee you, I can become your age instantly if it makes you feel better. You see… I'm four hundred years old. Now, I won't ask you again. Do you wish to be my mate or my victim?"

Tim's eyes opened wide in amazement. "Are you serious? How is that possible?" Catching the fire in the crone's eyes, Tim gulped and gave an enthusiastic nod. "If what you say is true and I could maintain my youth for hundreds of years, then yes… I'll join you."

Eva closed the distance between them, running a finger down Tim's chin before locking his lips to hers. Tim's face glimmered with golden light when she broke the embrace, and his eyes sparkled in anticipation of their future together. Taking his hand, the crone led him back down the path. "We should rejoin the group."

Nodding in obedience, Tim followed her without complaint. They rushed down the lane to catch the group before anyone noticed their absence. Several minutes later, they reached the group as their guide finished describing the Pinnock's haunted history.

"But don't worry… the miller only appears before a severe thunderstorm. Luckily, the storms rolled through last night, so we're safe for tonight, but the gypsy and highwayman are something else entirely!" Adam directed their attention to the crossroads. "A hundred years ago, an old gypsy woman named Abigail Nicholas was known to sit here at the crossroads next to Pinnock's Bridge in a horse-drawn wagon, smoking a pipe and selling watercress. One day, she accidentally caught herself on fire and burned to death in her wagon. To this day, locals still spot her misty apparition when crossing the bridge."

Eva slipped her arm around Tim's as their guide finished his speech. "Our last ghost is none other than Robert DuBois, famed highwayman of the 18th century. A massive Oak stood in the centre of the crossroads and became known as 'fright corner', all because DuBois would hide behind the tree to rob travelers who dared to cross his path. Unfortunately, DuBois came to a sticky end when he attempted to rob several rival highwaymen. They attacked him and drove a sword through his body, pinning him to the tree. There, he bled out and became food for wild animals, but to this day, witnesses claim to see his shadow when passing through the intersection. Tonight, we'll tempt fate as we pass the highwayman on our way to our final destination: Dering Woods."

Eva cleared her throat, drawing attention to herself for the first time. "Excuse me, but why the woods? What's so special about them?" Her eyes sparkled beneath her hooded cowl as Adam's face brightened to her query.

"That's an excellent question! Follow me, and I'll explain the mystery of the woods as we cross the field." Together, they passed through the crossroads without encountering the miller, gypsy, or highwaymen. After several minutes, Adam brought the group to the edge of the field, overlooking the woods. "We now stand in the exact spot where a grisly murder occurred exactly seventy-five years ago. The Dering Woods is known to locals as The Screaming Woods, because those living nearby hear screams of terror coming from the midst of the woods."

Adam pointed to a stone marker situated several meters away. "On November 1, 1948, a hunter discovered twenty corpses from five local families on Smarden Bell Road running through the midst of Dering Woods. The bodies, young and old, were drained of blood and stacked up like cordwood. There were no marks on the bodies and no suspects. Even today, The Dering Woods Massacre remains unsolved." He pointed to each member of the group in succession. "It's no coincidence that there are fourteen members in our group, including me. We need an even number of guests to reach our next destination: The Witch Shack. I want you to stay with a buddy as we enter the woods, so I'll number you all off."

Traveling down the line of tour guests, Adam began with himself and numbered each person as he passed. "6… 7… 8… 9…" When he reached Tim, Adam stopped and scratched the back of his head. "Ok, hold on now. Raise your hand if I've given you a number already." To his astonishment, everyone raised their hand. "That doesn't make any sense. We had fourteen members when we first started, so what happened to the other five teens?"

Tim glanced over his shoulder at the empty lane. "They may have stayed behind to search for signs of the gypsy or highwayman."

Adam nodded and tapped his chin in silent contemplation. "Well, I suppose it's possible. You and your date disappeared from the group for while back there. You two weren't the first couple to stay behind at a tour site and I daresay you'll be the last. I usually catch them doing it, but no matter." He gave Tim a good-natured thump on the back. "I'll just join you and your friend, to keep you two from getting into any more mischief."

Leading the group forward, he directed their attention to the distant treeline. "Watch out for the fairy lights. The legends say anyone who sees the lights in the woods will never leave there alive."

As they plunged deeper into the woods, Eva and Tim fell to the back of the group without Adam noticing their disappearance. Silent as death, Eva reached out and brushed against each group member, changing them into figurines. Placing them in her purse, she pushed forward, with Tim following close behind. He gaped in open-mouthed astonishment as each victim shrank in size and plunged into the crone's purse.

At last, they came to a halt at a dirt path leading to a ramshackle cabin. "On October 31, 1998, four college students entered these woods on a dare, but they all disappeared. Their bodies have never been recovered to this day. Some say an old witch lives in the woods and is responsible for all the murders and disappearances. Nobody has ever provided any proof to substantiate that rumor, but a lack of proof doesn't make the rumor untrue."

Adam turned to face the group and froze, finding Eva and Tim staring at him.

She fixed a cold smile on him. "I'm sorry, darling. You've been a wonderful guide, but you're wrong on one point. There *is* proof that an old witch lives in the woods, and *I* am that proof." Grasping his wrist, a golden mist enveloped Adam and his screams hung in the air as he shrank in size, dropping into the crone's palm.

Tucking his figurine within her purse, Eva took Tim's hand and led him down the dirt path. "Come along, Timothy, darling. Tonight is the beginning of a new chapter in your life."

Tim blinked several times and shook his head, breaking Eva's spell over him. "Whoa! What happened to my friends? Where's Bonnie?" His eyes grew wide in shock, and his face drained of color. "I remember now. I remember everything. You're the evil witch that haunts Dering Woods!"

Eva's fingers locked around Tim's wrist with lightning reflexes, and she fixed her murderous glare on him, chilling his soul. "You're going to wish you'd never said that." She spoke in a low hiss, forcing Tim to strain to catch her next words. "Men... they're so incorrigible..."

I claim your soul.

At these words, a golden mist enveloped Tim, filling the woods with his agonizing screams as he shrank into a miniature figurine.

Pinching his head with her long, boney fingers, Eva lifted Tim's figurine from her palm and stared at him with the utmost loathing. "I'll save you for last, so you can watch the others die."

Turning her back to the deserted woods, the crone followed the dirt path to the edge of the hovel and disappeared within a mass of fairy lights.

CHAPTER 4: TROUBLE IN PARADISE

The Ashford police station swarmed with visitors, pressing against the other to reach the desk sergeant first. The officer struggled to subdue the crowd and picked up the phone for help.

"Hello, sir? This is Sergeant Ritchie. I have a bit of a situation here, and I could use your help, sir." Replacing the receiver, he took a step back to avoid the grasping hands reaching over his desk.

Detective Chief Inspector Phillip Matthews entered the room and shook his head. "A bit of a situation, eh? That's the understatement of the century, Sergeant." He held up his arms and waved them to get the crowd's attention. "Okay, now folks, I'm DCI Matthews. Let's settle down first, and then I'll listen to your complaints one by one." Still, when the clamor continued, he placed two fingers to his lips and gave a shrill whistle. "Oi! Shut it!"

The boisterous crowd subsided with that, plugging their ears to block the unpleasant sound. The detective crossed his arms over his chest and glared at the assembled guests. "Look at you lot, fussing and fighting like hooligans. Now, I want one person at a time to tell me what's going on."

The crowd erupted again as each person tried to drown out the person next to them. The detective's shrill blast returned the room to order. "I can see manners have been lost on you and your lot. I'd swear you were a load of Yanks from the way you carry on. Now, I'll point to one person, and I want only that person to answer. If anyone else opens their yap, they'll get to spend the night in a lonely cell. Am I making myself clear?"

Several angry glares met his eyes, but the assembled congregation nodded. The detective took a deep breath and pointed to a middle-aged woman at the front. "You, ma'am, how can we help you?"

The squat, frumpy woman sniffed and wiped her eyes. "Thank you, detective. My name is Jackie Schultz. Last night, our son, Tim, and his girlfriend went missing in Pluckley. Tim called to say they were going on a ghost tour, but he never returned home. So, I assumed he spent the night with Bonnie, but she never returned home either."

Before DCI Matthews could stop her, a tall, bony woman pushed her way to the front to stand next to Jackie. "I'm Debbie Walker, Bonnie's mother, and we need you to find our daughter, too, detective!"

A tall Asian man called out from the back of the room. "And our sons!" The detective patted the air to quiet the growing uproar, but the commotion built as another person called out to him.

"Our sons, too, detective!" This was followed by, "Don't forget my husband," and "My wife is missing too!"

DCI Matthews stared at the crowd in disbelief. "Are you saying all of your family members disappeared in Pluckley last night?" A dozen heads nodded, causing a pit to form in the detective's stomach. "Okay, by show of hands... who is here today to report a missing person in Pluckley last night?"

Eighteen hands shot into the air.

The detective staggered backward into a filing cabinet, knocking a potted plant to the floor with a crash. He paled and licked his dry lips. "Okay, here's what we're going to do. I want to conduct interviews with each of you and gather the details for each case. Please be patient as I take you all in groups of two. Mrs. Schultz, we'll start with you."

A tall, black-haired woman called out to the detective from the back of the room. "Which one? Me or Jackie?"

"Jackie? Wait, what? There's two of you?"

"Yes, detective. As I was trying to tell you before you burst our eardrums with your whistle, Betty Schultz is my sister-in-law. She and her husband are here with us. Their two boys, Josh and Caleb, are missing also."

Running a hand through his thinning hair, the detective grew annoyed. "Fine. Jackie and your husband, come with me. The rest of you, find a place to get comfortable and quit annoying my desk sergeant."

Opening the hallway door, the detective ushered the Schultz family down the hall to the interrogation room. "I apologize for the location, but space is limited here. Now, please start at the beginning and tell me what happened to your son."

DCI Matthews interviewed two people every 30 minutes for the next five hours. At 1:00 pm, the last two people left the room, and the detective leaned back in his chair, releasing a massive sigh. But a light rapping on the door forced him to regain his professionalism. "Enter."

Sergeant Dennis Ritchie poked his head into the room as the door opened. "Uh... excuse me, sir. Do you have a moment?"

Waving him inside, the detective directed the sergeant to shut the door and have a seat. "What's the problem, Ritchie?"

"Well, sir, it's about these disappearances." The detective raised an eyebrow but said nothing, allowing the sergeant to continue. "As you were conducting the interviews, I couldn't help but overhear the crowd speaking, sir, and..."

DCI Matthews rolled his eyes and unscrewed his bottle of water. "Yes, yes... get on with it already. After dealing with this lot for the last five hours, I'm famished."

Sergeant Ritchie gave a hard swallow and nodded. "Uh, yes, sir. Well, you see, sir, the stories reminded me of the case my grandfather worked on seventy-five years ago when he was DCI."

The detective gagged and spluttered on his water. "Hold on a minute! Chief Constable Marshall is your grandfather?"

Nodding, the sergeant regained a measure of confidence. "Yes, sir. He's my grandfather on my mother's side."

"Does he live nearby? I wonder if he'd remember anything about the original case."

"Yes, he lives nearby, but he's ninety-five and has dementia. He doesn't even remember me anymore. I doubt he'd be able to help you."

A wry grin spread across the detective's face. "I wouldn't be too sure about that. When dementia sets in, the most recent memories are the first to go. This happened seventy-five years ago. He may still remember something. Can you take me to see him?"

"Aye, sir. I'll pull the car around, shall I?"

DCI Matthews nodded, lost in silent introspection.

This might just be the break I need. If I can crack this case, they're bound to promote me!

Donning his jacket, the detective left the station to find the sergeant waiting for him next to the car.

"After you, sir." When the detective settled himself, Sergeant Ritchie slid into the driver's seat and turned on the car.

"Where's your grandfather living now, Ritchie?"

"He's in the Hawthorne Estates Senior Living Centre in Pluckley, sir.

We should be there in 15 minutes."

"Pluckley..." The detective rolled his eyes and stared out the window, muttering to himself under his breath, "What do people see in that backwater dunghill anyway?"

Sergeant Ritchie stiffened in his seat, his fingers gripping the steering wheel with building anger. When he replied, he spoke through gritted teeth. "What makes you say that, sir? Pluckley is a historic town."

DCI Matthews started, unaware the sergeant caught his dark mutterings. "Oh, don't mind me, Ritchie. Pluckley is filled with ghosts, including the ghosts of my past. It's a place I don't enjoy visiting." When the sergeant did not respond, the detective shrugged and stared out of the window again.

Fifteen minutes later, they pulled into the parking lot of a sprawling complex composed of large, gray cobblestone walls. "Welcome to Hawthorne Estates, sir."

Exiting the car, the detective admired the building's craftsmanship as they approached the front door. "I love how they framed the edges with bricks. It defines the contours of the building and gives it a stately disposition."

Sergeant Ritchie cocked his head to the side, giving the detective an amused grin. "Not bad for a backwater dunghill, eh sir?"

DCI Matthews flushed at having his words used against him but swallowed his pride and proceeded through the front door into a lavish foyer. A small service bell stood next to a guest book situated on a side table. The detective strode forward and gave the bell two smart taps.

Sliding past his boss, Sergeant Ritchie grabbed a pen to sign the guest book. "We need to sign in, sir." An orderly wearing navy blue scrubs entered the foyer as the sergeant added their names to the register.

"Good afternoon, gentlemen. How may I help you?"

DCI Matthews reached into his jacket to retrieve his credentials, but Sergeant Ritchie laid a restraining hand on the detective's shoulder, taking charge of the situation. "Yes, ma'am. We're here to visit my grandfather, Connor Marshall. Depending on his condition today, he may or may not remember me."

The orderly fixed her sympathetic eyes on the sergeant. "Yes, I'm afraid the poor dear is in frail health at the moment, but if you follow me, I'll let you speak with him."

"Follow me, sir, and please... let me do the talking." Sergeant Ritchie fell in step behind the orderly, leaving the gobsmacked detective to catch up to him. They walked to the end of the hall and took the lift to the second floor. When the doors opened, the orderly led them to the left, down the hall, until they reached room 203. The nameplate on the door read: **C. MARSHALL.**

"Please let me see if he's willing to accept visitors today." Knocking twice, the orderly disappeared inside the room, securing the door with a sharp **click**.

"Now we wait, I suppose. Either Papa will meet with us, or he won't. I wonder why she locked the door, though. How strange..."

DCI Matthews bristled at the remark. "Oh, no. He'll meet with us one way or another. I'll let you try your method, but this is still an official police investigation. He'll cooperate whether he wants to or not. Unfortunately, he's our best hope of solving this case."

The sergeant's anger flared at his superior's flippant remark. "Or else what, sir? Are you ready to throw the former Chief Constable in irons for refusing to assist in an investigation he doesn't understand? You heard the orderly, sir. He's gaga these days."

Stiffening under his junior officer's rebuke, the detective's face flushed crimson. "He may well be gaga, Ritchie, but if he doesn't help us, we'll lose another eighteen people, and I daresay he won't want that on his conscience after he blundered the first investigation!"

Sergeant Ritchie squared off with the detective when the door opened, and the orderly reappeared. She took in the situation with bemused intrigue. "I'm not sure what's going on here, but if you two can remain civil, Mr. Marshall will see you now."

As the officers entered the room, the orderly closed the door behind them for privacy. Connor Marshall glanced up from his armchair, setting his newspaper aside. "Ah! If it isn't Oberon and Puck coming to visit me after all these years."

The sergeant knelt beside the chair, holding his grandfather's cold, frail hands. "I'm not Puck, Papa. This is Dennis, Mary's son. I'm your grandson. Don't you remember me?"

Connor Marshall turned his wizened face upon his grandson, staring deep into Sergeant Ritchie's eyes. For a moment, recognition flickered in the pale eyes, and the old man pressed a tender hand to his grandson's cheek.

Not wasting any time, the sergeant pled their case. "Papa, do you remember the disappearances at Screaming Woods in 1998? It's happened again. We need your help to find them before it's too late."

The old man's hand trembled, and he spoke in a hoarse whisper, "In the hall where time has ended, think on this, and all is mended. To find the truth before they die, you must expose their greatest lie."

CHAPTER 5: CONNECTING THE DOTS

An instant later, Connor Marshall's hand fell to his side, and he turned his attention to the detective again. "Oberon! You're still here?" He waggled a finger at DCI Matthews. "You can't have her, you know... Titania chose me. Go on now! Leave this place and take your trickster son with you!" The old man gave a dismissive wave and returned to his newspaper.

DCI Matthews seethed at the rejection. "He may be your grandfather, but he's nuttier than squirrel droppings." Then, marching up to Connor Marshall, the detective jerked the newspaper from his hands, causing the sergeant to cry out.

The old man stood and raised his cane in a single, fluid movement, poised to strike the detective, but Sergeant Ritchie was faster. Flying across the room, he grasped his grandfather's wrist with an iron grip. "Let me go! Let me go! He's not taking my Titania away from me! She chose me!"

The commotion caused the orderly to throw open the door and burst into the room. "What in blazes is going on in here? Why are you attacking Mr. Marshall? I demand an explanation!"

"Titania!" Connor Marshall dropped his cane and stretched out his arms to the orderly. "Titania, my darling! Oberon is trying to take you from me."

"Come now, darling... I won't let the jealous king spirit me away. I have foresworn his bed and company." The orderly jabbed her finger toward the hall and guided the old man back to his bed. "That's right... just rest, and you'll feel right as rain in a few hours."

Taking her cue, the officers left the room and waited for the orderly to reappear. When she did, her face was livid with rage. "Okay, I don't know what was going on here, but poor Mr. Marshall doesn't need this much excitement at his age. Let him live out his days in peace, the poor dear."

"I wish we could, ma'am, but we're on an official investigation." DCI Matthews reached into his jacket and produced his credentials. "I'd love nothing more than to leave Mr. Marshall to his delusions, but we have an investigation, and the knowledge locked away within his addled brain may be our only hope."

Sergeant Ritchie produced his credentials as well. "I wasn't lying, you know. Connor Marshall is my maternal grandfather, but I hoped he'd remember me and talk to me. I haven't visited in years because it breaks my heart to see him like this. I thought he recognized me briefly, but then he slipped back into his delusions."

He paused for a moment, considering another occurrence that bothered him. "Speaking of delusions... why does Papa think you're Titania? That's not your real name, is it?"

The orderly swallowed hard and shook her head. "No, it's not. Come with me, and I'll explain." She led them down the stairs to a private, family consultation lounge.

When the officers joined her, she closed the door and sat behind a desk. "My name is Tonya, but in his condition, Mr. Marshall believes me to be the fairy queen, Titania, from *A Midsummer Night's Dream*. When he admitted himself, he was already suffering from these delusions. Mr. Marshall claimed the fairies were after him and had this newspaper clutched in his hand. He spoke of Puck, the trickster, and believed the sprite caused him to fail the families of those college students who went missing in 1998. He also firmly believes Puck was behind the original murders fifty years earlier when he was DCI of the Ashford Police Department. You see, Mr. Marshall has bipolar disorder. During a particularly manic phase, he suffered a psychotic break with reality and now casts all visitors as characters in that particular play."

DCI Marshall mulled over Tonya's explanation in his mind before glancing down at the newspaper in his hand. **The Kent Messenger, Sunday, November 1, 1998.** A cold chill ran down the detective's spine, and he shoved it, face-up, across Tonya's desk. "What about this newspaper? Suppose he's living in a fictional reality based on *A Midsummer Night's Dream*. What do these disappearances have to do with that play?"

Tonya spread her hands out in an apologetic gesture. "I'm sorry, detective. I wish I could tell you more."

Sergeant Ritchie leaned forward, interested in learning more about his grandfather's debilitating illness. "And here I thought his failure to solve these cases drove him mad."

"That's partially correct, sergeant. The doctors believe his failure to obtain closure for the disappearances and murders, coupled with the Dering Woods' haunted history of fairy lights, caused his psychotic break."

"Does he have any personal effects? Anything that may shine some light on what he was working on before this insanity claimed him?" When Tonya hesitated, DCI Matthews gestured toward the newspaper again. "Please… this is all we have to go on. Eighteen people are missing. History is repeating itself, and Connor Marshall's years of research may be our only hope in solving it. Perhaps solving the case will give him some peace of mind."

Tonya's shoulders sagged in defeat, and she nodded, rising from her chair. "Very well. Follow me." She led the officers across the hall to a library, but the shelves were filled with safes instead of books. Tonya took the rolling ladder, moved it into position, and climbed several steps until she found a safe numbered 203. "This is Mr. Marshall's safe and contains all of his worldly possessions when he entered our facility." She pressed her palm against a scanner on the door, and the safe swung open. Removing a drawer, Tonya returned to the library floor and carried the tray to a nearby table. "This is all he had in his pockets when he arrived ten years ago."

The officers sifted through the personal effects, pushing aside keys, money, pocket knives, and other sundry items. DCI Matthews pushed the drawer away in frustration. "I don't see where this helps us. It's just another dead-end, and now we've wasted the better part of a day chasing phantoms rather than solving this case."

"Hang on!" Sergeant Ritchie withdrew a cast iron skeleton key and held it up to the light. "Have you seen anything like this? It doesn't look like any of the other keys on his key ring."

"Let me see that." DCI Matthews took the proffered key, examining it in detail under the overhead lamp. "This is an old key… very old. I'm not an expert, but I'd say it's an 18th-century skeleton key from its weight. It's quite heavy for such a small metal object, and iron objects were made of denser metals before the 19th century."

Tonya peered over the detective's shoulder and gasped. "Do you think it fits a lock at Surrenden Dering?"

Sergeant Ritchie glanced up in confusion. "What do you mean? My grandfather never lived in the Dering Manor. He's always lived in Pluckley Thorne, in the southwest corner near Dering Woods. Dering

Manor is in the northeast corner of Pluckley."

The orderly shrugged and returned to her seat, followed by the officers. "I don't know what else to tell you, sergeant. When he arrived in 2013, Mr. Marshall gave his address as Surrenden Dering. There was no mention of a home in Pluckley Thorne."

"Well, this is a quandary." DCI Matthews stroked his goatee as he contemplated the situation. "Mr. Marshall is the only person with experience in this case, and even his own grandson doesn't know where he lives." The detective patted the air to calm his junior officer. "Now, Ritchie, don't go off your nut about this. You know I'm right. If his own grandson didn't know about him living there, it's clearly meant to have been a secret. He probably slipped up and mentioned it by mistake. His rocket isn't exactly firing on all thrusters, you know."

Sergeant Ritchie calmed down, accepting the detective's logical reasoning. "At least we have a place to start now." Digging into the drawer, the sergeant removed his grandfather's keyring. "If we're going to run down this lead, we need to borrow his keys." Rising to his feet, he extended his hand to the orderly. "Thank you, Tonya, for showing us these items. You may have helped break this case wide open!"

Tonya blushed and retrieved the drawer from the table. "I'm glad to help. Just promise me you'll return these items after you've searched his home for clues. I really shouldn't let you take them at all."

"We'll be very careful with them, ma'am. You have my word." DCI Matthews rose and shook her hand in appreciation. "Now, sergeant, let's check out this manor your grandfather tried so hard to keep hidden from the rest of the world."

Bidding Tonya farewell, the officers returned to the car. "Well, Ritchie, you seem to know how to find this place. Lead the way!"

Sergeant Ritchie revved up the engine and pointed down the road. "Actually, sir, Surrenden Dering is less than a mile down Swan Lane." Minutes later, they pulled into the circular driveway in front of the estate. "It looks pretty dilapidated. I can't imagine Papa ever living in this squalor."

"Well, there's one way to find out." Taking the keyring, DCI Matthews unlocked the carved oak door, allowing it to swing open with a loud creak. "After you, sergeant."

Entering the manor, Sergeant Ritchie flicked on his torch to scan the premises. White sheets, covered in decades of dust, lay draped over the furniture. Spider webs clung to the corners of the ceiling and stretched across the doorframes. "This can't be right, sir. This place can't have been lived in for at least fifty years. There's no way my grandfather lived here."

DCI Matthews entered next, scanning the home with his own torch. "If that's the case, Ritchie, why does your grandfather's key open the front door?"

The sergeant opened his mouth to reply but shut it again, smacking his forehead with the palm of his hand. "Of course! How could I be so stupid? If he did live here, there must be a clue somewhere."

"I think he already gave it to us, Ritchie." The detective smirked as his torch illuminated an elegant grandfather clock in the hallway. "Do you remember what your grandfather told us? He said, 'In the hall where time has ended,' but did he mean a hall like a manor house or a hall like a hallway? Time certainly ended on this grandfather clock, but he also said to 'think on this, and all is mended.' How can thinking about a dusty old clock mend anything? And what's to be mended anyway? I don't see anything broken. Everything appears to be preserved and intact."

Sergeant Ritchie gave a boisterous whoop, causing the detective to drop his torch.

"Bloody Hell, Ritchie! You gave me a fright!"

"I've got it, sir! At least, I think I understand part of it. The line 'think on this and all is mended' comes from Puck at the end of *A Midsummer Night's Dream*. Papa was obsessed with that play for some reason, so somehow, the Puck character is involved in the clue."

Acting on impulse, the sergeant scanned the hall with his torch, revealing draped paintings along the walls. "This has to be it." Removing the first drape, Ritchie discovered an oil painting of a woman dressed in Victorian garments. He rubbed the nameplate at the bottom of the frame, reading it aloud. "Lady Elizabeth Tufton Dering."

Following suit, DCI Matthews removed the drape from the oil painting across from Ritchie and read the nameplate. "Sir Edward Dering. This must be the original owner of the manor. There are only three more. What's under your two paintings, sergeant?"

Not wasting any time, Sergeant Ritchie removed the drape from the other two paintings. The first revealed a dark-haired woman dressed in a bright red gown. The second painting revealed a blonde woman in a brilliant white gown. He gasped in surprise, pointing at the painting with unrestrained excitement. "It's the Red Lady, sir! Rose Dering! And her sister, Lilly Dering! They were the daughters of Edward and Elizabeth Dering. The legends say Rose got pregnant out of wedlock and had a stillborn daughter, so she's buried at St. Nicholas without a headstone and her spirit wanders the cemetery searching for her grave."

DCI Matthews gave a snort of derision. "Bullocks! I don't believe those old legends. I'm sure the tart got knocked up by some random tosser, but who knows the whole story. Families like this tried to keep their scandals all hushed up to avoid disparaging the family name."

"Sir, that's it! Quickly... remove your drape. I'll bet it's a woman with long, dark hair!"

Baffled by the suggestion, the detective shrugged and entertained Sergeant Ritchie's strange request. "Sure... why not?" DCI Matthews gaped at the woman's portrait as the drape fell to the floor. She wore a long, white dress, and her dark hair fell down around her shoulders. "How'd you know, sergeant? That was an impossible guess!"

"It was no guess, sir. It's the Dering family legend. What does the nameplate say under the woman's painting?"

Shining his torch on the plate, the detective read the single word etched into the metal. "Eva. That's all it says... just Eva. There's no last name. Eva must be the name of the Red Lady's daughter."

"The other part of the clue, sir!" When the detective returned a blank stare, Sergeant Ritchie gave an exasperated sigh. "Sir... Papa's clue. The last line of it said, 'To find the truth before they die, you must expose their greatest lie.' What if Eva's parentage is the Dering's greatest lie?"

DCI Matthews withdrew the cast iron skeleton key from his pocket. "Maybe this key is what will reveal their greatest lie. I wonder..." Shining the torch along the edges of Eva's painting, the detective pushed the portrait sideways and chuckled with delight. "Bingo! There's a keyhole hidden beneath this painting."

Inserting the key into the hole, the detective turned the key, causing the wall to turn inward. With a giant leap, Sergeant Ritchie landed on the turning floor next to the detective moments before the wall finished moving, plunging them into darkness.

Their torches revealed several candelabras situated in strategic positions around the room. Locating a box of stick matches, Sergeant Ritchie lit the first candle and proceeded to light the others until the room was filled with light.

The officers stared in wonder at the pictures, maps, and newspaper clippings lining the walls, connected by a tangled web of colored strings leading to a single location; Dering Woods.

CHAPTER 6: SEX, LIES, AND FAIRY TALES

"Would you look at this place? Papa must've been piecing together the clues in secret for decades. Why didn't he tell anyone?"

The detective switched off his torch and traced the lines with his fingers. One line led to a 1948 newspaper headline from The Smarden Post. "Sergeant! Check out this newspaper article. **Twenty Dead Bodies Found in the Woods.** This was seventy-five years ago."

Sergeant Ritchie pointed to another article further down the wall. "Here's another one! **Children were found murdered in Dering Woods.** This article is from 1973... That was fifty years ago."

"Are you kidding me?" Turning his attention to the sergeant's discovery, DCI Matthews confirmed the observation. "You're right. They're exactly twenty-five years apart. Each of the disappearances occurred on Halloween night, even the teens who vanished in 1998. The headline of that paper said something eerily similar. **Four Students Vanished in the Screaming Woods.**"

"Do you know any other details about that case, sir? Had you joined the police force by then?"

DCI Matthews gave a harsh, barking laugh. "Good Lord, Ritchie! How old do you think I am anyway?" The sergeant opened his mouth to reply, but the detective cut him off. "On second thought, don't answer that. For your information, I was only 20 years old in 1998."

The detective paused and narrowed his eyes, glaring at his junior officer. "Do you remember when I said Pluckley was filled with ghosts, including the ghosts of my past? Well, I was speaking literally."

DCI Matthews collapsed into a nearby armchair with a heavy sigh. The sergeant pulled up a seat opposite him, eager to learn the detective's hidden truth. "The memories still haunt me, even if their spirits don't. On Halloween night in 1998, several of my college mates decided to investigate Dering Woods on a dare... my dare. I told them I'd meet them at the edge of the woods, and we could perform a séance in the witch's shack, located in the centre of the woods."

A tear rolled down the detective's cheek, but he brushed it away with a growl of annoyance. "Look at me... blubbering like a baby over some prank I pulled decades ago."

Sergeant Ritchie leaned forward with interest, speaking in a sympathetic tone. "It's alright, sir. I won't make fun of you or think less of you for showing emotions. Please keep going... the information you have about that case could help save lives today."

The detective shrugged and glanced up at the wall of clues. "There's not much more to tell. I dared them to go to the woods, but I never showed up. I set up a video camera to record them, intending to ridicule them later, but they didn't wait for me. They crossed the field to enter the woods when an old crone emerged from the trees, touched each one of them, and they disappeared in a flash of golden light. The old crone disappeared back into the woods, and even after an exhaustive search, we never found her. Only an abandoned hovel, the witch's shack. This was too much to handle, so I transferred to a different college. I left Pluckley and the Dering Woods behind me forever; until now, that is."

Sergeant Ritchie absorbed this new information in silent contemplation, glancing back at the colored strings lining the walls. Aside from the newspaper clippings, several strings connected to photographic stills. And some other photographs resembled the paintings in the hallway.

The sergeant scratched his head, trying to piece the clues together. At last, his eyes flew open as sudden clarity illuminated his reasoning. "Sir, these ghostly images on the wall... are these still shots taken from your video camera in 1998?"

"Aye, but I don't understand why they'd be included with pictures of the Dering family portraits unless... no, it's a crazy idea. There's no way that could be possible."

"Wait... what? Which part? What can't be possible?"

DCI Matthews laughed, shaking his head. "No, it's impossible. For a moment, I wondered if the old crone could be the mysterious 'Eva' painted in the hallway, but she'd have to be at least 400 years old!"

The sergeant shrugged, accepting the hypothesis at face value. "Why not? This is the most haunted village in England. People call Dering Woods the 'Screaming Woods,' and the local legend says a witch lives in the woods but can never die. What if she found a way to preserve her life through dark magic?"

"How? By taking the lives of her victims every twenty-five years? Rubbish! You've been watching too much television."

"Then how do you explain everything here in the room? Why would Papa send us here? For a jolly good laugh? Somehow, the Dering family is connected to the Screaming Woods, the old crone, and the witch's shack. Papa said we needed to expose their greatest lie. What if the only way to destroy this witch is to call her by her birth name?"

DCI Matthews leaned back in his chair, covering his face with his hands. "Alright... I still say you're as barking as your old gaffer, but let's say you're right about all this. Where does it get us? How do you learn the crone's true name? Let's piece together what we know."

Grabbing a sheet of paper from the desk, the detective scribbled down their clues for further examination.

1. ***Dering Woods is called the Screaming Woods.***

2. ***People disappear in the woods on Halloween every 25 years.***

3. ***Eva could be the illegitimate child of Rose Dering.***

4. ***The Dering family is connected to the woods somehow.***

5. ***An old crone lives in the witch's cabin & can't die.***

6. ***Connor Marshall's cryptic clue:***

    a. ***In the hall where time has ended.***

    b. ***Think on this, and all is mended.***

    c. ***To find the truth before they die.***

    d. ***You must expose their greatest lie.***

Tapping his chin, the sergeant poured over their list of clues. "I think Papa's clue is key to this, but time is running out if we're going to save these people. The hall where time ended could be Surrenden Dering. Maybe 'their greatest lie' refers to the Dering's greatest lie that Eva was illegitimate. I say we head out to Dering Woods to investigate before it's too late."

The detective slapped the side of his chair and stood with a determined set to his jaw. "You're right, Ritchie. I've been trying to avoid those woods, but it's clear our answer lies there."

He crossed the room to Eva's portrait and waited for the sergeant to join him before twisting the key and revolving to the main hall.

Returning to the car, the officers sped down Surrenden Road and criss-crossed several side roads until they reached the Dering Woods, each one lost in speculative silence.

"Sir, I had a crazy idea."

DCI Matthews gave a derisive snort. "This entire case hinges on crazy ideas. Why should yours be any crazier than a four-hundred-year-old crone haunting Dering Woods who murders people every twenty-five years on Halloween?"

"Well, when you put it that way, you do sound like a bit of a nutter." The sergeant attempted to suppress his amusement as DCI Matthews rolled his eyes.

"Go on, then, let's have it. What's your crazy idea?"

The sergeant licked his dry lips, unsure of voicing his theory. "It's this business with *A Midsummer Night's Dream*, sir. What if the characters in the play are somehow inspired by the Dering family? They were alive during the same timeframe, and William Shakespeare was the same age as Sir Edward Dering's father. London is only eighty-five kilometers northeast of Pluckley, which was a day's travel on horseback. What if there was a love triangle between them?"

"An interesting theory, Ritchie, and not crazy at all. It's possible, and there's clearly something we're missing in the connection of Shakespeare to the Dering family. He couldn't be Eva's father because Shakespeare died in 1616, well before Sir Edward Dering married Elizabeth Tufton. Still, Shakespeare may be Edward Dering's biological father. That's definitely a possibility to explore."

When they turned onto Smarden Bell Road, DCI Matthews directed the sergeant's attention to the grassy shoulder. "Pull over here. We'll walk the rest of the way. I've had twenty-five years to review my video footage, and I believe the old crone has some form of early alarm system. We need to watch our footing and avoid the main paths."

It was late afternoon when they entered the woods, but the heavy canopy blocked most of the sunlight. Occasional rays of light rained down from the treetops, but they used their torches to locate tripwires or anything that may alert the crone to their arrival. After half a kilometer, Sergeant Ritchie caught his foot on a wrought iron fence post and crashed headlong into the brush.

DCI Matthews froze, glancing in every direction for the mysterious crone. When she did not appear, he relaxed and helped the sergeant to his feet. "Bloody Hell, Ritchie! Why don't you just invite the crone over for tea and biscuits?"

"I'm sorry, sir. I don't know what I tripped on. Whatever it was, it wasn't visible in this light. Help me clear away the weeds and rubbish to see what I tripped over."

Unstrapping his boot knife, DCI Matthews sliced away the vines and foliage to reveal a short, meter-tall fence surrounding an ancient tombstone. He removed a handkerchief and cleared the grime from the stone face to reveal: **Robin Goodfellow**. Below the name was a date: **2405 BC to 1644 AD**. The epitaph read: **Here lies an honest Puck. Killed by Sir Edward Dering.**

The detective emitted a low whistle. "That's the piece of the puzzle we were missing... Puck."

Sergeant Ritchie furrowed his brows staring from the ancient stone to the detective. "What do you mean, sir? I thought Puck was a fictional character written by Shakespeare?"

DCI Matthews nodded and pointed to the stone. "Aye, Puck was a fictional character, but Robin Goodfellow was a real person. He must've used magic to sustain his life the same way the old crone sustains hers. It all makes sense now. Puck, or Robin Goodfellow, must have seduced Rose Dering, producing Eva. She was a young, unmarried maiden, and Sir Edward Dering would have moved mountains to avoid sullying the family name. Rose must have had Eva at home, allowing Edward Dering to claim the baby was his own daughter. He may have avoided a scandal, but he knew the truth. It's also interesting that Robin and Edward died the same year. They must have mortally wounded each other in a fierce battle over Eva."

"So, her real name is Eva Goodfellow, not Eva Dering?"

"It must be, Ritchie. I think we've just discovered the crone's father."

CHAPTER 7: ASHES TO ASHES

Returning to her home deep within the Dering Woods, Eva moved to the back bedroom to examine her prizes.

Tonight has been a productive night!

Entering the bedroom, she frowned as she counted the two-meter-tall steel cages lining the room.

Ten... now, what am I going to do?

An instant later, a sly grin played at the corners of her mouth.

I know... I caught them in pairs, so I'll cage them in pairs like I did with those pesky neighbours so long ago.

Opening her purse, Eva dumped the contents on the floor to sort through her treasured figurines. She placed the teens into the first four cages and the adults into the next five cages, leaving a single cage empty for troublemakers.

There's always one, it seems...

Closing her eyes, the crone caused a soft, golden mist to flow from her fingertips and envelop the cages. An instant later, seventeen confused people stood staring at her from behind iron bars.

"Welcome to the beginning of the end of your life. I want to thank each of you for the sacrifice you're about to bestow."

Enraged and hysterical, the captives screamed, cried, and banged on the cage doors in a futile attempt to free themselves. "Now, now... settle down, my little poppets. I don't want you to use up all of your energy before I can drain it from you."

"Let us go, you barmy old hag!" Bonnie's grating voice rose above the din, causing Eva to growl in frustration and advance on the uppity teen.

"Old, am I? I'll have you know I'm only 30 years old, darling."

Bonnie rolled her eyes and blew a raspberry. "As if... you're old enough to be my mother. I can't believe you tried to steal my boyfriend. At first, I thought you were some random slag, but you're just some crusty old cougar trying to recapture her lost youth."

The crone peered into a mirror to examine her features and gasped to find herself aged several decades since her meal at the restaurant.

I must've used too much magic tonight. No matter... I can recover my youth instantly, and I know just who to pick.

Her eyes burned with hatred, turning coal-black like her father's.

Eva advanced on Bonnie's cage, and when she spoke, her lips curled into a sneer. "You're right, darling... I have aged since you last saw me. I suppose I need to fix that." The crone reached through the bars with lightning reflexes and fastened her left hand around Bonnie's wrist. When the teen struggled to free herself, the crone jerked her against the bars, causing her forehead to crash against the cage.

While Bonnie stood dazed from the blow, Eva's right hand shot out and clutched the teen's chest, her fingernails digging into the supple flesh. Seconds later, Eva stood erect in her teenage body and released Bonnie's lifeless corpse. Her body hit the floor, collapsing into a pile of ashes next to Tim Schultz.

Tim cried out in dismay, falling to his knees on the steel floor. "She's gone! You killed her! I hate you!"

A smirk played at the corner of the crone's mouth. "Oh, come now, Tim. She was a horrible person and treated you like vermin. Wouldn't you rather spend your days with someone who adores you?"

Tim spat at the crone's feet and flipped her a rude hand gesture. "I could never love an evil witch like you. I don't care how young and attractive you make yourself. Inside, you're still rotten to the core."

Fire danced in the crone's black eyes. "So mote it be, Tim. On your head, be it... I'll save you for last, so you can watch everyone you've ever loved or cared for return to the dust from whence they came."

"No... please God... no!" Tim's face paled as the crone approached Josh and Caleb's cage.

Josh and Caleb pressed their backs against the steel cage in a futile attempt to escape their doom. Eva stopped at their cage, glancing at Tim while she spoke. "You two were quite rude at St. Nicholas. I believe you referred to a man of God as 'father pickle poker' and called my mother a twat."

She eyed the teen boys with satisfaction as the realization of their error hit them. "Yes... that's right. I'm the 'demon's whelp' mentioned in the story, and the 'Red Lady' as you call her, was my mother: Rose Dering."

Clutching her ruby pendant with one hand, the crone reached through the bars and plunged her fingernails into Caleb's chest, draining his life force into the pendant. She repeated the same process with Josh, leaving two piles of ashes on the cage floor.

Tim wept bitter tears as he shook the cage door. "I'm sorry! I'll be your mate or lover or whatever you want me to be. Just bring them back!"

Eva continued to the next cage, ignoring Tim's pleas. She eyed Jonathan and David Coletti with a hungry desire. She pointed to David, who whimpered as they made eye contact. "You tried to steal from me, and you, Jonathan, tried to bribe me with a free meal rather than owning up to your sins. You and your brother were both stealing from the customers. I could read the truth on your worthless faces. Now, it's I who will be doing the stealing." Repeating the same process, Eva drained the life from the twin brothers and stored their vitality in an emerald ring.

Next, she approached the cage of Bryan and Ryan Long. She glared at the teens as they pressed their backs against the cage. Ryan cowered and whimpered, hiding behind his brother for protection. "What's the matter, darling? I thought you were invincible. Ghost stories are 'just a load of tosh to scare tourists,' right?" She reached through the bars, jerking Bryan into the cage door.

Blood ran down the teen's forehead as his vision swam from the concussion. "Come along, Ryan. You're a strong young man. Stop me, if you can..." When Ryan remained crouched at the back of the cage, Eva gave a sigh of regret. "Oh, you're no fun at all, darling. Maybe you need some motivation." Bryan arched his back an instant later, screaming in agony as the crone drained his energy into a sapphire necklace.

"Stop it! You're killing him!" Concern for his brother's welfare had galvanized Ryan against his own fear, but it was too late. As the teen reached his brother, Bryan's body collapsed into a pile of ash. "No!"

The crone plunged her fingernails into Ryan's chest in the blink of an eye, cackling with delight. "You said you didn't believe in ghosts, eh? Well, now's your chance to prove that theory wrong." With a twist of her wrist, Eva channeled Ryan's life force into the sapphire pendant to mix with his brother's energy. When the teen's body collapsed to a pile of ashes, the crone moved on to Tanika and Robert's cage.

Through the rest of the day, Eva drained the life of all her victims, storing their energy in various pieces of jewelry. In the end, Tim stood alone, the last of all her victims. As she approached, he tried to cry out, but his hoarse voice failed to make a sound.

"And now, we come to the man who refused my love, not once… not twice… but thrice. I hope this experience has taught you to take the opportunities life presents you when you have a chance."

Crossing to the wall devoid of cages, Eva stood at the base of a painting, admiring the image of a young boy with shaggy blonde hair, cream-colored skin, and dazzling emerald eyes. "Do you like him, Tim? This is my father, Robin Goodfellow. Despite his age, he always enjoyed a youthful appearance. I keep his painting on the wall to protect my most precious heirloom. You should be honoured!" Eva slid the painting aside to reveal an alcove containing a carved wooden box.

Returning to Tim's cage, the crone opened the box to reveal a diamond-studded amethyst broach encased in gold. "This was my mother's. She gave it to my father before she died, and he used it to trap the life force of those who offended him until I was old enough to perform the process on my own. Of course, my father was a pure-blood Fairy, so he didn't need to siphon off human energy to maintain his youth. If only my grandfather, Edward Dering, hadn't come seeking revenge, my father might still be alive today."

She shook her head, clearing away the distant memories. "Listen to me… boring you with details of my life when you're not worthy enough to hear them. No matter, your life will be mine soon." Reaching through the bars, the crone drained Tim's energy until his body collapsed, turning into a pile of ash at her feet. "Now we can be together forever, darling."

Snapping the lid shut, Eva returned the wooden box to its alcove and replaced her father's painting over the opening. As the portrait slid into place, the crone stopped and listened.

Someone is crashing through my woods. It appears I'll get to use that last cage today after all.

Eva retrieved her purse and left the shack, gliding through the woods, searching for the intruder. In the distance, two male voices drifted toward her. She continued forward, straining to catch their conversation. "It must be, Ritchie. I think we just discovered the crone's father."

The crone grinned to herself and moved forward into the clearing. "Congratulations, detective. You've learned my secret. I guess not every member of the Ashford Police Department is a complete moron."

"Halt!" DCI Matthews held his boot knife extended, keeping the crone from advancing on his position. "You're under arrest for the kidnapping of seventeen people. I'll seek a lighter sentence if you release them."

The woods echoed with the crone's laughter. "My dear officer, I take it back. The Ashford Police Department *is* composed of complete morons!" Ignoring the detective, she turned her eyes to the sergeant. "Oh ho! And who do we have here? Your face seems familiar to me, but I can't place where I've seen you."

Swallowing down his fear, the sergeant stepped forward, hands raised in a sign of non-aggression. "Hello, Eva... Eva Goodfellow. My face may seem familiar to you because I believe you knew my grandfather, Connor Marshall."

A dreamy state filled the crone's eyes at Sergeant Ritchie's mention of his grandfather. "Ah yes, DCI Marshall. I knew him well. It's a shame he refused my offer. We could've been very happy together."

The color drained from the sergeant's face. "Wait a minute! You... and my grandfather... Papa? He... you and he..."

Eva laughed again, her young, vibrant voice drifting through the trees. "Well, you may have inherited your grandfather's dashing good looks but not his eloquence. Yes, young man, your grandfather and I were quite happy for a few days. He discovered me after I murdered my neighbours. They learned my secret and tried to force me to leave my home, but I taught them a lesson. I drained their life and left their empty shells stacked up like cordwood in the field. It was a silly mistake, drawing attention to my activities."

The crone shrugged, advancing toward the officers. "It was a mistake I never made again. After Connor left me, I returned to draining my victims to ash and scattering their remains at my father's grave. It's a fitting legacy to those who offend me. As for your grandfather, he found me, and we fell in love, but he abandoned me when he discovered the truth about my past and my secret to aging. Now you've come to take his place. How lovely..."

As Eva approached the officers, DCI Matthews lunged at her, but she deflected the knife with her purse, securing her wrist around his.

Your soul is mine.

Plunging her free hand beneath the detective's shirt, the crone dug her sharp fingernails deep into his chest. His agonizing scream filled the woods, scattering birds and wildlife. She channeled his energy into her ruby pendant, turning his body into a pile of ashes. The crone faced Sergeant Ritchie with a playful grin. "Are you ready to join me or join your superior?"

"I could never join someone as evil as you. You're a murderer! You're a homicidal maniac! What did Papa ever see in you?"

The crone's eyes flashed, and her hand shot forward, grasping the sergeant's wrist. "I'm trying to live, just like you. I just happen to require human energy to survive. I'll enjoy consuming your energy, but I wish your grandfather were here to witness my retribution."

"Your wish is easily granted, my dear."

Spinning around, Eva's eyes grew wide with surprise and hatred. "You've gotten old, Connor."

CHAPTER 8: ONE LIFE TO LIVE

"And you're just as lovely as the day we first met, Eva."

Sergeant Ritchie gaped at his grandfather, standing unencumbered at the edge of the woods. "Papa, how'd you find us? How do you know this lady? Did you know she murdered DCI Matthews?" His questions poured out in a flood of curiosity, exasperation, anger, and disbelief.

"You've got it all wrong, Dennis." The old man grinned at his grandson's shocked expression. "Oh yes, I know your name. I'm not as senile as I appear. I did all that for your benefit. All the world's a stage, is it not?"

"You... what? My benefit? Why would you pretend not to know me?"

Eva remained silent, taking in the discussion and weighing Connor's words in a way the sergeant could never understand. Their connection remained deep, even after seventy-five years.

The old man chortled with glee. "When you followed in my footsteps and became a police officer, I knew this day would come. I knew you'd eventually discover my secret and, perhaps, attempt to kill Eva. I couldn't allow that to happen. Each time we met, I pretended to suffer from dementia, knowing you would stay away to preserve your memory of me."

He glanced down at the detective's pile of ashes. "When Tonya informed me of your arrival, I knew I needed to put on the performance of a lifetime. It was only a matter of time before you uncovered my secret or stumbled blindly upon Eva. If you were going to meet her, I wanted you to understand her the way I do. So yes, when you arrived, I played the role of a doddery old man for your benefit and that of the detective. You must understand that Eva didn't kill him; she absorbed his energy. When you place a sponge in water, do you kill the water? No, of course not! You absorb it and channel it into a new purpose. Humans are 70% water, are they not? I'm sure the people Eva absorbed were rude and detrimental to society. Isn't that right, my dear?"

The crone stood in stony silence, unsure of her response without revealing her troubled and confused emotions. At last, Eva responded with a curt nod but maintained her grip on the sergeant's wrist. She did not divert her gaze from the old man, but the hardness in her glare lessened. Her eyes filled with a mixture of hurt and remorse, which she blinked away in a flash.

Sergeant Ritchie pressed a balled fist against his temple in a futile attempt to make sense of the situation. "So, do you love Eva, Papa? If so, what about Grandma? Did you ever love her? Did you ever love any of us?"

Connor's jovial façade vanished as he realized how much the depths of his betrayal hurt his grandson. "Of course, I loved you all, especially your grandmother. Don't be naïve. I met Eva after the incident in 1948. I was only twenty years old then, freshly returned from serving in WWII, where I was stationed at the China-Burma-India theatre. Your grandmother waited for me, and we married in 1946 after I returned home. Your uncle, Harry, was only a year old when I met Eva."

The old man's eyes glistened with tears as he recalled the memories of those days. "When I met Eva during my investigation in 1948, she offered to make me like her rather than kill me. I wanted to and even promised I would, but I was already married and couldn't abandon my family. While she slept, I crept from the house and returned to my former life."

Withdrawing a handkerchief from his pocket, Connor dabbed the tears from his eyes. "When the children disappeared in 1973, I planted evidence and obtained a conviction against a known paedophile. Nobody questioned my conclusions. They were well shod of him. In reality, I couldn't face Eva's wrath, and blaming a known paedophile seemed like the best choice at the time. When your grandmother died, I considered returning to Eva, but I was too old. I feared Eva no longer loved me and wouldn't accept me."

"You were going to come back to me?" Eva's soft voice floated in the breeze, filled with tender love. "I thought you abandoned me forever."

"No. I could never abandon you. Not forever, at least."

"But… but Papa, I still don't understand. Why did all the murders…" He stopped as the old man lifted his finger to correct him. "Okay, fine… why did all the life force transfers occur on Halloween? Why exactly twenty-five years apart?"

Connor swept the air with a dismissive wave. "That's easily answered, my boy. Eva was born on October 31, 1623, during the pagan festival of Samhain. You know it today as Halloween. Because she's half-human, she is still subject to mortality, so she must renew her life force every twenty-five years."

Sergeant Ritchie stood gobsmacked by the confession, trying to gauge his grandfather's sincerity based on the available facts.

"Shakespeare!" The sergeant strained against Eva's grip, hoping the crone would be caught off-guard by his sudden movement, but she tightened her grip, glaring at him with unrestrained hostility.

The old man shrugged, oblivious to his grandson's discomfort. "Yes, Shakespeare. What about him?"

"Well... how does the playwright fit into all this? We knew that Lilly was the 'White Lady' and her sister, Rose, was the 'Red Lady,' but we failed to connect Eva and the Dering family to Shakespeare. Was that all misdirection, or was Eva's true parentage the 'greatest lie' you said we should uncover?"

Connor winked at his grandson, tapping the side of his nose. "Ah, that's a fly in the ointment, isn't it? Yes, you're right that Eva's father was Robin Goodfellow, better known as Puck. The sprite seduced Sir Edward Dering's daughter, Rose, and fathered Eva. Although Sir Edward Dering is Eva's grandfather, he convinced the world that Eva was his daughter, not Rose's. Unfortunately, the connection goes deeper than that. William Shakespeare is Eva's great-grandfather. He met Sir Anthony Dering's wife, Frances Dering, backstage during a particularly drunken stupor and fathered Sir Edward Dering. So, genetically... Eva's father and grandfather both have a connection to William Shakespeare. The nave even created *A Midsummer Night's Dream* based on his affair with Sir Edward's mother."

"You know then... you know all my secrets." The bitterness in Eva's voice was replaced with a sense of awe. "You're the first to ever make the connection between my father, grandfather, and William Shakespeare. You must've spent years researching the truth."

"A lifetime, my dear. I've spent a lifetime pining after you." Stretching out his arm, Connor quoted Puck's most famous line. "So, give me your hands if we be friends, and I shall then restore amends."

Releasing Sergeant Ritchie's wrist, Eva extended her arms to the old man, welcoming him back to her. As the two star-crossed lovers drew nearer, the sergeant stooped down and collected the fallen knife, tucking it into his belt behind his back. He waited for his grandfather to draw the crone into a warm embrace before launching himself at her.

"No!" Connor's cry rang out through the countryside, piercing the sergeant's eardrums. With strength belying his age, the old man shoved Eva to the ground as the boot knife plunged into his chest. Dropping to his knees, shock registered on Connor's face as blood spurted from his grievous wound.

Sergeant Ritchie stood frozen in horror as his grandfather coughed and spewed blood at his feet. "I'm sorry, Papa! I'm sorry! I didn't mean to hurt you. Forgive me, Papa... forgive me!"

With a herculean effort, Connor pulled the knife from his chest, dropping it to the ground as he attempted to stem the flow of his lifeblood spilling onto the woodland floor.

"You fool!" Eva's agonized shriek filled the air, latching one hand around the sergeant's wrist and the other around the old man's wrist. Closing her eyes, a golden glow enveloped both men as Sergeant Ritchie's life force transferred into Connor's.

The old man opened his eyes with a gasp to find his wound healed, and his youth returned. He glanced at the crone, whose dark hair was streaked with gray. "Eva? What did you do?"

She fixed Connor with sympathetic eyes, resting her palm against his cheek with gentle affection. "I did what was necessary." Resting her hand on an emerald ring, she absorbed a portion of its stored life energy to recover her youthful figure. "Shall we retire to my shack?"

Connor gave a wan smile, gesturing to the pile of ashes at their feet. "Was it necessary to take my grandson's life?"

Eva cupped Connor's cheeks in her hands, fixing her gaze on her lost love. "Sometimes, sacrifice is necessary to achieve your goals in life. I planned to spare his life for your sake since he hadn't offended me, but when he tried to kill me and risked your life, he sealed his fate as surely as if he'd plunged the knife into himself."

"I understand..." Hot tears rolled down Connor's cheeks, mixing with his grandson's ashes. "In a way, Dennis gave his life for me, and while I'm still alive, a part of my grandson will live on inside me."

"Oh, how I've missed your wisdom and insight. It's a shame I had to wait four hundred years to find you."

Extending his hand to Eva, Connor helped the crone to her feet. "Gather your things and come with me. I have a surprise for you."

Eva eyed him with leery hesitation. "You won't disappear on me again, will you?"

Connor laughed and shook his head. "We're bound by a stronger bond now, my dear. My grandson died to save me. Don't think his sacrifice is easy to forget or discard. I'll be here when you return."

Kissing him on the cheek, Eva rushed back to her shack to retrieve her jewelry and Puck's portrait. While she packed her belongings, Connor crossed the clearing to Robin Goodfellow's tombstone. "I promise to take care of your little girl, sir."

Reaching down into the ashes, Connor retrieved the detective's wallet and credentials. He returned to Sergeant Ritchie's ashes to retrieve his grandson's keys, wallet, and credentials. "I'm sorry it had to end this way, my boy. I'd have loved for us to be a family once again."

When Eva returned, she dragged two suitcases behind her. Connor eyed the bags as a mischievous smirk played at the corners of his mouth. "Did you pack enough? I think you might have left your cauldron behind."

Eva chortled at the joke, shoving one of the bags in his empty arms. "Here, make yourself useful. I couldn't leave behind my trophies or my father's portrait. So, now that I've done what you asked, what's the surprise?"

"I'm taking you home, Eva."

"To your home, don't you mean, Connor?"

He smirked again, guiding Eva back toward his grandson's car. "Yes, something like that." After securing her luggage in the boot, the couple turned the car around and returned to Surrenden Road. When they pulled into the driveway, Eva squealed with delight.

"My home! You're actually taking me to my home? But how?"

"I bought your home years ago after my wife died. I always wanted to find a way to come back for you, but if I failed, I hoped my grandson might be a good surrogate."

Kissing his lost love, Connor opened Eva's car door and escorted her to the front door. "I've been looking forward to this moment for decades!" Unlocking the carved oak door, Connor swept Eva off her feet and carried her across the threshold.

They lost themselves in the moment as time stopped within the shrouded walls of Eva's ancestral home. When Connor set Eva back on her feet, she wrinkled her nose in disgust. "And here I thought my shack was filthy!"

Connor winked, wrapping his arm around Eva's shoulder. "I'll admit... it needs some work, but we have all the time in the world."

On Jensen's Farm

The Autumn of 1690
Somewhere in the Hudson Valley

The ropes cut painfully into Emma's wrists. Though her eyes were bleary with tears, she could still make out the masked figures that encircled her. These figures held torches in their hands, the flickering lights casting a surreal illumination on the proceedings going on around.

Emma knew that under the masks were friends and neighbors, people she had interacted with since she was a small child, people who she had always greeted with a smile and kind words. Many of them, she was sure, she had grown up with, played with as a child, laughed, and learned with.

It was, after all, a small settlement.

Beyond the torchlight, Emma could barely see the *poppetje*, carefully built and lined up by the villagers as part of the ritual. They were simple things, really, just bits of cloth and corn husk, with sacks of potatoes as rudimentary heads. The craftsmanship was not very good, but Emma knew it didn't need to be. They would suit the ritual just fine the way they were, and the ritual would protect everyone in the village.

Everyone except *her*.

One of the figures broke through the circle of torches, tall and strong, and stood in front of her. While the other members of the procession wore their everyday clothing, this figure was dressed in a long white robe, its mask more detailed than its brothers' and sisters'. Yet, despite the mask, Emma recognized it at once as the colony's governor.

Surely he won't go through with this. Emma thought to herself. *He, of all people!*

Surely he will take pity on me and cut me down. We can always find another way to end this nightmare, a way that doesn't involve bloodshed.

The governor started to circle the pole that Emma was lashed to, intoning a prayer softly under his breath. It wasn't a prayer that Emma had heard before, and no matter how much she struggled to hear, she couldn't make out the words. Once the circling stopped, the governor pulled something from his belt, something that glistened and glimmered in the torchlight. Only when he brought the object to Emma's neck did she recognize it as a blade, the same blade that had cut her countless meals of lamb, pig, or game fowl.

"Please," Emma whispered, gathering every inch of sadness and desperation she could muster into her eyes. Surely it would be enough. "Please, father..."

"Forgive me, daughter," The governor apologized with a heavy tone. "I am truly sorry for what I am about to do. Still, it must be done."

With a tear in his eye, the governor slit his daughter's throat.

* * *

Somewhere in the Hudson Valley
Six days before Halloween
Present Day

Micah exhaled, the smoke from his cigarette temporarily obscuring the framed movie poster advertising Fellini's *La Strada* that hung on the common room wall. Of course, it was against the rules to smoke inside any of the school buildings, but they had disabled the smoke alarm, and as long as one of the R.A.s didn't come by to check on them randomly, nobody would know.

"You're kidding me!" Tara couldn't believe what she was hearing. "You're really going to sit there and say that Argento's films are better than Bava's?"

"Yes," Micah replied simply before taking another drag of his cigarette. "That's what I'm saying."

"C'mon! Mario Bava revolutionized Italian horror in the 1960s, and without his use of color, Argento's films wouldn't even *exist*." Tara rolled her eyes like a tween.

"Maybe so..." Micah rebutted. "But this is one of those cases where the student far outdoes the master."

"Wow, you two," Saar said with disbelief. She sat on the sidelines, quietly polishing her glasses, every now and then taking a sip from a metal flask emblazoned with an Eye of Ra she always carried with her.

"Oh," Tara remarked, voice full of sarcasm. "And where do you land on this?"

"I don't watch horror movies," Saar mentioned, despite looking very much like she fell out of a Hammer film. "So I wouldn't even venture a guess. I just know that you two always get fired up about this stuff, and it bleeds over until it becomes a real argument. The last time this happened, you guys didn't talk for a week, and we can't have that right now with this project looming over our heads."

Micah and Tara looked at each other, shaking their heads. As usual, Saar would get the last word and was probably right, but it was clear from the looks on the two friends' faces that this conversation was far from over.

"So, let's talk about the project then. If it's not *too horror* for you." There was no real venom in Tara's voice when she said this; there never was between them. Even when they fought, there was rarely any seriousness in it.

Saar raised her hands in mock surrender. "Hey, I don't play around with you two's creative processes. I just play with the cameras."

"And we thank you for it." Micah smiled. Saar was a wizard cinematographer and could probably write her own ticket after college, while the other two would most likely spend their lives begging for a second-rate distribution from a third-rate streaming service.

"They're really going to let us shoot at Jensen's Farm?" Tara asked skeptically, not for the first time.

"Yup," Micah replied, popping the p. "I cleared with the couple that runs the place. They'll even let us stay overnight for a few nights as long as we don't move any of their displays around."

"Man, this is going to be so boss." Tara grinned excitedly. One of the reasons the others liked her so much, even though she dressed like something out of Jersey Shore, was that she said things like "boss" unironically.

"We're gonna kill this project." Micah pointed out. "Professor Klein is going to gag when she sees it."

***

Noah and Lucas sat on the floor of Noah's bedroom, staring intently at the television on the shelf before them. On the screen, a man dressed in leather armor whipped a seemingly endless stream of zombies and skeletons, jumping from ledge to ledge. Then, suddenly, misjudging the trajectory of an oncoming bat, the man slipped into a hole. After that, the screen went black, with red lettering telling the two boys that the game was, indeed, over.

"Oh, man!" Noah lamented. "I was so close!"

"My turn!" Lucas declared, holding his hand out for the gaming control. Noah passed him the controller, and the little man started his adventures anew.

"I can't believe your parents are letting us go to Jensen's Farm this year," Lucas stated, deftly playing the video game as he talked. "And by ourselves too! My parents wouldn't ever let me go."

"Yeah, they figure we're old enough now," Noah replied, somewhat feeling proud of himself.

The boys played the game in silence for a while, passing the controller back and forth after each ignoble death of their onscreen hero.

Finally, Noah spoke up, "I heard that place is pretty scary..."

"Naa," Lucas defended. "It's just a bunch of dummies and stuff. I think the old people that set it all up go out in costumes sometimes and jump out at you, but that's it."

"I don't know. Maybe." Noah shrugged. "But I talked to Julia during recess the other day, you know, the girl with the braids?"

Lucas nodded, half listening as he commanded the armored man to dodge a series of scythes tossed by a massive Grim Reaper.

"Well, she went last year with her sister, and she said there was this thing... this demon thing. She called it Deer-Head..."

"Old man with a mask, I told you..." Lucas piped in, stopping Noah in the middle.

"No, she said it was really scary, so scary that her sister won't even talk about it. She pretends she didn't even see it. Julia said she had nightmares about Deer-Head for months..." Noah was trying, but Julia's words scared him.

"Julia was just trying to frighten you, man."

"Yeah, I guess so..." Noah mumbled, not at all convinced.

* * *

Five days before Halloween

Tara hated coming out here. She had grown up outside the city, in a small town very much like this one. A place where dilapidated houses flew faded flags, tireless cars sat on cinder blocks, and the idea of fun was a bonfire in the woods behind the old high school. Even as a child, she had longed for something more, something far from the closed minds and sealed fates of these people. The day she escaped to a big-city college was one big relief, though it always made her heart sink a little when she had to leave.

Tara focused on the music playing from the car's tinny-sounding speakers. A woman's voice, pretty and fragile, contrasted against chugging guitars and machine-gun drums; yet she didn't recognize the artist, she liked it. She turned in her seat to ask who the artist was when Micah started to speak.

"That's the turn, right there. Help me keep an eye out for the place."

"Shouldn't be hard to miss," Saar commented from the backseat. "They say it's pretty done up."

"Help me look anyway, guys. You know how I miss things sometimes," Micah asserted.

Tara thought that was a bit of an understatement. In the time she had known Micah, she had seen him, on separate occasions, step into traffic, walk into a tree, and trip over seemingly thin air itself. For a director, he wasn't very perceptive.

A few minutes after the turn and driving down your typical under-lit rural street, they found it.

"Holy crap!" Saar gasped, putting her phone down on the empty seat beside her.

"Would you look at this place?!" Micah exclaimed in excitement. "It's freaking perfect! I can already tell."

The house itself wasn't anything special, your typical country farmhouse, a bit better up-kept than the standard, on several acres of farmland. What was done with it, however, was fantastic.

A metal fence, Gothic and imposing, had been erected around the property. Hanging from it, in seemingly random intervals, were realistic dummies, each uniquely shackled or tied, as though they had been taken prisoner and displayed. A tin sign hung over the gate, which read,

Jensen's Farm

A Hudson Valley Harvest Tradition

Come inside and be scared!

"I'm already impressed." Micah smiled. "And we're not even inside the gate."

The property beyond the gates was huge, far bigger than it had seemed from the road. While her friends were excitedly talking, Tara looked everywhere; maybe she would see something else, a new display or detail that could send her mind reeling.

Here a skeletal pirate crew pulled treasure from a hole in the ground, there a deranged-looking doctor operated on a patient with a face frozen in a silent scream, and in yet another corner, a spider's web held suspiciously human-shaped cocoons.

Most impressive, however, were the scarecrows. Like many of these things, the yard and surrounding farmland were divided into a simple maze, but instead of wooden slats or rows of corn, the path was designated by hundreds and hundreds of scarecrows hanging from wooden crosses, each with a uniquely painted sackcloth face. Unlike the other dummies, which seemed store-bought, these were clearly hand-made with care.

Though difficult to see from the car, the path seemed to make its meandering way to a small black building, set some good distance away from the farmhouse itself. Tara pondered on what horrible wonder existed there and figured it was probably where visiting kids got their candy, not to mention their final, nightmare-inducing jolt.

"Oh, my freaking god," Micah muttered excitedly, parking the car at their designated place. "Could this place be any more perfect…"

"Right?" Tara said nonchalantly, and Saar nodded in agreement, though her face betrayed a touch of nervousness.

A woman dressed in a white button-up shirt and light blue jeans came out of the farmhouse, seeing them arrive, and made her way toward the waiting car. She appeared to be a young sixty, with salt-and-pepper hair that looked like it had recently been cut and styled. She moved with the easy grace of one who had some dance or acrobatics training and wore a soft smile. When she reached the car, she waved, and the students all got out in turn to greet their host.

"You must be the movie kids," the woman said. Her voice carried a slight accent, though the students could not place it.

"Yes," Micah confirmed as he shook the woman's soft hand. "I'm Micah, the director, and this is my writer Tara and camerawoman, Saar."

The woman nodded and shook each of their hands in turn. "I'm Mila. My husband Shem and I run this place."

"A pleasure," Micah gave her a warm smile as he spoke.

"No actors?" Mila questioned, looking around the car as if more students were there, hiding in the shadows.

"We're all acting in the project," Tara offered. "And doing sound. We only get a group of three for this project."

"Ah, I see," Mila mused. "Come inside and meet Shem, and we can talk about everything over some tea and cookies."

All but shaking with excitement, the three of them followed Mila into the farmhouse.

* * *

Noah lay in bed staring at the shadows cast on the ceiling by the meager glow of his nightlight. *'It was funny how his mind could make so many things out of shadows'*, he thought to himself; they were not "ha-ha" funny, but weird funny, the sort of funny that crept into your stomach when you stood in a high place or hit an especially nasty bump in the car.

At first, the shadows were snakes writhing and twitching on the ceiling in a deadly mass, and then, before his mind could process, they became the tentacles of an alien being, reaching and grasping toward his bed. He ducked his head under his Spider-Man sheets before they could change again.

Why am I such a chicken? He asked to himself, feeling stupid while huddled there, as though there was really something dangerous in his room and a simple cloth could defend him if there was.

I'm too old for this crap. He insisted. *And besides, I love scary stuff!*

He truly did, at least when the sun was up and there were other people around. At night, however, things were different. Movie monsters and spooky video games weren't real by daylight, but they just might be after everyone went to bed.

"Stop being stupid," he called out loud, forcing himself to uncover his face and stare at the ceiling again, at the shadows that were now making a spider's web impression.

For a moment, Noah considered shutting off his nightlight and taking away the soft illumination causing the shadows in the first place but realized that the plunge into total darkness would be far, far worse.

"They're just dumb shadows," Noah assured himself, willing it to be true and finding, much to his surprise, that it *was*. They didn't even look that much like spiderwebs anymore, and he was a total goose if he thought they had *ever* looked like tentacles or snakes. If he tried, he could find what was making the shadows in the room, which toy, game, or decoration was casting the darkness. None of this was particularly scary, though.

He was just being a chicken.

And was better now.

Noah laughed at himself, snuggling in and almost finally falling into a restful sleep.

Something, though, was standing outside of his bedroom window.

It was big, tall, and man-shaped. Something that wasn't just a stupid trick of the light, not just a random shadow mutated into a horrible being by the mind of an overactive eleven-year-old. Something that had big, forked horns on its otherwise human-shaped head, which stretched to the starless sky.

Julia's sister had nightmares about Deer-Head for months...

* * *

"I think it's so neat that you're doing a horror movie for your school project," Mila praised. "We both love horror movies."

"Always have," Shem agreed. "Ever since I was a little boy going to the ten-cent pictures. Did you know that, back then, you could see two movies for only ten cents?"

"Two movies and a Superman cartoon," Mila added with a bright smile.

Shem nodded. "Yup. Now you gotta take a second mortgage on your blessed house just to see one movie."

"And they're not as good as they used to be anyway." Mila laughed.

Micah, Tara, and Saar laughed along politely.

"Is that why you do the haunted farm?" Micah prodded for more insight as to why.

"It's part of it," Mila answered, taking off her bottle-thick glasses and polishing them on her flannel shirt. "But it's also tradition for Shem's family, isn't it, love?"

Shem nodded. "The Jensens come from Holland, originally, a little town that you've probably never heard of called Hertvorst."

Tara had never heard of it in Holland that she was aware of, but she kept that information quiet. After a momentary pause, Shem continued, "Hertvorst is, I guess, a very traditional place, you'd probably call it superstitious and backward, but they have their traditions. One of the biggest ones is The Harvest Ritual, and our humble home haunt is sort of a modern version of that."

"That's fascinating," Micah commented. "The movie we're shooting is about a pagan cult hiding in modern society, so this is perfect!"

"Oh, I wouldn't call the people of Hertvorst a cult," Mila said, her voice suddenly firm and curt.

"Of course not..." Micah spoke up, trying to make sure they weren't offended.

"We didn't mean to imply..." Saar started but got interrupted by Shem's slightly raised voice.

"Of course not. We didn't mean to make it sound like we're accusing you of anything. You seem like fine young people. All my beautiful wife was saying is that the good men and women of Hertvorst have their ways, just as you and I do, and it's best to leave it at that."

"Best to leave it at that is right," Mila said, her voice now as unreadable as the marks on a sidewalk.

"Tell us a little bit about what you have set up here," Micah asked. "I'm really curious. I don't think Halloween is a big deal in that part of the world, right?"

"Not really," Shem replied. "We have *Sint Maarten*, where we have parades and bonfires, kids going door to door looking for candy and stuff like that, but that's not really what our show is about. Their Harvest Festival is a lot older than that."

"Older than Christians?" Tara asked, now more intrigued than before, and Shem nodded before continuing.

"Their harvest festival was all about the elves, what they called the *Alven*. I know what you're thinking right now, little guys with floppy hats making toys, but believe me, the *Alven* are nothing like that. Well, some of them are a little like that, but most of them are taller than us. They aren't all cute either; some are downright horrible to behold. All of them, however, are trouble."

"What kind of trouble?" Tara asked, almost moving to the edge of her seat.

It was Mila who responded to this. "Well, most of the time, they are just tricky, not dangerous. Doing little things like hiding keys or tying young maidens' hair in knots. Every once in a while, though, especially in the fall, they can get downright nasty."

"That's why they have The Harvest Festival," Shem explained. "These elves like parties, and they like decorations. So during the festival, the people of Hertvorst would put together elaborate displays of dummies and scarecrows, which they called *poppetje,* for the elves to embody."

"Embody?" Micah asked out of curiosity.

Mila nodded. "Oh yes, the *Alven* could take their own forms in our world, but it was easier for them to just take over something that was already here. That's why they would sometimes steal our children and replace them with changelings, so they could have a willing body to jump into whenever they wanted to pay a visit to the silly humans."

"Sometimes they'd even change these children into things like themselves," Shem added. "If they felt the child was wild enough at heart."

Mila nodded once in agreement with her husband.

"So, what sort of things did they do during these festivals?" Micah asked, wanting to understand the breadth of things.

Tara had never seen such a big smile on Micah's face.

"Oh, the usual. Dancing, feasting, playing music," Shem informed. "But it would always end with something a bit more unusual."

"What's that?" Saar inquired curiously. Despite herself, she had been drawn into the story.

"Blood sacrifice," Mila said simply. "That was the important thing. The *Alven* demand sacrifice."

* * *

Four days before Halloween

This has happened to Noah before. Not very often, but now and then, scattered throughout his young life, he had visions, little images that came to him when he was thinking of something else, especially when his mind was occupied with the day-to-day minutia of kid life.

Like the time his dad lost his wallet. They had torn the house apart looking for it, creating a wake of near devastation from the front door to the basement. Even the tiny crawl space of the attic was ransacked, but the wallet failed to turn up.

But then Noah had one of his visions.

He was totally engrossed in getting his video game robot across a particularly hazardous stretch of a wasteland when a small, winged figure flitted through his closed window—without breaking the glass or screen, nonetheless—catching his attention. Noah couldn't remember what the creature looked like anymore, but he remembered it flickered like a firefly, drawing his attention away from the video game and toward a small pile of scrap wood in the backyard. There, under a splintered, nail-covered board, was his dad's wallet.

Ever since, now and again, he would see something, things that he knew weren't *really* there but would nonetheless lead him to something which was real, in the true world that would be important to him.

He knew the Deer-Head outside his window was one of those things, and it terrified him. None of his other visions had been scary, but this one... this one had been different.

"Man, it's going to be so figgin' cool!" Lucas exclaimed. They rode their bikes out to the comic shop after school and were currently opening packs of trading cards, each depicting a different monster from myth or legend. After video games and scary movies, collecting 'Monster Cards', as they called them, was their favorite thing.

"Figgin'?" Noah questioned, raising an eyebrow.

"Yeah, Figgin'. Got a problem with that?" Lucas grumbled in defense.

Noah shook his head.

"But it's gonna be totally sick, isn't it?" Lucas said, hardly containing his excitement. "I hope we get so scared that we wet ourselves!"

Noah nodded. He thought about saying something about his vision, maybe even trying to talk his best friend out of their Halloween trip, but kept silent. He didn't know how Lucas, whose parents were all into the whole 'God and church' thing, would react to his visions, besides, it *did* sound pretty sick. And his visions had never portended anything bad before. Just because the vision had scared him, it didn't mean that the message was sinister.

* * *

An old and rusty car paused for a moment on the street, and the window started rolling down. Tara briefly saw the driver, a woman in a blue windbreaker, raise her cell phone and hold it in front of her face for a moment, presumably to snap a few pictures, before the window went back up and the car rolled on its way.

"We're gonna get a lot of that in the next few days," Shem spoke with smugness in his voice. He was sitting beside Tara on the porch swing, nursing a seemingly endless mug of coffee. He offered one to Tara, but she politely refused since she liked her coffee strong enough to build a city on, and the concoction that the Jensens brewed looked more like slightly murky water. "Hope it doesn't interfere with your movie."

Tara smiled and shook her head. "We're filming everything in the back, by the shed, so traffic is no big deal. If it gets loud, we can even edit out the sound in post-editing. Just let us know if you're showing it to anyone."

Shem nodded. "No chance of that, at least if Mila gets her way." He laughed a sharp, raspy laugh. "She's all about the big surprise on Halloween night, won't even let me put the more neat stuff near the road where you can see it. The keenest stuff, the things in the shed itself, didn't get seen by anyone at all until the night of—not even by me."

"Really?" Tara's eyes grew wide in response to what he said.

Shem smiled at her reaction. "Yup, I lug all the stuff out there, and she works her magic. So I get to see it 'bout five minutes before when 'erybody else does."

"Don't you ever get curious?" Tara asked, knowing full well that if she were in the old man's shoes, she'd be in that shed about ten minutes after it was set up.

Shem laughed again, and when he did, his voice no longer sounded old, no longer contained the rasp and wheeze of the ages. "Now mebbe I do, a little, and mebbe I don't. But what I would never, ever do, not even if I was so curious that I couldn't sleep well at night, would be sneaking in on Mila's work when she doesn't want me to. It'd kill the magic."

Shem gave her a peculiar look before repeating himself, but this time his voice was old again and full of gravity. "It'd kill the magic."

* * *

Micah was surprised at how well the shoot had gone today, and when he closed his eyes to nod off, it was with contentment.

He knew the film they were making was nothing special plot-wise, the same sort of overdone *'evil artifact falls into innocent hands'* plot line of a million direct-to-video horror films. But he was confident that they could elevate it into something special with their combined talents, especially when they had such an awesome location to shoot. *Sure saved us a few bucks on set dressing,* Micah thought to himself. The Jensens had insisted that the students not pay them 'a red cent' for the privilege of shooting in their home, only asking that they don't disrupt anything while filming. Obviously, he intended to add a small thank you note at the end of the film, but even that was met with some resistance from the elderly couple.

"We didn't do nothing that we weren't gonna do anyway," Mila had said. "No reason to thank us."

Now they were lying there inside sleeping bags purchased that week, in the middle of a nondescript living room that could have belonged to anyone's grandparents, sitting on a gold mine.

Why stop at getting a good grade on the project? Micah thought to himself as he drifted off. *When this thing was finished, it would be easy enough to start showing it at festivals, maybe even ask some of the art theaters to give us a night to screen it. It would obviously have to be in the middle of the week, far from peak theater times, but still... one never knew what sort of person would be watching a promising student film in such a place. One never knew...*

"Did you hear that?" Tara asked softly, her voice pulling Micah back into the world of the waking.

"Hear what?" Saar swallowed. From the sound of her voice, she had been on her way out as well.

"I thought I heard something at the window," Tara said, a little spooked. Though it was pitch black in the living room, Micah could tell that Tara had sat up in her bag and was nervously scanning the room as though her eyes could pierce the darkness.

"What kind of something?" Saar inquired with a bit of dread.

"I don't know," Tara replied. It was obvious that she was trying to keep her voice calm, and even though she was doing a fair job, edges of child-like panic were leaking out. "Like a tapping."

There was a rustle in the darkness, and Micah imagined Saar also sitting up ramrod straight, hands clutched into fists. "Something is tapping at the window?!"

"I don't know... I just heard a tapping..."

"C'mon guys," Micah said matter-of-factly. "You're letting your imaginations get the best of you."

"I *heard something*," Tara panicked. "I know I did. Something was tapping somewhere outside."

"Tapping on the window?" Saar asked again.

"I can't say for sure. But it was tapping on something."

Micah could feel the look he was getting, cold and dangerous. If there was a person on Earth that could weaponize a look, it was Tara.

"Guys," Micah stated evenly. "We're city kids, and there are all sorts of things out there that we just don't hear. For all we know, there are some sort of critters out there that tap around all night. No big deal."

Though Micah's words communicated calm rationalization, his thoughts displayed nothing but the opposite. He was nervous, that much he could admit to himself, but more importantly, he was excited.

This was the sort of story reporters loved to hear, the sort of story that ended up in headlines—*Local Horror Filmmakers had a Real-Life Scare at a Horror Attraction.*

Micah fell asleep that night dreaming about how he could spin this eerie event, simple and innocuous as it was, into marketing gold.

* * *

Three days until Halloween

Everyone was surprised that Lucas and Noah were friends, not to mention best friends. Lucas was tall, lightly tanned, and popular, with sandy blonde hair that seemed to stay in place no matter what mischief the rest of his body got up to. Noah, on the other hand, was pale and skinny, with not-quite black hair that stuck up at odd angles no matter how much he tried to cement it down with hairspray or gel. Though both smart in their own ways, Noah was the only one considered a 'geek' by the other kids, while Lucas got away with being 'kinda weird, but cool'.

Even with these differences, there had been a bond between them ever since meeting by chance on the playground years before. For one, they both were into horror movies and comic books, which led to an acute interest in Halloween that went far beyond their peers. Where the other kids saw the night as a chance to get candy and cause trouble, for Lucas and Noah, it was a different, almost sacred celebration of everything that they both held dear.

"It's the one-time every year where everyone acts like us," Lucas said at one point, and Noah had to admit he couldn't have said it better himself.

Now they sat once more on the playground, oblivious to the other kids and their team games. Lucas quietly sketched in his notebook. Noah leaned over to see what his friend was drawing.

"It's Deer-Head," Lucas pointed out. "Or what I think he looks like, anyway."

Noah nodded. The drawing was pretty good in a preteen boy, muscles, and gore kinda way.

"Would your parents flip over this?" Noah questioned. He hadn't told Lucas about his vision and was hoping that maybe he could find a way out of going to Jensen's Farm on Halloween without explaining why.

"What do you mean?" Lucas asked, adding a few more cakey blobs of gore below the creature's gaping maw. Despite having the head of a deer, Deer-Head seemed to have the teeth of a wolf in Lucas' mind.

"I mean, isn't that thing like... a demon or something? I mean, your parents are sort of weird about that stuff."

Lucas laughed. "That's why I don't tell them."

"I don't want you to get in trouble, is all," Noah stated softly.

Lucas set his notebook down on the grass beside him and looked directly at Noah.

"Do you not want to go to The Farm?" he asked. There was no teasing in Lucas' voice, playful or otherwise, and Noah realized that if he said no right now, that he didn't, in fact, want to go, there would be no more discussion. They would simply move on to the next thing, no matter how much Lucas really seemed to want to witness this place.

He was that sort of friend.

And what sort of friend am I? Noah wondered to himself. He blinked once, twice, took a deep breath, and spoke, "Sure, I want to go. Don't be stupid."

"If you're sure, man. I mean, it's no big deal..."

"I said I want to go." Noah tried to fill his voice with conviction. After all, it had probably just been a stupid nightmare, not a vision at all.

Suddenly, Lucas' eyes filled with mischief. Noah had seen this look before and learned over the years just what it meant. It meant they were about to do something crazy that they could probably get in quite a bit of trouble for.

"Hey... I have an idea." Lucas grinned with a twinkle in his eyes.

* * *

Saar huddled in the corner, eyes wide with fear. In her white-knuckled hands, she gripped a fireplace poker, ready to strike. From around her came the sounds of banging and slamming, as though many people (or things) were trying to bash their way through the fence she leaned against. Suddenly, a gloved hand ripped through the wood and grasped her shoulder. She let out a piercing scream...

"...Aaand cut!" Micah shouted, from behind the fence, taking his hand off Saar's shoulder. "That was great!"

"Yeah, I hope we can fix that fence before the Jensens notice that you blasted through it." Tara scoffed, shutting off her camera.

"Don't worry... I was careful, only to knock out one board, and it was already loose. We're doing them a favor."

Saar rolled her eyes, making her way to the small blue cooler, pulling out bottled water, and drinking from it deeply.

"Besides fixing the fence..." Tara looked meaningfully at Micah. "What else do we have to do before calling it a day?"

"Just the scarecrow shots," Micah replied. "I wanna get a few establishing shots while it's still twilight."

Tara nodded, taking another sip of water. "I'll be ready in five if you guys wanna go and make sure everything looks the way you want it."

"...Step ahead of you," Micah said, his voice coming from somewhere in the scarecrow path. Tara was always in awe at how fast Micah could move when he really wanted to. "Whoa, wait a minute..."

"What's up?" Saar asked as she picked her way through the maze toward her partner's voice.

"Did one of you guys screw with the scarecrows?"

"I didn't," Saar said. "Tara?"

"Nope," Tara responded. "Wouldn't move anything without clearing it with you guys and the Jensens."

"One of them must have done it then," Micah grumbled. "I *asked* them not to change anything without telling me. Now I have to re-visualize the rest of tonight's shots."

When Saar and Tara found Micah, he was standing before a trio of scarecrows that were, without a doubt, not there before. They hung, almost shoulder to shoulder, in a row, far removed from the others that made up the rudimentary path, showing a display of their own. Though still simple, these three were a bit more detailed than their siblings, with carefully painted faces and clothing that went a bit beyond the usual plaid shirt and farmer jeans. Instead, they dressed somewhat similar to the outfits the three students had worn when meeting the Jensens. Painted in coppery red across the figures' chests were a series of runes that looked to Micah like they may be Norse in origin, though he was no expert.

"Those old fuckers are screwing with us," Tara pointed out. "They gotta be."

"That's not even remotely funny," Saar muttered. "I'm gonna go have a talk with our hosts."

"No, wait!" Micah exclaimed. "We can ask about this later. Hell, it's probably a tribute to us or something, a little inside joke to chuckle at. I bet people who set stuff like this up put all sorts of Easter eggs into their displays."

"They still should have told us," Saar grunted in irritation. "This is creepy."

Micah and Tara nodded in agreement.

* * *

All of Noah's life had been like this for as long as he could remember. Lucas would come up with some crazy plot, which he would shoot down with what Lucas called 'good boy logic', only to find himself doing whatever madness had been suggested, to begin with.

It seemed like his life was about to repeat itself.

"Are you *crazy*?" Noah asked. "We'd get nailed and be in *so* much trouble for this one."

"Oh, c'mon, man. You know me better than that. I never get caught."

"But I do!" Noah insisted.

Lucas laughed. "I'll protect you, lil' buddy."

Noah hated it when Lucas called him things like that but never had the guts to tell him.

"How would we even pull this off?" Noah asked with the vain hope that this time would be different, that this time his friend would listen to the words of sanity.

"It's easy-cheesy." Lucas beamed. "All we gotta do is have a sleepover at your house tomorrow night. Your parents go to bed at stupid o'clock anyway, so we wait for that, then sneak out the window and ride our bikes to the Jensen place. I bet that iron fence they've got is super easy to climb too. So we will just hop over, take a look around, and then, when you're not so worried about the place anymore, we go back. That way, it won't be so scary on Halloween, and we can focus on just how cool it all is with everything going and people in costumes and stuff."

"I mean..."

"C'mon. It's not like we're gonna wreck anything. We're not that kinda kids."

And for once, Lucas was telling the truth. Of all the messes they've been in, Lucas has never intentionally damaged anything, never played mean tricks or stolen anything. He was trouble, all right, but not the bad kind.

"Well..."

"A deep subject, lil' buddy."

Noah rolled his eyes at this old joke. "I guess it wouldn't be so bad. And besides, I'm not afraid of the place anyway."

"So it should be no problem to sneak in then, right? It will probably only take an hour or so, and then we can come back, and I can kick your butt at *Blade Warriors*."

Noah, despite everything, found himself nodding in agreement.

* * *

"I don't know anything about scarecrows that look like you," Shem said. He then turned to his wife. "Do you?"

Mila shook her head. "Nope, I put some new stuff up, but nothing like that."

"We saw them." Micah looked at his friends. "All of us did, right?"

The girls nodded.

"Well, I know that sometimes your mind can play tricks on you out there, especially when it's all decorated," Shem remarked.

"I know mine has," Mila agreed.

"It wasn't a trick. They were wearing clothes just like ours."

"How about you show us what you saw?" Shem got up from his seat and started walking towards the scarecrow display.

"Yes. I bet the display won't look anything like you said now that you'd gotten a chance to really think about it," Mila said kindly before following her husband.

So they half-marched, an elderly couple in tow, to the place where they had been setting up their final shoot of the day, to the circle of scarecrows and the mysterious three...

"It was right here!" Micah almost shouted. "I *know it was.*"

"Well, there's nothing like that here now." Mila pointed out mildly.

Micah opened his mouth to speak, but Tara put a hand on his shoulder. After seeing the look on her face, Micah closed his mouth again and stood silently.

"Like I said before..." Shem started. "This place can play tricks on your mind, especially when it's all decorated like this."

* * *

Two days before Halloween

Micah had gone to bed shaken, his mind racing, his body jumping at every shadow. After finally falling asleep, however, he awoke feeling quite different.

Happy.

Hopeful.

Sure, last night's events had been a bit creepy, especially at night, but what a great bit of publicity for the movie!

Maybe he would even shoot another short film to present before the feature, a documentary about the odd events that had occurred during the filming. He certainly had enough subject matter, and it would be simple to interview the girls, get them acting all weirded out about everything, toss in some establishing shots of the farm, and some voice-over. He had a creepy bit of supplemental material. Hell, maybe he could even 'leak' the footage online, send it to one of those 'weird video' channels and see if it takes off organically from there.

He wondered if the Jensens would give an interview too, get them talking about how 'nothing happened' and edit it to make their answers creepy and mysterious. He couldn't imagine them being bothered by this, as it would probably drive even more traffic to their little Halloween show.

"You guys awake?" Saar asked, sleep still dripping from her voice.

"I am now," Tara mumbled.

"Yeah." Micah also joined. "I've been up for a while. I had a great idea..."

* * *

"Do you think they'll be all set up?" Lucas asked as his on-screen muscle man knocked Noah's scantily clad warrior woman to the ground.

"I don't know." Noah shrugged, half-heartedly putting in the command for his girl to stand up.

"I mean, it's close to Halloween; I'd think that most of the stuff would be out by now." Another barrage of onscreen strikes.

"I guess."

"You sure about this?" Lucas asked.

"Yeah."

Another barrage hits Noah's character, who falls to the ground once more.

"I know you, man. You ain't actin' normal. I mean, this is one of your favorite games, and you are hardly even playing. And it's like you don't even wanna talk about tonight."

"I told you, I'm fine." Noah put in a series of commands that made his warrior-woman do a pathetic-looking series of punches and kicks, which didn't even land.

Lucas paused the game. "Listen, if you really don't wanna go, we don't gotta. I mean, it's no big deal. Halloween is for little kids anyway."

"You don't mean that," Noah argued. "I know you well enough to know that you don't mean any of that, especially the part about Halloween."

After a moment, Lucas responded, "You're right."

The two boys fell silent again.

Finally, Lucas spoke, "This isn't about what I told you, right? The stuff about Deer-Head?"

Noah shook his head.

"'Cause if it was, you know I was screwing with you, right? Just trying to make it sound scarier than it was?"

Noah nodded. "Yeah."

"I mean, yeah, Julia said all that stuff, but she's nuts. You *know* she's nuts."

"Yeah."

"And I bet her sister is one of those girls that screams when she sees a worm; it probably doesn't take much to scare her."

"Right."

"So, do you still wanna do tonight?"

At that moment, Noah almost told his friend everything. He actually saw himself, in his mind's eye, unloading all of the secrets he held. Everything about the visions and feelings, about how he was always 'different' and had kept it silent so Lucas wouldn't think he was a freak. He almost told Lucas that no, he didn't want to go to the stupid farm... that he had already seen, actually seen, Deer-Head, and that even though it had only been a shadow, it was worse than they had ever imagined. Worse than the worst thing they had ever seen in one of their horror movies, worse than an awful boss monster in the scariest video games, probably even worse than the Devil in Lucas' parent's fire and brimstone God stories.

Instead, he just nodded his head. "Yeah, I still wanna do tonight."

* * *

The Jensens were nowhere to be found. Instead, a note was left on the kitchen table, written on a piece of flowery stationery in a neat, practiced hand.

Left to run errands.

Should be back late.

Food in the fridge.

Have fun with your shoot today!

M & S

"Well, damn," Micah muttered, choking down the urge to crumple the note into a little ball. Instead, he set it carefully back down on the table, as close to its original position as he was capable.

"We'll catch 'em later," Saar said. "I mean, how late can two old people even stay out?"

"We should be taking this time to shoot anyway," Tara reminded. "It's not like we have a ton of time left if they want us out before Halloween."

"Yeah, you're right," Micah agreed. "Let's get rolling."

* * *

Noah was supposed to be brushing his teeth; instead, he was standing in the bathroom, trying to keep himself together.

You need to stop this. Noah thought to himself. *You know that things are going to be bad if you sneak out.*

Noah took a deep breath, trying to center his thoughts. He focused on the faint sounds of the video game that Lucas was still playing up in the bedroom, hoping that the familiarity of the digitized noise would help calm him. But, instead, it seemed to give a mad cadence to his worry, causing it to dance untethered through his mind.

"My visions could be wrong," he shouted to himself. "It could have just been a dream. I was scared."

You know it wasn't a scary dream. It was a vision. And you also *know that your visions are never wrong, never, not once.*

Behind Noah, the shower curtain moved. It was a subtle movement like a gentle breeze blowing the vinyl, but he knew there was no such breeze.

Something was behind the curtain, trying to stand still and failing, like an over-excited child playing hide and seek.

"You're not real," he screamed, turning to face the curtain. "You're just in my head."

Suddenly, the curtain bulged, like something standing in the bathtub had struck it violently. At that moment, a shadow appeared tall and grotesquely shaped, with large antlers reaching to the ceiling from its oblong head.

Then, there was a rapid banging on the bathroom door.

And the shadow was gone.

The curtain stopped waving.

"Hey, man. You okay?" It was Lucas' voice.

"Yeah," Noah replied, trying to even his breathing. "I'll be right out."

"I gotta use the facility."

"Cool. I'll be out in a second."

"Yeah. Your folks are getting ready for bed too, so... yeah."

Noah nodded and then realized that his friend couldn't see him and repeated again. "I'll be right out."

He knew that no matter the visions he received, no matter the knots in his stomach, he wouldn't deny his friend tonight. They were going to sneak out, and they were going to sneak into Jensen's Farm.

* * *

It was now nine o'clock, and the Jensens still hadn't returned home. The filming had gone quite well, and since they would have no problem finishing the shoot the next day, the students were in good spirits.

"I hope nothing happened to them," Saar said.

"I'm sure they're fine," Micah responded. "Probably got carried away on their 'big trip to town' and lost track of time."

"I don't know; I'm kinda worried," Saar said playing with her fingers.

"They are pretty old..." Tara added.

"Yeah, but they're still pretty sharp," Micah reminded. "I'm telling you, they just got carried away. They probably stopped somewhere for a late dinner or some drinks."

"They should have called us, let us know they were going to be this late," Saar chastised.

"What are we, their parents, now?" Micah scowled. "And besides, do you think those fossils have cell phones?"

"Probably not," Saar agreed. "But..."

Their conversation was interrupted by two noises outside. Small, soft thuds, one after another, came from somewhere in the backyard.

"What the hell was that?" Tara hissed, jumping up from the overstuffed couch.

"Maybe it's the Jensens," Saar said, walking toward the house's back-facing window.

"Why would the Jensens be back there?" Micah pondered. "And why wouldn't we have heard their car pull in?"

Micah and Tara joined Saar at the back window as she pulled back the curtains.

"What... the... crap?" Saar almost shouted and the others stood in silent agreement.

The scarecrows were back, the ones that looked like them.

They were standing right outside the window, posed to appear as if they were peering inside.

* * *

Lucas cleared the fence without a problem, landing on the other side with a soft thump. Seconds later, he was joined by Noah, who had taken that short period of time to attempt to choke down the last vestiges of doubt and fear that twined around his heart and stomach, making him feel like he was at the top of a roller-coaster hill waiting for the inevitable descent.

"We're in," Lucas whispered, taking on the voice of one of the television military heroes as he flicked on his penlight, covering the lens with the palm of his hand, so it gave a bit of light while still being hooded.

Noah didn't intend to turn his flashlight on, half convinced that the almost silent *click* would bring people running from miles around, but with the beam of his friend's light covered in the way it was, there was not nearly enough light without it. So nervously, he clicked his light on. Nobody came running.

"Wow, this place *is* pretty cool," Lucas was clearly impressed.

"I bet it's cooler with all the lights and stuff on," Noah said. "Maybe we should just go back home."

"Naaa. The whole point of this is seeing everything without all that stuff, so you can see it before it gets all scary and won't have to worry when we come back on Halloween with all the actors running around, remember?"

"I don't know. It's kinda scarier this way," Noah complained. To him, the odd shadows and relative silence made the hundreds of looming figures seem real in a way he imagined they wouldn't when properly lit.

"But we came all this way, snuck out of your house, hopped the fence, and now you wanna go back? Without seeing anything? The hard part is over, man."

"I guess so," Noah agreed halfheartedly.

"Yeah, let's check it out," Lucas spun around to take everything in. "This farm is really awesome, huh?"

And it *was* pretty cool. The part of Noah that loved Halloween, loved all things horror and macabre, admitted such, even as the other part of him shrank back, begged him to turn around, hop back over the fence, and leave. *We need to just look around a little.* This brave part, filled with Freddys and Draculas, Godzillas and Jasons, whispered. *You'll regret it if you don't.*

So Noah looked around and, honestly, was impressed. He had expected the usual, old clothes stuffed with newspapers and leaves, topped with drugstore masks wrapped over basketballs, and though such things were present, the majority of figures were of higher quality, many of them looking like they were made from department store mannequins, repainted and dressed until they became the stuff of nightmares.

Most impressive, however, were the scarecrows. It seemed like every inch of the huge farm lot that wasn't the setting for a particular scene was full of scarecrows, all of them hanging on their own crossbars. In one section, it even appeared that rows and rows of scarecrows set the boundaries of the path that viewers were supposed to walk, though from where Noah stood, he couldn't see where it led.

You're not a kid anymore. Noah's brave voice—which honestly sounded a bit like Lucas—shouted. *You need to stop thinking that nightmares are anything special. They're just bad dreams, and you aren't a superhero.*

"Let's see where all those old scarecrows lead," Noah spoke up, trying to sound somewhat braver.

Lucas smiled and patted him on the shoulder. "Right on, man!"

* * *

"Not fucking funny, guys!" Tara shouted, projecting her voice like a community theater actress, making sure she was heard by anyone that might be lurking in the woods with wrinkled hands covering laughing mouths.

"Really? This is getting old," Saar growled, voice not quite as loud but doubly angry. She turned to look at Micah and was surprised to see that he was filming with one of their hand cameras, sweeping the lens between the girls and the scarecrows, making sure to take everything in.

"Seriously?" Tara asked, trying to snatch the camera from her friend.

"Awww come on," Micah begged, excitement bleeding from his voice. "Don't you see? This is great!"

"Yeah, really wonderful," Saar fumed, turning away from the window and beginning to roll up her sleeping bag.

"What are you doing?" Micah asked, spinning around so the camera was pointing at Saar. "We can't leave yet!"

"The Hell we can't!" Saar snorted. She had finished with her sleeping bag in record time and now was angrily shoving her things into her backpack.

"We aren't done filming yet," Micah argued. "We have a couple of crucial scenes for tomorrow."

"We can film somewhere else," Saar said with finality. "I'm out."

Micah swung the camera to face Tara. "You're gonna stay, right?"

Tara shook her head. "I don't like this, Micah."

"C'mon. This is actually really cool," Micah pleaded. "I was thinking about all of this, and I think this will make everything so much cooler. We can shoot the movie like planned, but tack all of this stuff on at the end, make it a film within a film! Remember those guys in the '70s? The ones that made that movie, *Snuff?* They started with a terrible biker movie that wasn't gonna make any money at all, tacked on some footage that made it look like the actress was actually killed, and then rode the controversy to success! We can do something like that, and we don't even gotta fake it!"

The girls looked at each other and then at Micah.

"If it gets any weirder, we're gone," Saar informed him.

"If it gets any weirder, I'll drive us out of here myself," Micah promised, putting a hand over his heart. "Besides, what can the Jensens do to us? They're just old people... they're just old people."

Tara sighed and slopped down on her sleeping bag. Saar, rolling her eyes, began to unpack.

Micah was right; this *could* work for them.

* * *

As they picked their way through the darkened yard, Noah began to feel better. Surely, if something were going to assault them, something huge with horns that cradled the sky, it would have by now. Maybe, for the first time ever, Noah's vision was just that, a phantasm with no meaning beyond his over-stimulated, horror-obsessed mind.

Maybe that's all it ever was. Noah's mind insisted. *Maybe you just imagined the connections.* Noah thought eht about all the times he had heard something mentioned, a certain colored car, a particular design on a t-shirt, and then saw it everywhere he looked. Like it had been conjured by the simple action of drawing his attention to it, even though the thing had been there the whole time. *Maybe your 'visions' were just you noticing things.*

The boys walked past another display, this one depicting an insane-looking dentist and his terrified victim, and stopped.

"I think that's it," Lucas said. "I think we saw everything. Feeling better?"

Noah nodded. Not only was he feeling better, he felt like something had fundamentally changed within him, like he had, for lack of a better term, grown up a bit that night.

"Wait," Lucas said, stopping Noah. "We haven't seen *everything* yet."

"Oh? What did we miss?"

"Probably the coolest thing." Lucas made an exaggerated gesture, pointing past Noah, who turned to look. The path of scarecrows, which the boys had been basically ignoring in their wild explorations, terminated just beyond their field of vision.

"We never walked to the end of the path," Lucas spoke excitedly. "I bet it leads to something cool, prolly where they keep Deer-Head!"

Where they keep Deer-Head...

Noah shivered, a twinge of old anxiety snaking back into his body.

"C'mon, man. Let's go!" Lucas grabbed Noah by the arm and raced down the path, observed by rows and rows of featureless figures passively bound to their crosses. Finally, they reached the end of the path.

There stood in front of them a small building, a large shed really, its lone front window covered with black construction paper. Scrawled on the door, in dripping red paint, were two words.

THE LAIR

"Too cool." Lucas turned to Noah for confirmation.

"I don't know. It just looks like a shed to me." Noah was suddenly struck with a thought as abrupt as his visions, though far less visual. He knew, without a shadow of a doubt, that whatever was going to happen to them, whatever event the warnings had been about, was going to happen there, in this simple shed. It was as though a voice was screaming in his head over and over again.

NO! NO! NO! NO!

Lucas made his way to the door, carefully pulling to test it. "Aww man, it's locked." He turned and looked at Noad with a pouting face.

"Oh well." Noah tried to sound uninterested. "We better get back home before my parents wake up and come to check on us or something."

Then suddenly, the shed door swung open, nearly striking Lucas in the back of the head.

"Whoa," Lucas mumbled. "Crazy."

"Yeah... crazy."

"Let's go!" Lucas had a huge, goofy smile on his face, which made him look even younger than his age.

"No." Noah almost yelled.

"What?!"

"I said no." Noah tried to sound tough and firm. He tried to channel every strict teacher, every no-nonsense mall security guard, and every hard-nailed cop in every movie he had ever seen. "We aren't even supposed to be here; I'm not going to go into a locked building."

Lucas blinked once.

Twice.

Took a deep breath.

"Fine," he snapped. Noah had never heard his friend, usually happy-go-lucky and rakish, sound so upset. "Stay here then. I'll be back in two seconds."

"No, man. Don't."

Lucas turned away from Noah, shaking his head. Before Noah could do anything, his friend stepped into the darkness beyond the previously locked door and was gone.

"I swear to God, man," Noah said, feeling even older than he had. "Come back here, or I won't be your friend anymore."

No response from the darkness.

"I'm not joking..."

Nothing.

"We're done, man. Just come back here..."

No answer.

Tears in his eyes, Noah took a step and then another.

The darkness of the shed ate him as well.

* * *

The Night before Halloween

No scripted footage was shot that day. Instead, the students spent the day going over every inch of the farm with a fine-toothed comb. If asked, none of them would have been able to tell you what precisely they were looking for, only that they were searching.

Micah, in particular, was man obsessed. With a hand camera plastered to his face, he scanned not only the props and motifs set up on the vast farm property but the contents of the house itself.

When he began to film the Jensens bedroom, throwing open wardrobes and closets, Tara tried to stop him. She cited privacy and ethics, the old rules that have guided filmmakers for decades, but the manic look on his face had frightened her, and she quickly stopped, going back to her own, far less intrusive searches.

They gathered as the sun went down, bringing with it an almost wintry chill. The Jensens still hadn't returned, dashing any fantasies the students might have had about them going on an adorable extended night on the town.

"Did anybody find anything?" Saar asked. "I got *bubkis.*"

"I'm not even sure what we're looking for, to be honest," Tara admitted. Even so, she had been caught up in a frenzy, hoping that things would start making sense if she was just proactive and kept rolling.

"I wanna get into the shed," Micah said. Part of his face was still behind the hand camera, its red light still illuminated, even though neither of the girls had seen him recharge its battery.

"We *tried* that," Tara reminded him, and they had. Micah had even tried to smash the padlock off the door with a boom-mic stand before being pulled away by the others.

"I wanna try again."

"Why are you still filming?" Tara finally asked. "Are we really that interesting, sitting here tired and dirty?"

Micah nodded the camera's red-eye bobbing before him. "You are. You guys are the story. I'm the story."

"We're supposed to be shooting a horror movie, remember? A made-up horror movie. We didn't even finish that, and we're gonna have to leave when the sun comes up," Tara reprimanded.

"If the Jensens even come home by then," Saar croaked. "If not, we might want to contact the cops."

"Yeah, yeah. I'll call 'em myself," Micah muttered, angling the camera so it could frame Tara's face against the backdrop of the scarecrows, still playing sentinel outside the window. "I just wanna get back into the shed."

"I'm not liking this whole thing," Tara growled. "We're tearing through these poor people's *home*. For all we know, they're on the side of the road dead or something."

"I don't think so," Micah said without any care.

"Oh yeah? Why not?" Tara arched an eyebrow. The other students knew this was a signal that she was gearing up for a fight.

"Because I think they're in the shed," Micah stated simply.

"In the shed?" Tara asked, her voice sarcastic.

"Yes. 'In the shed'," Micah mocked. "Coming out just long enough to move stuff around and screw with us."

"Why would they even do that?" Saar chimed in.

"Because they like screwing with people." Micah turned the camera toward Saar as he spoke. "I mean, who runs a place like this unless they like messing with people's heads?"

Tara deflated somewhat. Micah might have lost his mind and might be acting like an obsessive artist from a bad Lovecraft story, but his explanation *did* make sense.

"Alright, guys. How about this?" Saar asked, putting on her best mama bear voice. "You and Tara go out and check the shed one last time, and I start rounding up our gear, putting everything away. If the Jensens aren't in the shed and don't come back by the time you guys do, we take off and tell someone."

Tara thought for a minute before responding, "Alright, so say we break into the shed, and they aren't there. And then they show up with some wild story about what has taken them so long? I don't think they'll be too happy."

Micah nodded, turning the camera back to Tara. "Well, then we apologize and offer to buy a new lock for the shed."

This plan had a mollifying effect on the students, and they began to prepare for their individual tasks. Micah had actually set the camera down for a minute, but Tara noticed its red eye was still alight from the bookshelf where it rested. They were about to head out when they heard Saar's voice from the other room, loudly shouting a series of profanities that would not have been out of place in a shipyard, and Tara ran back into the room they had used as a base camp. Taking a moment to retrieve his camera, Micah followed.

"Someone trashed our shit." Saar faltered. She was standing in what appeared to be the aftermath of a tornado. Pieces of metal and plastic littered the floor, intermixed with what looked like miles of wire, frayed and cut.

Not cut. Tara's mind insisted. *It looks chewed.*

"We are in so much deep shit with the school," Saar fretted, sounding like she was on the edge of tears. "This is thousands of dollars of gear..."

"I'm going to fucking kill them," Tara fumed, fists balled at her sides.

"Kill who, darlings?" The mature but somehow melodic voice that came from the direction of the farmhouse's front doors was unmistakably familiar.

It was the voice of Mila Jensen.

* * *

At first, Noah was surrounded by darkness, his little flashlight doing nothing to break through the gloom. His eyes adjusted quickly, however, what he saw was astonishing.

The rest of the farm was pretty cool, he had to admit, with its careful attention to detail and the overall quality of the props. However, it all held an air of artifice, a falseness that betrayed the fact that it was really just all for fun, a gag for Halloween.

The scene inside The Lair was different.

The walls were covered in branches, twisted and knotted around each other making strange patterns that almost looked like foreign words. Here and there, amidst the tangle, Noah saw other things, more animal than plant, scattered antlers, hooves, and yes, even bone. All of these were bound to the branches with tanned leather. Unlit torches also hung from the walls, and Noah wondered if they would give illumination during the show tomorrow, even though he knew you weren't supposed to have a real fire at things like this.

On the floor stood several adult-sized figures, features obscured with white robes and hoods. Noah found himself looking at these figures over and over again, assuring his racing imagination that they were, in fact, no more real than the less realistic props outside.

Hesitantly, Noah moved forward, the fragile blade of light created by his flashlight cutting deeper into the darkness. Taking a few steps forward, the light revealed Lucas, and Noah let out a sigh of relief. His friend was, in fact, here and hadn't been eaten by the awful darkness or anything that dwelled within it.

But something was wrong.

Noah figured he'd find his friend standing there, hands cockily on his hips, a goofy smile on his face as he checked out this new tableau. But, instead, Lucas was on his knees, head bowed. He was rocking back and forth and muttering something over and over again that Noah couldn't quite make out.

"Luc!" Noah called his voice somewhere between a strange whisper and a quiet shout.

Lucas didn't answer.

"Lucas?"

Nothing.

"Hey, dumb ass!" Noah figured that Lucas would react to his usually proper friend swearing, nodding, and smiling, maybe even turning and patting Noah on his shoulder, talking about how 'His little buddy was all growed up'. or some other nonsense. But, instead, Lucas just kept rocking, muttering.

Noah walked even closer to Lucas, the flashlight penetrating even further, revealing more of the room. Lucas was kneeling before a large throne, and sitting on the throne, huge and powerful, was another figure.

It was Deer-Head.

And it looked just as it had in Noah's visions.

* * *

The three students whirled to face the voice. There in the doorway stood the Jensens, but instead of the normal flannel and denim outfits worn by farm people worldwide, they wore crisp white robes, hoods obscuring their hair and most of their faces.

They don't look frail anymore. Tara thought to herself. *They used to move and stand like old people, healthy old people, sure, but still old people.*

Now...

"Where were you guys?" Saar asked, feeling a little uneasy.

"We had to make some preparations," Shem responded.

"Sorry to be rude," Mila added. "We didn't figure it would take so long."

"Preparations for what?" Tara questioned. She glanced toward her friends and was unsurprised to notice that Micah was still filming, shooting the robed figures and then panning back to his classmates to get their reactions. Tara had a sudden urge to tear the camera from his hands and smash it against the wall until it was as much a pile of useless parts as the rest of their gear, screaming the whole time.

"Why, for the ritual, dear." Mila smiled, but something was different about it now.

"I thought you'd figure that part out by now," Shem said. "You being smart, city college kids and all."

"Maybe you should explain it to us," Micah prodded, his voice cold, passionless. It was the sort of voice that one put on while conducting an interview.

"Micah..." Saar hissed. "Maybe we should..."

"No, I want to hear this," Micah insisted.

The old couple looked at each other and smiled, then turned their attention back to Micah.

"I think we already did, dear." The smile on Mila's face did not falter. "Way back at the beginning, when you first came to us."

"The elves, you mean?" Micah asked. "The... what did you call them?"

"The *Alven*," Shem replied. "Yes, this is all about the *Alven*."

"Micah. We need to *go*." Tara tried to pull him by the arm, but he didn't budge.

"I'm afraid not, dear-heart." Mila shook her head. "I'm afraid that you aren't going anywhere until we get this whole thing settled."

"And one of you isn't going anywhere, ever." When Shem spoke these words, his voice didn't change at all.

It should have been easy. Even without Micah's help, two healthy young women should not have had any problems pushing past two septuagenarians. However, when Tara and Saar surged forward, it was as though they had hit twin brick walls. Without putting forth any sort of visual effort, Mila and Shem were able to hold them in place by simply placing firm hands on their shoulders. No matter how much they struggled, they could not move forward.

"Micah!" Saar shouted, but their friend simply stood there behind the camera's red light, filming the unlikely event that was occurring before him.

"Now, now, kids. Please hear us out. We aren't monsters." Shem's voice was calm, almost friendly, the voice of a man who was talking to a troublesome neighbor he didn't wish to offend.

"The *Alven,* however, are," Mila said with a laugh. "And that's why we need you, young folk."

"At least one of you," Shem added.

* * *

It's just a statue. Noah thought to himself, with something like disappointment. Sure, with the visions and bad feelings, everything had been a bit scary, but nothing bad had really happened. Lucas was right there, and though he was acting weird—no big surprise there—he was unharmed. This whole thing had just been a spooky adventure, the sort that kids were supposed to have at Noah's age, and now he was standing right in front of the thing he had feared most; it was just a statue. And not even a very good one.

Its body was a mannequin, the sort that was stark white, with chiseled chest muscles and six-pack abs. The old people that ran this place had placed it in a sitting position on the ornately carved throne and put a cloak over it, but it was still glaringly obvious that a mannequin was all it ever was and all it would ever be. The mannequin's head had been removed and replaced with a work of taxidermy, a snarling deer head with wild, rolling marble eyes. It was a little startling, sure, but compared to what Noah had been expecting, it was nothing.

The whole place was nothing, really.

Just a goof for Halloween.

"C'mon, Lucas. We saw it; now, let's go home."

Lucas didn't respond. Instead, he just knelt there, head bowed.

"Lucas?" Noah placed a hand on his friend's shoulder. "Let's go."

"No," Lucas said. His voice sounded weird like it was coming from the bottom of a swimming pool. "Can't you *hear* him? He wants us to stay."

"Knock it off, dork-face. It's not funny." For the first time, maybe in his entire life, Noah wasn't scared. In fact, he was a little bit annoyed.

"*Listen!*" Lucas pleaded, his voice becoming more insistent but still just as weird and distant. "He's talking to me. Come down here, and he'll talk to you too!"

"Come off it, moron. He's not talking to you. He's just a stupid doll."

"*Sometimes* he is," Lucas agreed. "But he's not right now."

"That's it, I'm gone," Noah said, turning to leave his friend. If Lucas wanted to be a dork, he could do it all alone in the darkness.

The shed door slammed shut to the sound of soft, melodic laughter.

Noah's flashlight flickered and then went out.

He heard the sounds of something moving, something standing up in the darkness and making its halting way toward him.

Something much larger than Lucas.

* * *

"You see, the *Alven* are all about transactions," Shem spoke, his voice calm. It was as though he was discussing something as simple as the local sports team, a trifling conversation to pass the time. "If we do something for them, they do something for us."

"More importantly," Mila chimed in, "If we *don't* do something for them, they *will* do something to us, and as we've discussed before, they can be quite... troublesome when they put their mind to it." Her voice was as calm and rational as that of her husband.

"So what, you're gonna give them one of us?" Tara asked. She had long since stopped struggling against the seemingly unbreakable grip of her elderly captor.

"Yes, dear," Mila said simply.

"What do they even want with us?" Saar asked. Tara noticed that she had not stopped struggling, but it was getting her nowhere.

"I don't rightly know." Shem shrugged. He had been silent for a moment before speaking as if pondering. "And I don't rightly think that it's any of our concern."

Tara's eyes moved to Micah, who was still silently filming the scene. "Are you seriously going to just stand there?" She sneered. "These people are talking about fucking killing us!"

"I gotta get this," Micah stated, his voice distant like it was coming to them from the opposite end of a long tunnel. "I have to."

"I'm pretty sure you don't." Saar scoffed. She jerked suddenly to surprise her captor, but, like everything else she had attempted in the past few minutes, it made little difference.

"What's the matter?" Micah still sounded distant, but his voice had taken on a bit of a sarcastic edge. "Isn't this the sort of thing you go for? You're always watching those Kenneth Anger movies, with all the rituals and stuff, and now you get to live one."

"Do any of you want to volunteer?" Shem asked, looking at Tara, who he still held in his grip.

"Bite me," Tara responded hatefully.

Shem sighed. "Always the way..."

"It'd be so much easier if people just accepted things," Mila claimed. "It would only take one selfless individual... I guess we should get this started. It will be midnight soon and a new day."

"Halloween," Micah sounded lost again. "What a wonderful day!"

* * *

Noah had felt this before.

It was the same feeling he had countless times, huddled under the false safety of blankets, pillow gripped tensely in his arms, head filled with whatever phantasmagoria his morbid curiosity had caused him to fill his day with this time. Only it was much worse now because the thing threatening him, the shadowy thing, was not made up. It was not something conjured from a movie, video game, or even the lurid cover of one of the paperback books that leered at him from the grocery store shelves.

It was a real monster.

No vision, real or imagined, but really real.

It was Deer-Head.

The beast knelt down before Noah, horns still towering over the child's small form. It placed one powerful hand on Noah's shoulder in a gesture not unlike that of a kindly grandfather, and then, it spoke. It took Noah a moment to realize that the voice, deep and powerful, wasn't coming from the creature at all but from Lucas.

Even so, it was obvious who was speaking.

"Child," the voice said, "What brings you here on this night?"

"I..." Noah's voice halted; whatever he was about to say was stifled by fear.

"It is alright, child," The Deer-Head voice assured Noah. "I have no cause to harm you. Children are sacred, after all." The beast squeezed Noah's shoulder slightly, and surprisingly, he found himself comforted.

"Have your elders chosen you?" The thing asked, something like reproach in its rich voice.

"I... I just wanted to see the Farm..." Noah stuttered. "I don't even know what's going on."

"Your elders offered a sacrifice this night, and you and your friend came here. Am I to believe this is a simple coincidence?"

"I don't know!" Noah found himself close to crying but managed to hold it back. "I don't even know who these *elders* are!"

The beast let go of Noah's shoulder and made its way back to the throne, carefully stepping around Lucas' kneeling form. Then it sat down, majestically moving in a form that wasn't meant to move at all.

"We have been promised a sacrifice, in the terms laid out long ago, when the elders to your elders first settled these lands. Yet I do not believe that the two of you are said sacrifice. My subjects tell me that there are others, more fitting."

Noah didn't know what to say, so he didn't say anything for a moment. Finally, however, his curiosity got the better of him.

"Subjects?" he asked.

Deer-Head nodded, vast horns scraping the ceiling as he did so. "A great many of us have come this night, one for each of the *puppetje* your elders have built."

Noah didn't know the word *puppetje*, but he could figure it out enough to get the idea, and it sent yet another spike of terror into his heart, which was already slamming against his chest like an enraged animal.

The displays were all alive. Each one was filled with things like Deer-Head.

* * *

Effortlessly, the Jensens took their young prisoners from the house to a spot behind it, somewhere in the vast field of gaudy phantasmagoria. Tara put up a token struggle to no avail, and Saar didn't even bother. Like a loyal dog, Micah followed along, the camera taking in the entire thing.

*It's like he's not in control anymore...*Tara thought to herself as Shem carefully arranged her in front of a row of scarecrows. *It's like something is guiding him with a wireless remote. There is no way he'd be acting like this if he was in control.*

Saar's thoughts, on the other hand, were far from Micah's strange behavior. Instead, she was paying attention to the scarecrows. Though she tried to convince herself that it was her imagination, she could no longer force her mind to deceive itself. When they had entered this part of the display, the scarecrow's heads had been haphazardly arranged, left untethered and at the mercy of the sometimes harsh New York winds. Now they were all uniform, all tilted at a slight angle as if to demonstrate curiosity.

They had all turned their heads to watch them while she wasn't looking.

"I wouldn't dare run anywhere," Mila advised kindly. "It wouldn't do any good and only tire you out."

"We'd catch you," Shem added. "Or *they* would."

"What did you do to Micah?" Tara finally managed to put words to a question that had been flickering through her head since the Jensens came back home.

"Why, nothing, dear," Mila smiled innocently. "Nothing at all."

"The *Alven* can have quite the effect on people," Shem defended them. "Some more than others."

"I don't know what you mean," Saar asked, furrowing her brows.

"What happened to him?"

"Nothing happened to me," Micah responded instead of the elderly couple. "I just want to get this, is all. It's going to blow *minds*!"

"He's being controlled, isn't he?" Tara stated matter-of-factly. She eyed the field behind her, wondering how much space she could put between herself and the Jensens if she broke into a sprint. She wasn't the most athletic person on Earth, but she was a lot younger, and that had to count for something.

All at once, Tara's mind filled with images of hands, of gloves stuffed with straw and wireframes wrapped in skin-like latex, all grasping at her as she ran; fingers that weren't meant to bend and twist doing so; blank faces, some almost real and some simply painted, leering at her as she was ensnared.

I don't know if my mind could take that. Tara thought to herself. *I think it would be just enough to send me off to Happy La-La Land for good.*

She didn't run.

"No," Shem's firm voice caught Tara's attention, reminding her of the question that Tara had forgotten she had asked. "Not controlled *per se.*"

"The *Alven*, from what I can tell, are all about desires," Mila said. "They like to feed off of us, especially when we want something really badly."

"Say you like hamburgers," Shem started to explain. "I mean, really, really enjoy them, Okay? You're sitting at home, watching television, not thinking about hamburgers at all, at least not with the front of your mind... the... what's it called, dear?"

"The conscious," Mila offered.

"Yes, that's it! Your conscious mind isn't thinking about them at all, but somewhere, deep down, all you want in the world is a hamburger, right?"

"Sure," Saar nodded, a little confused; not sure where this was going, but hoping that if she could get them talking, get them to pay more attention to their words than their captives, a situation would present itself that could lead to escape.

"Now, you're watching television, and your show is interrupted by commercials," Shem started to explain. "One of these commercials has a shot of a big, juicy burger, all fresh and flame boiled. Suddenly, a burger is all you can think of, right?"

"We've all been there," Mila said with a smile.

"The *Alven* are or can be anyway, like that commercial. And I think that for your friend, this movie project is just like that hamburger." Shem finished with a satisfied nod.

"It's going to be so great," Micah murmured, voice still underwater.

"Now, let's get to this," Mila announced.

From within their robes, the old couple produced simple white masks with the same odd lettering on them that had been on the doppelganger scarecrows. Tara noticed that Shem's mask had horns while Mila's did not.

The Jensens put on the masks and began to chant.

* * *

Noah felt something pressing on his mind, far back in the place where his spinal column fused with his skull. The sensation somehow reminded him of a moth flapping madly against the glass surrounding a streetlight. He realized at that moment whatever this thing was, it wanted inside of him, wanted to take him over, as another of its kind had undoubtedly taken Lucas. He also realized that, unlike Lucas, he could stop it from coming inside.

Am I stronger than Lucas? Noah's mind wondered, and then more bizarrely, *Have I always been stronger? Was Lucas pretending to be tough and cool? Was he actually just as scared as me? Even more so? Was the Devil-May-Care attitude just a mask, as fake as those that stare from the Seasonal racks at Walgreens every October?*

"Stop it!" Noah hissed, with steel in his voice. "And leave Lucas alone too."

The mind flutter stopped. And in the darkness, Noah saw Lucas' cold blue eyes focus, looking around with confusion.

"Leave the others alone too. Whoever you were talking about before, the people that are 'more worthy', let them go."

From behind Noah, Deer-Head laughed. It was a deep laugh from the bowels of the thing's powerful belly. It was the laugh that he imagined would be laughed by one of the pagan gods he had learned about in school, Zeus maybe, or Odin.

"You demand much," Deer-Head mocked. "For such a small child."

"I do," Noah agreed. He wasn't sure where all of this strength was coming from. But he imagined it had something to do with everything that had happened that night—from sneaking over the fence to the realization that the static, narrow world he was told he lived in was a lie. And finally, the realization that Lucas, once a signal-flare of power in his little life, was just as confused and scared as he was.

Noah, at that moment, had grown up.

"A deal is a deal," Deer-Head announced. "And this deal was sealed decades before your parents were born. 'For prosperity and success in the coming year, one must be taken'. "

"Maybe," Noah negotiated. "But I don't think you have to hurt anyone."

Lucas blinked again and stood up, his awed gaze never leaving Deer-Head.

"You are correct," Deer-Head agreed. "It is your elders that have always insisted on bloodshed. Though we do enjoy such vulgarity... it is not necessary."

Lucas spoke up then, and the words out his mouth stunned everyone involved, be they human or *Alven*.

* * *

Tara and Saar both struggled when the Jensens bound them, kicking, biting, and flailing like caged beasts. But, no matter how they struggled, it was in vain as they found themselves tethered to wooden poles, just two more decorations in the vast diorama that was Jensen's Farm on Halloween.

Micah still stood unbound, still recording, making no attempt to flee.

Mila knelt for a moment, taking a few deep breaths. Then Shem put a gentle hand on her shoulder.

"You alright, ma?" he asked.

Mila nodded. "Yes, dear. I'm fine. Just not twenty-five. This gets harder every time, even with *their* help."

Shem patted her shoulder before letting go. "This would be so much easier if they'd just listen to us. If one of them would just give in without a struggle."

"If wishes were horses," Mila stood back up with her usual kind smile. "Beggars would ride."

"So, which one of you will it be?" Shem asked. "Or do we have to just pick one of you?"

"Micah," Tara replied coldly. "How about you take Micah?"

"Yeah," Saar said, shooting daggers from her eyes.

"I don't think they will," Micah said. "I think they like that I'm recording this."

Mila and Shem looked at each other for a moment and then at the rows of scarecrows as if for confirmation.

"Unless he wishes to volunteer?" Shem turned expectantly to Micah.

"I'm good," Micah gave a dismissive wave. In front of his face, the camera light continued to glow, despite its constant use without charging.

* * *

"I want to go with them," Lucas revealed. His voice was that of a much younger child, a child meeting Santa Claus for the first time, or perhaps a beloved celebrity. It was a voice free of cynicism, free of the weights and chains that bogged down a person with age. If the surrounding events weren't so terrible, Noah would have been happy to hear such a voice coming from his best friend, but here it was somehow surreal and disturbing.

"Have you lost it?!" Noah hissed. "What are you saying?!"

"I'm *saying* that I want to go with Deer-Head and the others." Lucas pouted a bit, adding to the de-aging effect. "I hate it here."

"Lucas," Noah called out, wishing that he could say something more, something that showed all of the feelings in his young heart, all of the confusion and fear, and yes, all of the affection too. He wanted to say he had taken this friendship for granted all these years, just assumed that his best friend, with his trouble and humor, his goofy grin, and loyalty, would always be at his side. Instead, he just said the boy's name again.

"Lucas."

"No, man. I'm serious. I hate it here. I hate how much my parents try to control me, try to make me something that I'm not. I hate that I always have to be tough and cool, even though on the inside, I just want to cry and throw a fit sometimes, you know?"

Noah knew very well.

Deer-Head knelt before Lucas, so his grotesque face—no longer a taxidermy piece, now something both more and less than that—was on an even level with the boy.

"Don't hurt him," Noah muttered, feeling powerless.

"I told you before, there is no need for bloodshed," Deer-Head reminded Noah. "That is an invention of your Elders and their limited understanding of sacrifice. Now, do you mean your words, child? Truly and honestly mean them?"

Lucas nodded his head.

* * *

Shem pulled a coin from the pocket of his jeans, which he wore under the white cloak. It was a half-penny that he had found as a boy and, for reasons that only made sense to a young child, had kept with him his entire life.

"Since nobody wants to make any decisions here, it's the only way," Shem said. Mila nodded in agreement, and he flipped the battered copper coin into the air. The coin came back down on his palm, the face of Lady Liberty facing up.

"Guess it's your lucky day." He said to Saar, pulling the cloak's hood over his head. Mila did the same, also producing a wicked-looking dagger from her cloak's folds. The couple began to mutter in a language that sounded to the captives a bit like Dutch but much, much older, more weighty, and primal.

Saar redoubled her efforts to escape, pulling and straining against the ropes that bound her to the pole to no avail, noticing that Tara had stopped struggling entirely and now wore the same vacant look as Micah.

Then Tara and Micah began to chant as well, their dopey voices adding to the Jensens'. Finally, Shem raised the dagger and brought it against Saar's throat, pressing slightly into the tender flesh as the chanting reached a crescendo.

Suddenly, a hand reached out and grabbed Shem's, preventing him from making the killing cut. He turned quizzically toward the owner of the hand, which was not his wife's, nor was it the unbound film student. Instead, it belonged to one of the scarecrows, which had somehow freed itself from its cross-bar and now stood, under its own power, next to the old man.

"Stop," The scarecrow commanded. Its voice was the high and clear peal of a young girl. "It is done."

* * *

"Are you crazy?!" Noah asked. "You don't even know what these... these *things* are!"

"They won't hurt me," Lucas assured his best friend.

"How do you know?"

"I just do, okay?"

"I told you true before... no harm or bloodshed is necessitated in this exchange." Deer-Head's voice broke into the conversation.

"But... I'll miss you, man." Noah knew that his words were an understatement, but he also knew how important they were and how powerful they could be if received properly.

The tears that formed in Lucas' eyes meant that it had been enough.

"I... I can't stay here, man. Besides you, there's nothing here for me. My parents are nuts, and you know that."

"I know. But you have lots of friends. At school, you're always surrounded by kids!"

"And they don't mean a thing," Lucas said a bit sadly. "I just pretend to be what they want, and they follow me around. Only you have ever liked me, the real me, I mean. Whatever's out there, whatever it's like where these things are..." Lucas gestured to Deer-Head as he spoke. "...I think that's where I belong."

"Have you made your decision, child?" Deer-Head asked. "The time grows near."

Lucas nodded to Deer-Head and then turned to Noah.

"I'm gonna try to come back. Even if just for a second. Just so you know, I'm okay, alright? I'm really gonna try."

* * *

The scarecrow leaned its head against Mila's for what seemed like hours but was most likely only a minute or two. Then, finally, it straightened its sackcloth head and made its way back to its empty cross-bar, where it slumped on the ground, lifeless once more.

"Welp. I guess the ritual isn't necessary after all."

"How's that?" Shem asked.

"I guess some kids broke in while we were occupied. One of 'em decided to go with the *Alven*."

"Well, don't that beat all," Shem commented, shaking his head.

Mila turned to Tara and Saar. "Looks like you're free, kiddos."

"You're just gonna let us go?" Tara asked, astounded.

"Yup," Mila nodded her head to confirm.

"No reason to keep ya," Shem affirmed.

"But what if we go to the police?" Saar asked, voice still full of impotent vitriol.

"You won't, dear," Mila said simply. "Because you won't remember any of this."

"That's the way of things," Shem revealed. "The way it always is."

Micah blinked once.

Twice.

Thrice.

"Wha..." Micah asked. For the first time in hours, he lowered the camera, which flashed its 'Low battery' warning.

"Let's get you kids home," Shem said finally.

* * *

Time passes.

"A '**B**'?" Tara asked. They had crowded around the grade sheets, along with the rest of their class.

"I'll take it," Saar beamed. "A '**B**' from Klein is like an '**A**' from anybody else, and you know it."

"Yeah," Micah agreed with a sigh. "I thought we had it with the Halloween farm stuff, though."

"I guess he wasn't impressed with a couple of scarecrows and some latex dummies after all," Tara quipped. "Let's just take the win and move on."

And they would move on.

In fact, they had already begun.

For some reason, neither of the girls really trusted Micah anymore. If pressed, they would say that he had acted weird at Jensen's Farm, but neither of them could quite describe how or why.

It had just been weird.

* * *

Time passes.

"Another good crop this year," Shem grinned, leaning on his shovel. He was getting a bit old for this manual labor stuff but wasn't quite ready to admit it.

"Yes'm," Mila remarked. "Guess they liked the kid."

"If only it were this easy every time." Shem shook his head.

"And if wishes were horses..."

"Fools would ride."

* * *

More time passes.

Noah sat on the uncomfortable wooden bench, waiting for a train. Around him sat other people, just as bleary, holding various cups of steaming coffee against the early hour. Every few minutes, a group of people would stand up, check their surroundings for forgotten possessions, and make their way to a train that would carry them away to wherever life's next event was going to be held. Noah had a half hour before his turn, so he reminisced.

After high school, he had been drawn away from The Valley, repelled as though from an oppositely charged magnet. He now found himself caught up in the blur of light and sound that was New York City, somehow comforted by the honking horns and blaring sirens, the random bass from passing cars, and the rattle of the above-ground trains.

It all made him feel safe.

If he was being honest, Noah had to admit that his hometown had started to feel dangerous when he was a kid, still scared of TV boogeymen and video game monsters. If he was being *truly* honest—which he was at that moment, waiting for his train to take him back to The Valley—it had started with Lucas' death.

It had been an awful accident. Lucas, who was prone to doing such things, had snuck out of his house one night and had fatally met with the bumper of a drunk driver. Noah wasn't sure how bad it had been, but he did know they had to bury a closed casket.

"It feels so light." He remembered Lucas' father saying as he hefted the polished wooden box with the help of a faceless group of uncles and cousins. "It's like he isn't even in there."

Noah took a sip of the too-hot coffee, letting its singe pull him from memory. By the time his train was called, he wasn't thinking of much at all.

Now he sat there, in and out of sleep, as tons of steel and plastic drove him back to the place he was born. When later asked by his parents, Noah would say that the trip was uneventful, boring even, and for the most part, it was.

Except...

About twenty minutes before pulling into Poughkeepsie station, where his parents were waiting to cart him home for a visit, he saw a man on the side of the road.

The man was tall, with careless blonde hair that blew wildly about his head. This man stood slightly elevated on one of the many small dales you would pass in this part of the world, just close enough to the tracks to be seen.

At first, Noah didn't recognize the man, who really didn't look much different from anyone and didn't stand out any more than any random stranger would.

But then he smiled.

It was not a man's smile.

It was the crooked, goofy smile of a troublesome eleven-year-old boy.

The man raised his hand and waved.

Noah jolted in his seat, leaning closer to the window to get a better look at this now familiar man.

The man waved once more and vanished, gone as though he had never been there.

In the final seconds, Noah could have sworn that the man had small horns on his forehead, like a baby goat. Or a small deer.

But surely, that must have been a trick of light and motion.

Noah closed his eyes and smiled as the train pulled into its station, taking him back to his place of birth.

Dead Wait

THE SUICIDE

Everyone knew Johnny Lang was a good kid. Of course, he got in trouble from time to time like other kids in high school, but all in all, he was a good citizen and a hard-working lad.

Johnny was a senior at Mill Grove High School. He played football for his school team, the Wildcats, and helped his father on the farm whenever possible.

In nineteen hundred, his great-grandfather, Jonah Lang, built the family farmhouse. It was a substantial three-story house to accommodate a large family. Many children would be needed to run the farm in the future, and this house would ensure plenty of room for them. Now there was no large family. It had dwindled down to only Johnny and his parents.

Other than playing football and helping out on his father's farm, Johnny liked to go hunting. But, mostly, he liked to spend as much time as he could with the love of his life, his girlfriend Christina Blanchard, who also attended Mill Grove High.

Johnny was six feet tall with a large frame. He had deep blue eyes, the color of an island ocean on a white coral sand beach, and wore his brown hair in the new style that Elvis Presley had started. When Love Me Tender came out, he began to slick his long locks back as Elvis did. The pomade made his light brown hair dark and shiny. He was a sensitive soul, but he hid it well lest anyone think him not manly.

However, what's more impressive was the girls were attracted to his solid physic, formed from the hard work of a farm boy and football player. But, as far as he was concerned, he belonged to Christina and no one else. Of course, he noticed other attractive girls, but his devotion was to her alone.

* * *

Christina lived in another town in the county but rode the bus to school. The day Johnny first saw her, he was a junior and knew he wanted her to be his. Christina had long blonde hair, a button nose, and one of the cutest faces he had ever seen. She was petite and a little shy, but she knew what she wanted. And what she wanted was fun and attention, nothing more.

Johnny and Christina had gone steady for over two years. He was so deeply in love with her. But what Christina had was a mere infatuation with his good looks and position as a quarterback for the Wildcats. At sixteen, she had no idea what love was, let alone feel it for a boy at school. On the other hand, Johnny knew how demanding work at home can be and learned what commitment and loyalty meant to a family business.

Everyone knew the two lovers at their school in that small town. The speculation was that they would probably get married one day, which pleased Johnny immensely. Though Christina thought it was funny and paid it little mind, including Johnny's plainly evident head-over-heels love for her. She was too oblivious.

When the 1958 high school senior prom began selling tickets, Johnny naturally assumed he would be taking Christina. However, Christina decided she was bored with Johnny and accepted an invitation from another boy, breaking off her relationship with him.

Johnny was more than devastated. It was as if she had reached into his chest, ripped his heart out, stomped on it, and coldly walked away.

Johnny stayed home from school for several days and spent most of it sobbing in his room. Christina shattered his poor heart into tiny little pieces. A girl who had no appreciation for his love and not a clue of its depth. He hoped, against hope, that she would come to her senses or that someone would point out to her what an awful thing she had done to him. No phone calls, no notes passed. Days passed; it had been over a week now. There was nothing from her.

* * *

Then one day, hopelessness turned into a hellish rage! Johnny paced his room for hours, seething about what she had done to him, how she had dumped him like a pile of garbage. He pulled at his hair while his mind was screaming about the injustice.

That fucking whore! That goddamn fucking whore! I was devoted to her and gave her anything she wanted! I took her to places and bought her nice clothes, jewelry, and dinners. And that's how that dirty bitch thanks me! I treated her like a queen, gave her all my love, and then she dumped me for someone else without the slightest fucking thought! That goddamn brainless, worthless cunt!

She'll be sorry when I'm gone, and wish she had been loyal to me and treated me like I deserved!

Johnny clutched his .357 revolver in his right hand while he paced his bedroom floor. He glanced at it several times as he ranted back and forth in his room. Tears of white-hot hatred and regret streamed down his face.

She'll be sorry, but it'll be too late. FUCK HER!

And with those final words, Johnny pointed the revolver at his right temple and pulled the trigger. The bullet smashed into his skull, tore through his brain, exited out the other side, and lodged into a two-by-four inside his bedroom wall. His brain lay on the floor, and his body was in a pool of blood.

Johnny never heard a thing.

At first, he thought the gun hadn't fired… until he saw his body slumped dead, lying on the floor, and the revolver nearby to the right of his arm. Johnny saw the permanent horror he had created and left on the floor. Instantly he regretted it, but it was too late. It was done. *He* was done. Johnny screamed the agony of the damned dead.

There was no light, no tunnel, no angels.

Nothing.

Just the hideous horror he left for his parents to find. He thought he had his heart ripped out, and now, because of what *he* had done, his parents would be filled with terrible grief that could ever be imagined and a sight they could never unseen. They would go to their graves with what he had done.

Johnny walked the halls of the house after his terrible deed. His parents never heard or saw a thing. He would throw things around his bedroom and kick objects as he walked through the house in a rage.

I'll bet the little slut didn't even bother to come to my fucking funeral! Too goddamn busy being little miss stuck-up and fucking the football team. I'm here for fucking ever, stuck in this house because of that piece of trash! I'll kill that bitch if she ever shows her worthless ass around here.

Johnny wanted revenge for his mistreatment by the girl he loved. He was in his own private hell, and he would never leave.

REGRETS

When Christina heard that Johnny was dead, she went to his house to give her condolences. Considering her part in it, one would have thought she ought to have had the sense to stay away. But instead, she paid a visit, and Johnny's parents quickly answered the door.

"What do *you* want?" His father asked, enraged.

"I wanted to pay my respects."

"Well, you and your respects can go straight to hell. You've got a lot of nerve coming around here after what you did to our boy!" He yelled.

"You're the reason he's dead!" His mother screamed, coming to stand beside Johnny's father. "I hope you suffer like his father and me someday."

Avoiding their accusatory eyes boring into her, she looked downward at her shoes, then the boards of their front porch, and sniffed. "I-I-I-just… I just wanted to say I'm sorry." She sputtered, panic welling up inside her like a volcano.

"Get out of here. Never darken our door again!" His father shouted, pointing toward the road before slamming the door in her face. They stood behind the storm door, making sure she left, all the while cursing at her through the door's glass window.

"She ever shows up here again, I'll kill the bitch," announced his father.

And with that, Christina ran to her car, her tires churning the gravel drive as she left their farmhouse for the last time.

THE FUNERAL

The dreary day of Johnny's funeral came. A long procession of vehicles entered the cemetery. It snaked along the winding, one-lane road until they came to the green canopy standing over a new grave. The seats lined up under it in short rows, facing the casket stand.

Johnny's parents exited the long, black limousine. His mother held a tissue in front of her face, quietly sobbing into it. His father supported her as they walked to their seats.

As they sat, waiting for the casket from the hearse to be placed on the stand, he tried to be strong for her. When it arrived and was now before them, he fell forward, collapsing on the ground, sobbing uncontrollably, yelling, "Why, why, why?! My baby boy! My baby boy!"

His mother was crying her heart out, just as painfully as her husband. Only the other mourners could help him off the ground and back to his seat. It was a terribly heart-rending sight no one would wish to see. As the minister read the twenty-third Psalm, they lowered the casket into the ground. Johnny's parents clung to each other, sobbing on the other's shoulders.

After the graveside service, some mourners, who were Johnny's classmates, helped his parents back into the limousine.

Almost every student and teacher at Mill Grove High School attended the funeral. Johnny's parents were amazed at the outpouring of love from everyone and didn't realize just how popular he was. It was a safe bet. Johnny never knew it either.

Christina had become persona non grata at Mill Grove. Everyone stared and pointed at her. They blamed her for his death. Finally, her family pulled her from school, and she spent the remaining high school years in another county. She didn't attend the viewing or the funeral. Maybe it was best, but it showed everyone who she really was. Christina and her family also had to move. Once everyone heard the story of Johnny's death, no one wanted to have anything to do with her, and school became impossible.

Johnny's parents moved out of the old farmhouse and away from Mill Grove. The memories were too much for them to take, day after day, in the house where he died. They couldn't bear to constantly walk past his room and be reminded of the horrific scene they beheld that day. But unfortunately, they were never able to sell the place, so they abandoned the house and farm to start a new life elsewhere.

Now they must live with the horror created by Christina and Johnny for the rest of their lives. Their only thought was that it wasn't right that Christina got to live on while he did not, despite the horrible thing she did to their boy. It wasn't logic but unrelenting, hellish grief that created the lens they now looked through.

The old Lang house sat vacant and abandoned for generations after that. It remained in a time capsule of the nineteen-fifties. The metal roof kept out the weather through many decades, preserving the homes interior just as it was left. Nothing lived there anymore. Never a light to shine again in the old house. Never a caring voice to utter, "I love you." Only the wind, howling through the shutters and cracks in the window frames, made the slightest sound. Its creaky, wooden floors, untrodden by human footsteps ever since.

THE TRESPASSERS

The years rolled on, but the old Lang house remained unchanged and uninhabited. Then, in the late nineteen sixties, three teenage boys got the notion to go out to the old, abandoned farmhouse and explore on, of course, Halloween night. Too old for trick-or-treating, this would be their ghost-hunting fun. No matter the generation, boys will be boys, and they typically like to challenge each other in their teen years, much of the time just to see if they can convince one another to do something stupid, dangerous, or both. Halloween night, 1969, was no exception, and in this case, they managed both the foolish and dangerous in one challenge.

They would go in and explore, and if one of them gave up in the middle of the task, then that person would have to spend the night alone in the immense house. They brought a blanket, pillow, sleeping bag, flashlight, and flash camera to supply to the "winner" of their unwise dare. The 'contestants' were Bobby Jessup, James (Jim) Crouch, and Troy Goodwin.

They were from Mill Grove and fighting against the small farm town disease among teens known as 'bored-as-hell-itis.' In 1969 Mill Grove, if you were suffering greatly from this horrific ailment, you either got on a bicycle or in a car, hoping you would stay out of trouble while trying to get into it. All while doing something you knew you weren't supposed to because there was nothing else in the entire town to do.

Mill Grove only had about eight thousand residents, and a good many of them were connected in some way to farming. There were two grocery stores, four gas stations, and various old chain stores that had long since sold out and closed. There were no lakes or amusement parks of any kind. Just school and work after school. So really now, who could blame them?

Someone certainly did, though. It started like this: Bobby, James, and Troy would hang out together at school and afterward. At one of these after-school get-togethers, they cooked up a thrill-seeking idea. Juniors in high school usually didn't go trick-or-treating, so they created their own ghost-hunting adventure. They would go ghost hunting at the old Lang house. They had heard many rumors since '*IT*' happened in the late nineteen fifties.

"Johnny Lang haunts the old house; he committed suicide over a girl and will attack anyone who dares enter."

"Better stay out of the old Lang House! Johnny don't like folks snooping around there, 'especially at night'!"

Some people don't believe in such things or must learn the hard way. No matter how sincerely and terrifyingly these incidents are told, there always seems to be plenty who refuse to believe or heed the warning.

This is a retelling of their unfortunate stories.

THE EXPLORERS

It was 1969, and the Lang Farmstead had been abandoned for ten years. It was the year that the rumors and legends of the house grew and took hold in the community.

Three juniors from Mill Grove High School heard about the legend of Johnny Lang and his house from their friends at school. They saw his name on some of the school's trophies in the display case and wondered how such a good student and football jock's life could end so tragically.

Bobby Jessup, a natural leader, *always* took charge of organizing their outings. The others deemed it as work they didn't want to do. He had relatively short hair for the time, only covering his ears with his medium brown locks, and his six-foot-tall frame added to his aura of being the boss. He always wore black jeans and a white T-shirt when he wasn't in school.

Troy Goodwin was a good lad and a good student. Other than when he was at church or a funeral, he never wore slacks, only beat-up, faded blue jeans. He was skeptical of the paranormal but had somewhat of an open mind and wasn't opposed to their planned adventure. In his mind, he figured, what the heck. Even if nothing happened, it would be fun. Troy also liked to play practical jokes, and nothing delighted him more than ribbing his rivals about their ghostly beliefs.

James Crouch, on the other hand, was a believer. He had his own experiences with the paranormal, but those he kept to himself, as he was a very private person, afraid of ridicule. James, though, wanted to discover the history behind the awful story of the Lang farmhouse. He wanted to delve into the sordid details, or he *thought* he did. It always came up in his conversations during Halloween, and this year was no exception. James convinced the others to scout out the house during the day and find a way in when they came back at night. It was right after school when they gathered to discuss it.

"Guys, are you up for checking out the Lang house today?" James asked, grinning like a Cheshire cat who'd caught a canary.

"Troy and I got homework, a shitload. We should do it this Saturday and then come back for the nighttime deal," Bobby said, though he wished he could chuck it all and go.

James nodded, a little bit disappointed. "Okay, I guess that would work. We'd be going back the same day, no surprises."

"Right," replied Bobby, pointing to the pile of textbooks next to him.

It seemed to all of them that Saturday would never come. The anticipation was almost too much. The thought of at least driving by the old place was deliciously tempting. Finally, the day came. It was bright and sunny, after all; what's to fear on such a day?

The boys drove on country back roads for twenty minutes until they found the Lang Farm and pulled onto the rutted gravel driveway that led to the house.

There it was, standing tall between overgrown bushes, paint peeling from the clapboard siding and front porch posts. It also had a metal-covered roof. The windows had collected over a decade of dust, but one could still see through them. Grass, weeds, and trees grew up all around the property, choking out the light coming into the windows. The wooden porch was rickety but still intact, though it, too, had weeds growing up through some cracks between the four-inch boards. The metal doorknob on the front door was so rusty that it would barely move and made a screech when anyone attempted to turn it.

Nothing about the house's appearance would warn anyone away, at least during the daytime.

The boys sat in the car, still idling, transfixed by the massive home that loomed over them.

"I found out some things about that day," announced James, his voice quavering as he looked up at the third floor of the house where he guessed Johnny had died.

"What day?" Troy asked, turning to James, who was still gazing at the building.

"*The day*. In nineteen fifty-eight or whenever."

Absorbed in the horrific history of the house, James finally returned his attention back to his partners-in-crime, "Come on, guys, this is important."

Bobby, still not appreciating the seriousness, chimed in, "So?"

"So, Johnny Lang blew his brains out in his bedroom. His mom and dad found his body. His brains were on the fucking floor! The bullet is supposed to be still buried in a wall. It was all over some stupid girl. Can you believe that shit? See the window at the very top? *That's* his room! According to the news from back then, there was a large pool of blood on the floor, still leaving a stain."

"Well, no shit, that'll happen when you blow your brains out," replied Troy, teasing him into reacting.

"I'm just telling you what the newspaper reported at the time, jerk." James sneered back.

"Okay, guys, we can't sit here looking at the place and jaw-jack all day. So let's get out and see where we can get inside," announced Bobby, trying to cool down the situation between James and Troy.

But they didn't move.

"You know, just because you don't believe in those kinds of things doesn't mean you have to be an asshole about it," James admonished.

"I didn't say I don't believe; I'm just fuckin' with you, lighten up!" Troy rolled his eyes.

"Or hey, how about this; how about you not be a snotty jerk?" James shot back.

"Troy! James!"

Startled, they turned to look at Bobby.

"You guys... knock that shit off! Let's hurry up and scout this place and get out of here!" Bobby repeated.

"Sorry. I was thinking about tonight, and I don't need Troy trying to piss me off," James replied hotly.

"I'm sorry, man, come on, I'll take it seriously, I swear," Troy pleaded.

"I hope so," said James. "This is potentially dangerous, and we need to be careful. I don't want any of us to end up in the hospital or jail for trespassing."

Remaining silent, Troy simply nodded that he understood.

"Let's try the front door. We'll go in, look at all the rooms to make sure we won't fall through the floor tonight or fall over or down the stairs in the dark," Bobby warned, slamming the car door closed on his side.

"Jesus! Are you trying to wake the dead?" James asked.

"Sorry, bad habit."

"Anyway, you guys, my dad is a master carpenter, and I've been to old homes he's worked on. A lot of abandoned homes have rotting floors and termite-infested stairs, banisters, and other parts of the house. You could be killed or seriously injured, taking the wrong step in the dark.

The boys walked up the deteriorating wooden porch steps and onto the creaky boards of the deck. So much of the white paint that once covered them had peeled and curled from the lack of maintenance.

Bobby stared at the old iron door handle for a minute before reluctantly reaching and turning it. The ancient metal handle screeched loudly. It was the first time any human had touched it since that awful time. The door was unlatched but stuck due to the years of warpage the wooden door had suffered. Bobby pushed it, but it didn't budge. Troy and James tried as well, but still, it wouldn't move.

Bobby reared back to kick it open when suddenly, the door opened wide, startling them.

"Holy shit!" Bobby exclaimed.

"Uh… you first, Bobby," whispered Troy.

Bobby turned back to respond to him but just scrunched his face in a mocking frown.

Turning back to the open door, he reluctantly took another step toward the door and stuck his head inside, "Hello? Hello? Anybody home?"

Looking back at Troy and James for comment, they merely shrugged their shoulders.

"Well, uh, let's… let's go inside and see what we have," Bobby said, moving behind his friends.

The three of them stood there for a few moments.

"Well, are we going in or not?!" Bobby asked again.

"We were waiting for you," James scoffed, noticing Bobby had moved.

"You guys are in front of me; what are *you* waiting for?" Bobby pointed out with a sheepish grin while wringing his hands.

Exasperated, Troy moaned, "fine" rolling his eyes, he continued, "let's all go in at the same time."

They were about to be the first humans to step foot inside the Lang farmhouse since Johnny's suicide.

"My research indicates that his parents turned a portion of the attic into a room for him." James started to show off his knowledge again. "So, really, there are only three floors because of that. The rest of the area up there is just an attic."

"Before we go *there*, let's check out the first floor first," suggested Bobby, stopping James and Troy from moving forward.

The old-fashioned, wide floorboards of a time long past creaked with every step. Weeds and saplings scraped against the windows because of the wind, rubbing an occasional clear spot in the film of dirt, allowing light beams to penetrate the gloom. Dust particles caught in the beams danced and shimmered as they floated in the stale air. The smell of musty old newspapers and magazines permeated every room. Teal-colored furniture, the kind that was popular at the time, was woven with glittering metallic threads throughout the upholstery. The accumulated years of dust hid the shiny strands. It covered the blond coffee and end tables so that only the legs revealed the finish.

The three of them had been inside for only two minutes when footsteps thudded on the second floor!

"Oh shit! It's Johnny, its fuckin' Johnny!" Bobby yelled.

"My ass is gone!" screamed Troy. "Come on, guys!"

James said nothing as he turned 180 degrees on his heel for the exit.

The footsteps continued from the third floor and down the stairs toward the boys.

Wasting no time, they bolted from the foyer and fled to safety outside.

Chests heaving and struggling to catch their breath, the three looked back at the front door, sure that someone was about to burst out toward them.

But no one did.

The house was silent.

Troy noticed a hard rubber ball quietly rolling toward the front door, but it stopped at the threshold and moved back a little.

"Holy shit! What the fuck was that?" James exclaimed.

Bobby, still trying to get over his fright, could not speak.

"Guys! Look! Look at the front door. That little rubber super ball rolled down the steps, sounding like footsteps when it bounced on each one. So you guys were afraid of a super ball?" Troy laughed while holding his stomach.

"Fuck you, Troy; you ran too," said Bobby, attempting to catch his breath while pulling out his asthma inhaler to take two puffs.

"Yeah, but I didn't freak out. It was just a ball." Troy gave Bobby a side-eye.

"Oh, really?" enquired James, pointing rigidly toward the front door. "Then what made the ball roll in the first place, and how did it make running footsteps sound by simply rolling down a flat hallway? How did it manage to roll straight the whole time until it got to the steps and then turned the corner?"

"Well, maybe there's a raccoon or other animal up there that knocked it off a table or kicked it," Troy reasoned.

Increasingly frustrated, James demanded, "And what about the footsteps running down the hallway up there?" He placed his hands on his hips, waiting for the answer.

Troy shifted from one foot to the other. "I dunno. Maybe it just seemed like that to us at the time."

"Right, all three of us made the same hearing mistake at the same time," intoned Bobby.

Troy shrugged his shoulders and replied, "Well… nothing came after us, did it?"

"So, it was just the ball moved by a raccoon or something?" James frowned, not buying it.

When no one spoke for a moment, Bobby offered his take.

"Look, maybe it was the ball. They don't call them super balls for nothing. They can bounce higher than trees. So, I say we act like men are supposed to act and explore this place tonight. We'll be the first. No one has been in there since… that kid, well, you know. So, are you guys in for this?"

"Yeah, sure," James and Troy answered in unison, but the look of revulsion on their faces, and quivering response, betrayed their confident words.

"Okay, then it's final; Troy, close the door. We'll be back tonight. Hell, guys, after all, it's Halloween!" Ignoring James's and Troy's wavering bravado, Bobby rubbed his hands together, psyching himself up.

Troy walked back up the porch steps, gave the little ball a slight kick inward, and closed the door.

While some of their other friends were planning Halloween parties,

Bobby, Troy, and James planned what they presumed to be a scary but exciting exploration.

As it began to get dark, the boys piled into an old sedan with all their supplies, including a camera and three flashlights with extra batteries. By the time they got to the farmhouse, the sun was almost set. Somehow, the farmhouse seemed threatening, lurking behind the cover of thigh-high weeds and overgrown bushes. The boys piled out of the car and looked up at the Lang house, silhouetted against the sky by the twilight. Soon it would be dark, and the waning moon would leave little light.

"It looks different," said Troy, a little puzzled.

"What looks different?" asked Bobby, confused, staring into the dark rooms of the upper windows.

"The house. It looks different. I don't know. I don't like it."

"It's the same house, Troy! Nothing has changed," insisted Bobby.

"That's not what I mean. It looks... like it's expecting us." Troy felt some trepidation in the pit of his stomach.

"*Now* you believe? What happened to laughing at us?" James sneered.

Troy, feeling as if they were being watched, gave a warning, "It doesn't hurt to be careful."

Bobby shot back, "Don't be ridiculous! We just got here, and we're not going back because you turned chicken!"

"I'm not chicken; I just made an observation. If anybody is being super sensitive, it's you, Bobby! I never said I didn't want to do this."

"Fine, Troy, I'm sorry. Are we okay now, all of us?" Bobby asked, and the other two nodded in agreement.

Once satisfied, Bobby took the first step up to the porch, but before reaching for the front door handle, he looked down at the threshold. He had kicked something dark and small, which rolled away.

He turned on his flashlight in search of it, thinking maybe some animal was resting there. However, it was the ball Troy had kicked inside before they left.

"What the fuck?! Is that the same ball?" Bobby exclaimed, not believing his eyes.

"What are you talking about?" James questioned, looking a little puzzled.

"Troy, didn't you kick that super ball inside before you closed the door?"

"Yeah, why?" He answered nonchalantly.

"It's outside on the porch now." Bobby turned and pointed toward the ball.

"Bullshit! Quit trying to fuck with me. I said I'm not afraid," Troy hissed.

"I'm not damnit, look!" Bobby pointed his flashlight at the ball he had just kicked.

"Is that, or is it not the ball you kicked inside?" Troy picked it up and looked at it, carefully examining it. "How the fuck did this get outside? I kicked this ball farther into the house; I watched it roll into the darkness and closed the fucking door!"

The boys said nothing for a few moments, staring at the ball Troy held in his hand.

"Well… what do you guys want to do?" Bobby finally asked, breaking the silence.

"Are you kiddin' me?" James remarked. "We *gotta* go in now! We gotta find the answer."

Bobby looked at Troy. "What do *you* say?"

"I want to know too. How *did* it get outside?"

None of the boys dared to back down now for fear of showing the others how afraid they were. But they were, and it was too late now.

Bobby again reached for the door, but this time, before Bobby's hand, reached the handle, it opened ever so slowly as if simply a breeze caught it and slightly pushed it open. They stepped inside, quickly doing a cursory scan, but Troy remained back by the door. Bobby and James tried looking into the darkness, focusing their eyes on an old wall clock with protruding metal petals hanging on a foyer wall.

Instantly, the door slammed shut.

James and Bobby spun around and grabbed each other, causing them both to trip and fall on their butts, with eyes as big as dinner plates! They looked up at Troy, who was only a foot or two from the door that slammed.

Standing just in front of it, Troy laughed so hard that snot flew out of his nose.

"You asshole!" James and Bobby shouted.

Troy continued to laugh until his sides ached.

"Fucking asshole!" Bobby cursed.

"Hey!" Troy teased. "I thought you guys weren't scared."

"Fuck you, Troy. You'd have done the same thing if it had been Bobby or me who did that to you."

Troy bent over with his hands on his knees as he continued to laugh. "You should have seen your faces. Funniest thing I ever saw!"

"Yeah? Do that shit again and see if it's so funny," Bobby warned.

Troy mimed Bobby's anger by making stupid faces, and Bobby returned the silent insult with his middle finger. Then, finally, Troy smiled a big Cheshire cat grin, satisfied with the reaction he'd expected, and Bobby turned back to the task at hand, which was building up the courage to walk further into the house.

The white paint on the walls was peeling from years of humidity and freezing temperatures. The dining room contained an old hutch full of antique pottery and glassware covered in dust. Next to the small wooden dining table was an old, warped, upright piano in the corner of the room; music sheets still sat on its easel. The curtains, yellowed and moth-eaten, hung above an assortment of dead flies, bees, and wasps that covered the windowsills.

In the kitchen, pots and pans sat on a porcelain gas stove and counters. With various paintings of chickens, the yellow wallpaper was coming unglued and curled up from the ceiling downward, forming rolls. White steel and porcelain cabinets still hung in place, slowly rusting at the chrome hinges and handles. A small white refrigerator, the kind with the circular cooling unit on top, stood empty across from the stove.

Suddenly, the lights in the kitchen flickered on and off for a minute. The boys looked all around for an explanation, but there was none. The flickering had stopped now.

"What the hell was that?" Bobby whispered to the others.

"There's no power here. I flicked a light switch when we walked in here, and nothing happened," informed Troy, a little uneasy. "I was told sometimes people have seen lights on when they drive by at night. Maybe it's on when *they* want it on."

Bobby inquired, "Who's '*they*' Troy?"

"Who do you think?"

"You know, Troy," Bobby announced, "I wish you'd make up your mind whether you believe or not. You act like you do, and then you pull an asshole move like the goddamn front door! Why should either of us believe anything you say? It's your own fault, you can't be trusted."

"Look, I'm sorry. This shit really scares me, and I guess it's my way of... to use one of my dad's big words, mitigating the fear. I'm afraid I'll panic, and joking around keeps that from happening. So... now you know the truth. I don't wanna look like a chicken-shit in front of my friends."

Bobby dead-panned. "If fear is good enough for us, it's good enough for you too."

"Come on, let's check other stuff, just to make sure," James chimed in, in an attempt to smooth over the angst between Troy and Bobby.

The boys began flipping switches on other kitchen devices and could find nothing that would turn on. So finally, they stepped out of the back door from the kitchen and checked the meter. It wasn't turning, indicating there was no power connected.

While outside, behind the house, they took note of a large barn, and ramshackle tool shed.

"Hmm, looks like we got more to investigate, huh?" said Bobby with all the enthusiasm of a grave digger.

James and Troy stared at the buildings but didn't respond.

The boys stepped back inside the house, looked over the kitchen once more, and headed for the rooms off to either side of the foyer they had first entered. One was a sunroom, and the other a large living room.

Just as they exited the kitchen, they heard a loud WHOOSH! They turned around to see what the sound was and found every burner lit on the gas stove with full force.

"Oh shit! Did you guys turn the gas on?" wondered Troy as he jumped back against the wall behind him.

"No! There is no gas!" Bobby declared.

"If there's a fire on the stove, there's gas," replied Troy matter-of-factly.

"Oh really?" Bobby sneered. "Did you notice a long, large concrete slab outside in the back?"

"What the hell does that got to do with it?"

Bobby reluctantly reached for the stove knobs and turned the burners off.

"Come back outside," ordered Bobby.

The three of them tromped back outside and approached the old, dilapidated shed.

"You see that concrete slab over by the shed?"

"So?" Troy replied.

"*That's* where a large propane tank would have set to supply gas to a furnace and stove. There IS NO gas!"

"Well, then how did…" Troy trailed off.

Facing Troy and James, Bobby asked worriedly, "Exactly. How *did* the stove turn on?"

The boys walked over to the slab and examined it. On either end were large, rusted mounting studs and bolts where a propane tank was bolted long ago. A capped pipe stuck out of the ground at one end that used to supply gas to the house.

"That's nuts." James felt a cold sensation creep up his spine. "Gas stove comes on with no gas. What kind of shit is that?"

"Maybe there was still gas in the line. The end was capped, so maybe it was trapped," Troy reasoned.

"Right, after ten or more years?" noted Bobby. "And who turned on the burners?"

"Beats the shit out of me," Troy blurted out.

"Yeah, it does. So I think we know something's not right," Bobby warned. "If we're gonna be the first to investigate this house, we'd better keep our wits about us. Don't go running blindly in a panic. That's how you get hurt."

"Let's go back inside. We'll come out later to check out the barn," suggested James.

Troy replied, "Maybe we should have gone to a Halloween party instead. Mighta got lucky with some hot babe."

"Yeah, we could be giving them a 'special treat' instead of rummaging around here," Bobby agreed.

"Special treat. Like you got one," James scoffed. "But, uh, yeah, I could go for that," he admitted.

At this point, the boys were getting the heebie-jeebies after the unsettling happenings around them. They began to imagine themselves anywhere but the Lang Farmhouse, but on the other hand, they were the first to go in. No one had ever seen the inside since that awful day.

They closed the door to the backyard and turned to go back to the living room through the kitchen. But stopped in the middle, looking at the stove momentarily, expecting it to light up again.

"Jesus Christ!" Troy yelled.

"What?! What?! What happened?" James and Bobby asked in fright.

"Someone touched me! Or something… something touched me!

"On your leg?" James inquired.

"Yeah, something touched my leg."

"That was me, dofus! My knee accidentally brushed up against you, sheesh," replied James, rolling his eyes.

"For crying out loud guys, you're clinging to each other, it's bound to happen," Bobby reminded them.

"Let's get out of here and check out the living room. We'll check out the house floor by floor," whispered Bobby.

"Why are you whispering?" Troy asked.

"I dunno. I guess, so we can hear if something happens, maybe."

"Or maybe someone is listening," James pipped up.

They left the enormous kitchen and went back into the dining room.

The boys were walking past the dining room table when James asked in bafflement, "Weren't those curtains closed when we went through here?"

"Which curtains?" Bobby asked, looking in the direction James was staring.

"The window in the middle. I could've sworn they were closed." He pointed at the suspected window.

"I don't remember," remarked Troy, desperately trying to recall.

"Neither do I," Bobby replied.

"I know they were closed," James assured, his eyebrows furrowed.

They stood there watching the curtains… waiting.

"Well...they aren't moving." Frustrated, Bobby ordered, "Come on, guys. This is a big house. Let's do this."

Inside each one, the fear was building, and the anxiety between them was showing.

Shifting his weight from foot to foot nervously, James asked, "Where do you wanna go next?"

Just then, the sound of old door hinges creaking came from the second floor.

"Uh... I guess we go upstairs to the second floor." shrugged Bobby with a pained smile.

Troy, uneasy and looking all around, suggested, "Hey, shouldn't we do the sunroom first?"

"There's just a bunch of old chairs in there." Bobby shook his head. "But hey, I'm not gonna argue."

"What about Johnny Lang's room?" James whispered slowly.

Troy couldn't believe what he had just suggested. "That's on the third floor, remember? You're the one who told us that."

"Oh yeah." James sheepishly smiled.

"Well, guess we can't go, too bad," quipped Troy.

Frowning at James, Bobby complained, "Sheesh, don't go goofy on us now."

"What do you mean 'now' Bobby? I think you're a little late," Troy shot back.

James mouthed, "Fuck you, Troy," and Troy mouthed back, "You'd like that," and cracked a big smile.

The boys looked around and eyed the staircase. Not a single step was cracked, nor a single rung in the wooden banister was missing. Except for the dust and insect damage, everything was intact as of the day the Lang's left.

Bobby shone his flashlight toward the steps. As it illuminated the floorboards, a gray mouse skittered across the floor and into a hole in the baseboard near the stairs.

"Damn, I wonder how many of those little guys are in here," Troy pondered.

As Troy spoke, they heard three notes played on the piano in the dining room, causing them to almost jump out of their skin.

"Shit! What the hell was that?!" Bobby asked.

"Gotta be mice like we just saw. They probably live inside the piano, running around on the hammers," replied Troy, as usual with his reasoning mind. "You wanna check it out?"

"Not really," groaned James. "I'll accept your explanation."

Bobby managed a pained smile and said, "Ditto for me. This shit might be funny later on, but it ain't right now. Let's get to the second floor and get it over with."

"What, we couldn't go trick or treating like other kids?" retorted James.

"Jesus, Jim! You're almost eighteen! What kids do you hang out with?"

"I was just kidding… kinda." James laughed.

Troy busted out laughing, and Bobby just shook his head in mock disgust.

"Come on, before you *do* turn eighteen." Bobby, wanting to get going, nodded toward the stairs.

Like scared rabbits on the lookout for hunters, they crept up the staircase to the second floor. The boys kept their heads on a swivel, constantly looking behind them, eyes wide as the hubcaps on their car. Bobby placed his hand on the banister as he climbed, sweeping some decade-old dust off, and quickly removed his hand as he felt the dirt. Then, brushing it off on his jeans, he kept his gaze forward and upward into the darkness of the next landing.

Reaching the second-floor landing, they looked back and saw that Troy was no longer with them.

"Shit," Bobby whispered for the first time, sounding somewhat frightened, "Where the fuck did he go?"

"He's probably pulling more of his shit," James retorted. "You know, he's skeptical of ghosts and all that."

"Damnit, we don't need his bullshit right now," Bobby seethed. "Troy!" he whispered as loud as he dared. "Where the hell are you?"

From downstairs came the reply, "I'm down here looking around. You guys go ahead."

"Idiot," Bobby murmured to himself.

"Well?" James asked, expecting Bobby to decide what to do about Troy.

"Oh fuck him. Maybe he'll run into Johnny down there." Bobby was getting annoyed.

"I guess that'll make a believer out of him."

"Serves him right for goofing around." James reckoned Troy would get what he deserved.

"When we step into the hallway, you shine your flashlight down to the left, and I'll shine mine down the other way," Bobby instructed, thinking it was the most efficient way to get this whole thing over with and get out.

"And then what?" James wanted to know what his friend was thinking.

Bobby spoke quietly, "Tell me what you see."

They reached the second floor, and each looked down the hallway closest to them.

"Well, whaddya see, Jim?"

"Jim?"

"Uh ...I see a door slowly closing by itself at the end." Jim swallowed hard, his heart pounding like a racehorse.

Bobby heard the creepy squeaking of the hinges and turned in time to watch the door close but not latch.

"That could be the wind." He hoped.

"What wind? There are no broken or open windows. We checked, remember? What did you see down your hall?" James had a dreadful feeling in the pit of his stomach.

"Doors. Four doors, two on each side. That's it." Bobby shrugged

"There's only two on my side. I suppose we gotta go see what made that door move," James bemoaned, hoping to check it out together.

"You go check your hall, and I'll check mine," Bobby countered pointedly, avoiding what could be behind that door.

James crept as silently as he could, considering the creaking of the floors. With each careful step, he noticed incredibly old family pictures on the walls, caked in a decade's worth of dust. Though, James could still make out the faces through the glass. One of those faces, he was sure, had to be Johnny.

He came to the room where the door had closed on its own and slightly kicked the bottom of it so that it opened slowly. He peeked inside and then stepped into the room.

Once again, the door slammed closed, but this time behind him. He was inside, unknown to Bobby.

Bobby heard the noise, quickly spun around, and dashed toward the room at the end of the hallway. It was closed and latched. Bobby watched the door for several moments, waiting to hear any sound. However, there was only silence. No screams for help. Bobby couldn't understand why James wasn't yelling for him.

He gripped the doorknob but stopped short of opening it.

Bobby took a deep breath, held it, and turned the knob.

It opened.

He peeked inside.

James was not in the room, nor was there any sign he had ever been in it.

"Jim!" Bobby yelled. "Jim! Where are you?!"

But there was no answer.

He went downstairs to look for Troy.

"Troy! Are you down here?! Troy! Answer me goddamnit!"

There was no response.

Bobby had enough. It was time to abandon this terrifying disaster while he still could.

A moan came from the sunroom. He knew that it must be Troy. He probably fell and injured or knocked himself out, he thought.

Bobby sprinted into the room, but there was no one there.

The French doors slammed closed.

Bobby screamed the agony of the damned, and no one could hear him.

THE INVESTIGATORS, OCTOBER 30TH, 1979

In 1979 there weren't a lot of paranormal investigators. In those days, if you faced creepy goings-on, there weren't many people to rely upon or call. There were a few famous investigators, but they were unlikely to take any case but the most extreme. There also weren't the plethora of investigative tools and electronics like today. However, there were students of parapsychology on some university campuses, and two such students decided they would look into the rumors of the Lang house and the missing boys. They'd make their mark and perhaps get national media attention if they could crack that case. It was worth a try, they figured.

Parapsychology didn't have a lot of electronic equipment at its disposal, and what they had available was big, clunky, and debatable on whether it actually worked.

Don Baumgard and Victor (Vic) Mead were fascinated by and interested in how ghost-related activities could be scientifically explained. Don was of average height, five-foot-ten, and a rather stocky build, but not fat. His straight, jet-black hair caused him to stand out in a crowd. A nice fellow, engaged to be married the following year to his long-time sweetheart, he'd hoped to make a name for himself in his chosen field.

Vic was a cut-up at times, but he took his investigations seriously. He wanted to use his education and experience to write a book someday. In addition, he desired to be a pioneer in the growing new field of paranormal investigations.

And both had borne the ridicule of the Psychology Department and their self-described *elite* class. Still, they verbally dismissed them to their faces as 'mere children calling names because they're intimidated by anything that goes against their preconceived ideas.'

When that didn't work, a simple 'Go fuck yourself!' sufficed.

Now it was time to go to work. To put up or shut up, as it were.

They were being dropped off at Johnny's home in a borrowed box truck by a fellow student. Don and Vic opened the truck's back door and began unloading their equipment in front of the house.

"So, this is the infamous Lang house," Vic confirmed while picking up a crate full of devices. "Doesn't look all that scary to me."

"Yeah," grunted Don, lifting the last piece of equipment out of the cargo area. "Just an old farmhouse."

"Supposed to be like a time capsule inside, from uh, let's see, the nineteen fifties, I think."

"You'd think the roof would've given way by now, and this place would be falling down."

"Didja see the roof? Galvanized steel or tin. It's not going anywhere unless there's a tornado. It's not pretty, but it sure lasts a long time."

Vic waved goodbye to the box truck driver after they had gotten everything unloaded and watched the truck as it went out of sight.

"Well, we're not going anywhere until Wednesday morning at six unless we walk somewhere first to make a phone call," Vic announced.

"You realize what day this is, don't you?" asked Don.

"Yeah, it's Tuesday."

"It's also the thirtieth. At midnight, it'll be Halloween and the witching hour," Don warned in a spooky-sounding manner.

"Ooh, scary! Should I shit my pants now or wait till later?" Vic aped.

"Later, much later. Like after you get home," Don answered while placing the equipment on a long table.

"Yes sir, captain! Shit my pants much later, sir," Vic snapped his heels together and saluted him.

"I hope the ghost of Johnny Lang kicks your ass," Don wisecracked.

"That's a pretty *shitty* thing to say," Vic shot back as he watched Don do all the work.

"You should go into stand-up instead of parapsychology, or better yet, see a psychologist."

"I'm going into stand-up parapsychology, thank you very much."

Don shook his head and laughed. "Let's get this equipment set up and running. I know we brought a generator and fuel, but let's check and see if there's still power. This place is in the boonies, so they might have forgotten to shut it off once everyone was... well, dead and gone. Like that old mental hospital last year. Remember that? Power left on all those years. You'd have thought they had turned it off when they closed."

Vic stepped onto the porch. The steps, rotting away, lying in moss-covered pieces in the dirt, were being reclaimed by the earth since the metal roof of the porch didn't cover them. Bricks supported the porch itself, so it remained intact, though many bare boards were split and cracked. The paint had mostly weathered away long ago.

Carrying two cases of equipment, Vic stepped up to the door. Almost frozen with rust, the hinges creaked and groaned as he pushed it open. He noticed an old push-button-style light switch on the wall to his right. He pushed the top button in.

"Holy shit, Don! The power is still on. I can't believe it. Well, I guess I have to. It's right in front of my face. Look, the foyer light came on." Vic pushed the antique light switch on, marveling at both.

"We won't have to deal with the noise of the generator. That thing contaminates every sound recording," Don replied, looking derisively at the generator.

"Where do you want to set up? How bout' close to the center of the first floor?" Vic suggested, pointing down the center hall.

"See if there's a dining room. That's usually the center of most places. We can run cords if there aren't outlets in it." Don directed as he hooked up the monitoring systems on the table.

"Hey, there's an old piano in here," Vic shouted, quickening his pace as he approached it.

"Did you expect it to be new?" Don chortled.

"Funny as a heart attack, Don."

"I don't have your sense of humor, thank God," he taunted.

Setting a box of cables on the piano, Vic clowned, "My mommy thinks I'm funny."

"At least you have one fan."

"Fine," Vic replied as he flipped Don the bird. "Nothing but seriousness from now on."

"Let's put our control center down from the foyer, but before the start of the hallway. It's a straight shot out the door and not far to haul all our stuff. I would like to set everything up in a semicircle and have our chairs inside that. The proximity sensor is on the left, reel-to-reel next to that, CCTV monitors in the middle, and the motion picture camera next. Put the 35mm loaded with infrared film on a tripod pointing to the living room for now. Next, we need to set up the video camera that we'd better bring back in one piece, in Johnny Lang's room. Oh, don't forget the infrared illuminators in the dining room and Johnny's room."

Vic's face turned pallid at the mere mention of the horrific scene of Johnny Lang's suicide. "Oh... yeah, Johnny's room. Uh, can you help me with that?"

"Sure, I wanna see it too, but not alone." Don smiled at him.

"Thanks!"

"Of course, buddy. Who'd wanna go up there by themselves?"

Looking up to the very top of the staircase, Vic uttered, "Well, it sure as shit ain't me!"

Dragging video cable behind them, Don and Vic headed up the steps with the infrared video camera they borrowed from the photography department and a large spool of coaxial cable to transmit video back to the monitor downstairs.

They arrived at the attic door, which opened to Johnny's room. The doorknob was the old glass type, black. Don reached for the knob, and it turned as if partially rusted and squeaked with the sound of metal on metal. The bolt withdrew. As he carefully pushed open the door, it groaned and squealed.

Don turned back to Vic and remarked, "Damn, that's not creepy at all, is it?"

Vic shuddered and looked in from the door jamb.

Stepping inside the sky-blue room, they looked around for any signs of the legendary suicide. Never made again after Johnny's terrible deed, the bed was disheveled and wrinkled. The bed cover, a heavy quilt, lay in a heap on the bed.

In the middle of the room, on the floor, was an ugly, dark stain where the blood soaked into the wood.

Vic looked up and down at the plastered walls for a tell-tale sign. About six feet up from the floor, over Johnny's bed, was a hole. As he looked closer, there were very tiny dark splatters near it.

Strewn on the floor at the foot of the bed were letters, cards, and notes in a girl's handwriting.

"Oh my God, Don. It's all true. He must have gone crazy over the break-up, torturing himself with old love letters, and then... well, there's the floor and the bullet hole."

"I wonder why this room never got cleaned up or anything."

"If it were your child, would you want to? Would you ever want to enter the room again?"

"Yeah, I guess not. God, his parents! What they must have gone through. Awful!"

"If ever there were a place for ghosts, this is it."

Using a wide-angle lens, Vic set up the camera on a tripod in one corner of the room to catch anything that might happen.

"With this camera, we will get clear video and in the dark to boot! I even have the infrared illuminator mounted on top of the camera, so we'll see everything in complete darkness," Vic assured.

"Let's just make sure we get it back to the photography department without a scratch, or they'll have our asses," said Don.

"You know it. Neither one of us has any money."

Vic lined up the camera to get an overall shot of Johnny's bed, the stain left on the floor, and as much of the wall with the bullet hole, as he could. Everything was now ready for the night's investigation.

"Well, I think we have everything set up unless we forgot something?" Don asked.

"No, most of our stuff is gonna be used downstairs. We hardly have any cameras to post anyway."

"Okay, I think we need to head back to our little headquarters downstairs and just wait and see what happens." For several uneasy moments, they stood there scanning the sickening scene before them and then headed downstairs to their monitoring station.

As nightfall came, they sat in the chairs inside their little semicircle of monitoring equipment. Don took half and Vic the other. At 11:43 p.m., a proximity sensor indicated something was moving in the kitchen. Unfortunately, there were no cameras in this area, so either Don or Vic had to check it out themselves. Vic decided to volunteer.

"You sure you wanna go? You don't have to," insisted Don.

"If I don't go, how are we gonna know what's going on and document it? I would have liked to have more investigators with us, but you know the school culture. Small people, small minds equal cowards," Vic scoffed and pounded the table with his fist.

"Yeah, I know. Next time I'll go if there is a next time."

Vic sighed, looked at Don, and got up from the perceived safety of the monitoring table. He walked at a slow, unsteady pace from the foyer until he reached the entrance to the stretch of hallway. Along the hall, there were several rooms on either side that would have been accommodated by the once large Lang family. As he approached the entrance, he looked back at Don, who gave him thumbs up. Vic, whose face had now become ashen, gave a pained look as if he'd swallowed a rock and turned back toward the hall.

Whether out of fear or superstition, he took every step as quietly as he could, looking into the pitch-black rooms along the way as he passed them. He had left his flashlight on the monitoring table. What he thought he might see with such an absence of light was a mystery.

As he neared the kitchen, a prickly sensation on his skin struck him, and he saw that the kitchen ceiling lights were flickering though off. By this point, his goose pimples had goose pimples.

Vic peered into the kitchen, straining his eyes to see if there was anyone inside.

He flipped one of the kitchen light switches, but nothing happened.

Something dark, darker than the surrounding night, shot across the length of the kitchen and into the opposite wall.

Vic bolted from the kitchen entrance and briskly walked back to the monitoring station.

"Well, what was it?"

Out of breath, Vic answered, "What was what?"

"The proximity sensor!"

"Yeah, right, uh, shit. I got a creepy feeling walking down that hall. It just washed over me, and I almost panicked. It was like something was waiting to jump out at me from every room, but as I got to the kitchen, I got this static electricity all over me. The lights in the kitchen were flickering even though they were off! I tried to turn them on, but nothing happened. Then I saw a black, I dunno, blob-like thing dart across the room! I said, fuck this, I'm gone!"

After Vic was done explaining to Don what happened, they both heard a pot or pan hit the kitchen floor.

"Man, I wish we had another camera! I mean, is that a rat or something else making that noise?" Don excitedly announced, with eyes as big as saucers.

"I'm not going back down there!" Vic declared. "That's enough solo adventure for me. I don't need rabies, either. There's something wrong in that fucking kitchen!

"That's cool, Vic; I wouldn't do it either. But look at it this way, we're not leaving here with no evidence. How many places have we been where nothing at all happens?"

Vic sat back down at his seat behind the monitoring station for a moment.

"I gotta go to the bathroom," he announced after a minute.

Turning to look back at Vic as he was walking toward the front door, Don reminded him, "Just don't forget, there's no running water in this place."

"I'm taking a leak, not a shit, dofus."

"Hey, bring in the cooler too while you're at it, and don't forget the portable potty, in case you crap your pants," Don harangued as he threw an empty pop can at him.

"You're hilarious," Vic deadpanned as the can tumbled onto the floor.

Don snickered and watched him walk outside.

As Don tried to keep an eye on all the equipment, the camera's proximity sensor caused it to snap off several photos in a row of the living room at which it was pointed. He turned back toward the open front door and called for Vic.

"Vic! Hey Vic!"

"I'm bringing the damn cooler," Vic yelled as he zipped up his pants.

"No! Th- the camera! It went off! Maybe we got something!" Don corrected, looking back toward the living room and to the monitors several times.

Don narrowed his eyes, lamenting, "I wish we could get a Polaroid that could be hooked up to the sensor so we didn't have to wait."

"We should get one next time so that we can take pictures at random anyway," Vic added, motioning as though taking a picture with a camera.

"Now that we have the cooler inside, you want a Coke?" Vic asked, rummaging through the ice and pop cans.

"Sure," he answered, holding out his hands to catch a tossed can.

Sitting at the monitoring table, Don propped his feet up on the table and remarked, "I'll tell ya one thing, out here in the boonies, it's fuckin' dark! No roadway lights out this far, and you can't see your hand in front of your face without a flashlight."

"Yeah, I was afraid it'd be dark before we got things unloaded and set up. I didn't want to use up all our Coleman lantern fuel before we even started, just to see to unload the damn truck.

"Well, we got it done, buddy," Don said with a satisfied smile.

Shifting his attention back to the equipment, Don asked, "Can you keep an eye on the reel to reel too? If the tape is close to running out, change it or let me know."

"I can do that," Vic assured, placing a new reel of Scotch recording tape in front of the recorder.

At 01:07 a.m., the film camera's proximity sensor kicked on and began filming the hallway toward the other rooms and the kitchen at the end. The sensor detected movement toward the camera. Don and Vic sat up in their chairs and watched the monitor and the hallway.

A mist that resembled cigarette smoke came from one of the rooms along the hall.

It wafted and swirled toward the camera in a vertical form. At times, portions of it seemed to form into shapes of a human arm, torso, and head but quickly reformed into a mist. The hallway lights on the ceiling flickered as it passed.

Then it came closer and closer to the camera and slowly faded until nothing of it remained.

"HOL-EE SHIT!" Vic exclaimed. "Did you see that?!"

"God yes! And we got it on film!"

As Don spoke the last syllable, every door along the hall slammed closed, one after another, and the whole house shook.

"What the fuck is going on?!" Don yelled.

"Jesus! This place is coming apart. We need to get the fuck out of here!"

"Wait! Just wait! Give it a minute, don't say anything."

They both stood up to run but stayed behind the monitoring table for a few moments.

But there was only silence—no lights, no mist… nothing.

Only the lights from the monitors on the table gave any light into the darkness.

"What now?" Vic whispered. "My heart is jumping out of my chest."

"I dunno," Don replied, his voice breathless, while his hands quivered like jello. "Maybe it's over."

"What's over?" Vic asked, his voice cracking.

"Whatever the hell that was."

"I sure hope so," he whispered again.

"Okay, okay, let's try to calm down, we have a job to do. We need to remember that," Don reassured.

Five minutes passed when Vic asked, "Are we staying inside?"

"I think so, for now, anyway."

02:45 a.m.: All was quiet at the monitoring table. In fact, they both drifted in and out of sleep, figuring the proximity sensors activating any of the equipment would wake them.

Don nodded off, and the call of mother nature woke Vic. Vic stepped away from the table and back outside, taking his flashlight with him. He found his spot and did his business.

Just as he was finishing, every proximity sensor went off, activating the motion picture film camera, 35 mm camera, and the video camera in Johnny's room, making a racket loud enough that Vic could hear outside.

"Don! Don! What the hell is going on?!" he screamed as he sat on a large firewood log.

Jumping up from his chair, Don shouted, "I got it! I'm gonna check it out. Get back in here and watch for me!"

"Hey wait! I gotta pull up my pants!"

Don didn't answer back.

Moving as fast as he could, Vic cleaned himself and grabbed his pants off the ground, fumbling with the buckle as he ran back into the house.

Don was gone.

The monitoring equipment was still running.

Vic scanned the immediate area, but there was no Don.

Shit! He ran up to Johnny's room by himself; goddammit!

"Fuck! Now I gotta go find him!"

Vic bounded up the steps to Johnny's room.

The door, partially open, slammed closed.

"What the fuck?!" Vic screamed.

Pounding on the door with both fists, Vic called out to him, "Don! Don! Are you in there?! Answer me, goddammit! Are you in there?!"

The door opened a crack.

"Don? Don? Is that you? Please answer me," Vic whispered.

In an instant, the door opened wide to reveal pitch-black darkness, as though everything inside was painted black.

Something behind Vic shoved him inside, and the door to Johnny's room slammed closed again.

Two black, amorphous shapes passed through Johnny's bedroom door and disappeared like smoke.

PRESENT-DAY, ALL HALLOWS EVE

It's been a Mill Grove tradition to drive by the abandoned Lang farm on Halloween night and stop for a few minutes on the road just to look at the old place. Of course, they want to see if they can spot Johnny Lang's ghost or anything spooky. But that's it. Never going in. They stay outside where they can speed away.

The past unexplained disappearances kept these curiosity seekers from doing any more than looking from what they considered a safe distance and with a quick escape. And like that, many decades passed since anyone dared to step foot inside the Lang farmhouse. But there was one intrepid soul who would attempt such a feat. She was old now and suffering from a terminal illness. She was facing a painful death. Fear was much less an enemy now that her end was near.

It was not until her thirties that Christina gained enough maturity from raising her family to realize what she had done to Johnny so long ago was a terrible evil. She had been such a narcissistic teen, but when she was responsible for her own children, the thought occurred to her, what if she had married Johnny?

It was then she admitted to herself that if not for her, Johnny would have had a family of his own.

Now that she would be meeting her Maker soon enough, she had to make amends to Johnny and his family. It was the only decent thing she could do now.

She gathered her family together to explain what she intended to do and why.

A tan car pulled up in front of her house. It was her son Thomas. His wife stayed home with their children. This was to be an adult conversation, not appropriate for kids.

Thomas opened the front door to his mother's house.

She was sitting in her favorite chair, surrounded by old pictures from her high school days. Christina's eyes welled with tears as she reminisced about her past and regrets. She held a dainty kerchief in her left hand as she went through her collection of old photos she had squirreled away in the attic.

There were pictures of herself and Johnny, along with old love letters she had stored in a tattered, white shoebox. She'd forgotten about the box in her attic. She had written in pencil on the lid *'My Box'* many years ago as a young girl and hidden it at the bottom of a trunk full of old clothes, no longer in style.

Christina thumbed through the fragile photos, stopping at each one to take in the lost memories. She punished herself with the secret regret she had kept inside most of her life. No one could convince her she did not deserve it.

As Thomas walked toward his mother, he couldn't help but wonder if this was about his dad or, worse, some terrible family secret.

"Mom, what's going on? Why did you say not to bring Candi and the kids?"

Holding a wadded tissue in her hand to dab her eyes, she answered, "When your sister gets here, I'll explain."

Confused, Thomas, nevertheless, sat quietly, waiting for his sister to arrive.

A silver VW Bug arrived within ten minutes, and his sister Terry came through the front door.

Terry, distressed at the awful possibilities running through her mind, hurriedly asked, "Mom? What's this all about? What's the big secret?"

She took a deep breath, scooted herself in her chair, and wiped her eyes as she sniffed, "I have a confession to make."

Incredulous, Thomas frowned, "What could you confess? You haven't done anything to us!"

"Yeah, mom, that doesn't make any sense," Terry agreed.

"It's not about you. It's about me. You know about the Lang farmhouse, right?"

Both nodded. "Yes."

"Please listen," she begged. "It got that reputation because of me."

"Mom, you're not making sense. It got that way because Johnny Lang shot and killed himself back in the 1950s, not you," Thomas insisted as he sat across from his mother.

Tears streamed from Christina's eyes, running down her cheeks. She bowed her head and sobbed into her kerchief.

"Mom! Why in the world are you crying?" Terry asked, placing her arm around her and wiping her eyes with her hanky. "Johnny killed himself. You're not responsible for that!"

Insistent on her guilt, Christina shouted, "Yes, I am!" and pounded her knees with her fists. "I'm the reason he killed himself! He'd still be alive if it weren't for me, but I was a selfish, conceited little bitch."

"Mom!" Thomas exclaimed as he scooted to the edge of the chair toward her, "What the hell are you talking about?"

"I'm talking about regrets, and I have a huge one. I must tell you this before I'm gone. Remember, I don't have a lot of time left, and you have to know.

"I was a good and faithful wife to your father, but I wasn't always so good. I was a very different person in my teen years."

"Okay, we all go through changes' mom." Terry put her face almost nose to nose close to her mother's. "But that doesn't make you a monster." She tried to assure her.

But Christina shook her head. "I *was* a monster at one time! I was Johnny's girlfriend, his lover. I thought he was so handsome, and being a school jock, I wanted to be seen with him. I wanted to be able to brag about being his girlfriend. He had a nice car, and I liked to be seen with him in it. We dated for several years. He was head-over-heels in love with me, and I loved it. I thought I was a big deal having such a popular boy in love with me. I bragged about it all the time.

Johnny would take me everywhere. He would buy me jewelry and take me out to nice restaurants. He spoiled me, and I was already spoiled when I met him.

I concerned myself with what I wanted and nothing else. I thought the world owed me. I look back on it now, and I don't recognize the person I was. I hate her! But it was me that was a snobby, self-centered, stuck-up little bitch, that wouldn't have recognized the importance of true love if it had bashed me over the head."

"Mom... you just grew up, is all. You became an adult," Thomas insisted.

"No! I knew how much Johnny loved me. He loved me that way for several years. But one day, I got a bug up my bottom and decided I was bored with Johnny.

He expected I would go with him to the prom, and why wouldn't he? We had been together... and intimate for so long. But no, I wanted to go with another boy, and I never gave it another thought. I threw Johnny away as if he was nothing more than a pet goldfish to me.

That was the day he killed himself. I felt terrible about it, but I was still more concerned with myself and what people thought of me. It's incredible that I had such a thick skull, but I did, and that's a fact. That's why I've kept it a secret. Who'd want anyone to know that about themselves?

I actually had the gall to try to pay my respects to his parents and went to his house to tell them I was sorry. But instead, they told me never to show my face again at their home and blamed me for their son's death.

Now I know I didn't pull the trigger, but there is no denying that he would never have killed himself if I had been a decent person. There is no denying that he would be alive if I had been faithful to him and not thrown him away like used toilet paper.

I'm the reason the Lang farmhouse is haunted, and no amount of arguing by either of you or anyone else will change that fact.

I'm dying. Cancer will kill me anyway, so what do I have to fear? I have to do whatever possible while I can to give Johnny peace. To release him from that house and step into the light. I can only pray he will forgive me and meet me when I pass. He deserves nothing less and a whole lot more."

Sitting down on the couch across from her mother, Terry asked, "So, what do you intend to do, mom?"

"You can't bring him back," Thomas said, standing up and pacing about the room. "And how do you expect to... 'explain' yourself to him?"

"He's in that house. He's *always* been in that house. Perhaps he's the reason for the unexplained disappearances surrounding the place." Christina got up from her chair and stood facing her son and daughter. "Whatever the cause, I know he's there, angry, hurting all these years from what I did to him. I *owe him* at least that, and I'm not missing my chance to pay part of that debt while I still can."

Thomas, scratching his head, asked, "So, then what exactly are you going to do?"

"I'm going to the house, and I'm going to talk to him... by myself." Christina, her fist pounding the palm of her other hand, declared, "This is *my* debt and mine alone. So, I wanted you both to know while I'm able to tell you."

"You won't take anyone with you?" asked Thomas.

"No. If I don't come back, you know where to find me. My car will be there. You can't stop me, so don't try. I'm doing this," Christina implored, clutching the keys to her old car.

"Dad would stop you if he were still here," Terry said, her eyes welling up.

"That's for sure," replied Thomas, handing his sister a tissue.

"I know he would, and that's because he loved me. He loved me as much as Johnny did, and thank God I was able to realize that! I have two beautiful children, grandchildren, and even great-grandchildren because of it. And those are all things Johnny never got to have and experience.

But now, it is time to do the right thing. This is one regret I refuse to accept on my deathbed."

Thomas looked over at his sister, "I think we understand, mom, and if we had to admit it, we'd probably do the same thing. You raised us right, mom."

Terry nodded in agreement.

"Mom, If this is what you really want..." Thomas agreed, running his hand through his hair, "...we won't try to stop you."

Placing her right hand over her heart, Christina gushed, "I knew you'd understand. I wish I'd been mature and thoughtful enough to have returned the love Johnny gave to me, but I can't change the past. I can only try to affect the future, and I don't have much time left to do that."

"When are you going to do this?" asked Terry, rubbing his chin.

"When it's time," she said mysteriously.

Disappointed, Thomas shook his head. "You're not going to tell us, are you?"

"No, I'm not." Christina smiled.

THE DEBT: A TRICK OR TREAT?

Christina sat that morning at the breakfast table, looking out at the angry skies and contemplating what she was about to do.

What would happen to her?

Would she disappear, too, like the others?

Did they disappear, or did something else happen to them?

What if she saw Johnny's ghost?

Could she keep from screaming?

Would she fight the urge to run out, or would she have the courage to speak, pouring out her heart, begging for forgiveness?

Having haunted his old house alone for so many years, what will he do when he sees her?

No matter, she thought. She must do this regardless.

It was time.

She adorned herself in the prettiest dress she owned and pinned on a beautiful brooch given to her by Johnny that she had not worn since that awful day. It was preserved in the same shoebox along with the love letters, photos, and other items from Johnny.

Christina wore her hair as close as possible to the same fashion as when they dated, though now it was mostly gray.

She looked at herself in the full-length mirror behind her bedroom door. Her youthful curves were gone. The dress hung on her tiny frame, but she was still attractive for her age.

She frowned at her reflection and said, "Well, this is as good as it gets."

Christina walked out her front door, wondering if this would be the last time she did so.

Then looked her old Buick over once.

Just get me to Johnny's house; that's all I ask.

The radio was switched on, tuned to her favorite rock and roll oldies.

Sam Cooke was singing 'Only Sixteen'.

Christina wondered if this was some sort of sinister message from Johnny.

She shut it off before the next lyric.

Traversing the winding and hilly back roads, she thought about what to say to Johnny's spirit and prayed that she would not goof it up but say all the right things.

Storm clouds were moving over the countryside. Expecting it to pour at any moment, she looked at the floor on the passenger side, spying on her umbrella.

The air filled with electricity from the approaching storm. She could see the lighting from far off, but there was no thunder yet.

Now she was on 500 W/700 N, the road leading to the Lang farmhouse. Christina saw coming into sight on her left the white clapboard house. It was overgrown with weeds and wild vegetation on the property. English Ivy crept up every side of the house and wrapped itself around the red brick chimney on the east side of the home.

She sat for several minutes looking up at the forlorn, abandoned farmstead. Its windows, opaque from the years of dust and windstorms, restricted much of the light of day. The screen door hung from one hinge, and its metal screen—time caused it to be covered in rust. The porch roof was still held up by flaking turned wooden supports. The front door still sported a mechanical doorbell that one could turn by hand to notify its residents.

Black storm clouds from a passing thunderstorm gathered over the Lang Farm, dumping a heavy deluge on the area.

Through the pouring rain, a bolt of lightning struck the large oak tree at the driveway entrance, causing a large section to fall and block the drive.

Undeterred by the threatening situation unfolding before her, Christina took a deep breath and stepped out of her car.

She dropped her umbrella in the weeds and ran onto the rickety porch. Her next step found a rotten part of the porch floor, and it gave way. She fell to the floor, the jagged board cutting her leg as it went through. Christina screamed in pain, and as she withdrew her leg from the porch floor, her shoe fell off underneath in the crawlspace. She sat down and with a grimace, strained to bring her leg up to look at her injuries. Blood ran down her leg from the scrapes. Having nothing to wipe them, she used her hands and stuck them out into the rain to be washed off.

She gathered herself up, and looking down at her other leg, she removed that shoe before walking barefoot into the house.

Christina opened the front door. It made a sound that, to her mind, was like a rusty casket. Perhaps it would not be long before she lay in one. One like Johnny was laid to rest-in.

She closed the door behind her. Dust fell from the threshold as it latched. The filthy windows forbade most light penetration, but now with the black thunderclouds overhead, it might as well have been night. It certainly was as dark as any night inside.

Christina had left her flashlight in the glove box, but she was not about to go back out into the storm to get it. Instead, she would wait until her eyes adjusted to what little light there was.

She looked to her left and right, now she could see ahead of her. Christina spotted a series of tables in a semicircle with various strange, dust-covered instruments. Looking them over, she could see that they were very old and covered with a thick layer of dust and cobwebs. A few soda cans and snack packages were strewn about and seemed to be from the same period.

Before the hallway of rooms, ahead of her, were the stairs that led to the second floor. She knew what was up there and beyond because of spending time in this house long ago with Johnny. Christina knew where his room was. She had made love with Johnny in it when his parents weren't there.

Like a movie in her mind, the memories came flooding back. Back when she was so young. Back when she and Johnny couldn't get enough of each other. Back when they were almost caught in the barn. They were exciting, thrilling risks, and their passion made it all the more intoxicating.

God, if she could only relive it, she'd do things so differently now. She'd love him right and stay with him. Marry him and have his children. But then, isn't that the human condition? she thought. She didn't appreciate what she had and lost it forever. Christina thought she didn't deserve the man she did have, and it was only by God's grace that she did.

Christina looked up the staircase to the second-floor landing. Carefully watching where she stepped, now that she was barefoot, and walked to the foot of the stairs. Holding onto the railing, she mounted each stair, one at a time, keeping her eyes up ahead.

Reaching the landing, she looked to the left and right down the hall, hesitating at the short steps to Johnny's converted attic room.

She had not seen his room since the late 1950s, and now she stood at the base of the steps leading to his bedroom door.

Up the stairs, Christina climbed until she was face to face with it. Dare she touch the doorknob? There's no backing out now, she thought.

Her hand reached for it. She hesitated for a moment but placed her fingers on its black glass handle. It turned. As rusty steel will, it squealed and made a 'clunk' sound as the bolt retracted into the door. She slowly pushed it open. The bedroom walls were still sky blue. Johnny's bed and everything else in the room were just as she remembered.

Except for the ugly stain on the wooden floor.

And the bullet hole in the wall, where it lodged after passing through his skull and brain.

Plus, the small splatters of blood on the quilt and white plaster wall.

Including the letters and cards she had written to him strewn about the room.

Those things she didn't remember.

Christina became sick to her stomach at seeing the aftermath, left lying in the places they finally rested after the awful tragedy. Nothing had been changed or moved. It was a time capsule dedicated to a horror beyond description.

The room where she had spent romantic times with Johnny could no longer evoke those pleasant times, those passionate liaisons. It only held the memory of a dead, once-living nightmare. A nightmare that one could never awake from.

Christina had readied herself for this moment. And had practiced it over and over again in her head. She had so much to say. So much forgiveness to beg for. So much repentance for the girl she had been, and hopefully forgiven because of the woman she had become.

Surely, if Johnny is really there, he'll see that I'm not the same person I was.

She was redeemed. If only Johnny could see that, maybe it would set them both free. She began the prepared speech and quest for forgiveness, "Johnny, I don't know if you can recognize me or not. It's Christina. I'm an old woman now. I have no right to ask you for forgiveness, but I am dying. I have cancer and very little time left. I wanted to use this time to get on my knees in front of you and beg for forgiveness. I-I-I'm… I'm sorry…" she began to sob. "I-I was a rotten, spoiled little bitch! I cared only about what I wanted and no one else.

I was too stupid and immature to realize that you genuinely loved me. Through my selfishness, I thought of only myself. Had I had at least one rational thought in my head, I would have known what a wonderful boy I had found and never let you get away from me! But I didn't. I was an undeserving brat. I want you to know I became a better person. I came to know just how awful I was, and I hated that person. I wanted to be… I wanted to be the kind of person you were," she cried. "I wouldn't blame you if you killed me or did to me whatever happened to the others that came here. Not since I changed my ways has a day gone by that I didn't regret what I did to you. I should have loved you right and married you. We should have had a family and grown old together. Do what you will to me, but please, in the name of God, please forgive me. When I die, I want to see your face, and I want you to have peace. A peace you deserve, no thanks to me. I want you to walk into the light at peace and with God. Please, Johnny, before I die, please forgive me."

Christina's face was reddened and swollen. The top of her dress soaked with tears, and her fixed hair, now hanging down in her face, she knelt on the cold, dirty floor of Johnny's room.

She continued sobbing, bent over so that her head was resting on the floor as she begged.

Suddenly, Christina felt a creeping coldness coming from behind her. She could feel the temperature drop. Her back became colder. She was sure of it.

Footsteps. Footsteps were climbing the stairs.

Now they reached the landing, getting closer.

She could see her breath in Johnny's room.

Christina could sense someone behind her. She could feel them glaring at her with a hatred she had never known. Someone was there, alright. Had Johnny come to make her disappear into nothing like the others?

She resigned herself to her fate. She had given it her best shot, and now it was over.

Christina turned around to face her doom, but there was no Johnny.

Before her eyes, she watched as an apparition formed.

The wispy visage of Johnny's parents.

She knew them both in life, but they were in front of her as spirits.

They glared at her with demonic hatred. There was no doubt that they wanted her dead in Christina's mind. But it couldn't be, could it? Yet, there they were, standing just outside Johnny's room, their eyes burning holes in her as she knelt on his bedroom floor.

They spoke to her.

"We've been waiting for you. Waiting for you since we were killed in a car wreck only two years after you killed our beloved Johnny! We knew you'd come. And knew you couldn't stay away forever. We warned you never to come here again. You're going to pay for killing our boy; you're going to be dead to everyone, just like all the others!"

However, before they did anything, Christina heard a voice from behind.

A voice she had not heard since she was a teenager.

"Leave her be, mom; leave her be, dad."

Christina turned to see Johnny standing before her.

He glowed, emitting a golden light around himself.

It was a beautiful aura that was coming from within him somehow.

"She's not the same person anymore. The girl she was, *is* dead. She is a woman. I can feel it from her heart. She's the woman I always wanted. I *chose* to end things the way I did. I am responsible for my actions. Each of us has our sins, and each of us must ask for our forgiveness. I can no longer hang onto this hatred, and you must do the same. I want to leave this house. Leave her be, mom and dad; leave her be."

Johnny looked at Christina and spoke the words she came for, "Christina, you are forgiven. Be at peace."

Christina, prostrated before Johnny, sobbed, but they were tears of joy this time.

A brilliant white light filled the room, yet it was not blinding.

Puzzled, Johnny turned and looked at it, but turned back to Christina.

"Yes, Johnny, that's the light. God's light. Walk into it."

He smiled at her, looked into the light, and turned back to her, "I'll wait for you."

Johnny walked into the light until all that left *was* the light, and it too faded away.

The ghosts of Johnny's parents were also gone. Only silence and the gloom of the house remained.

Christina lay on Johnny's bed, falling asleep until she too saw the light where Johnny was waiting for her.

Covenstown

Deenya Vaughn stared at the front page of the Covenstown Press. She scowled at the picture of Officer David Hine on the page. She really hated that man. The headline above his head made Deenya want to laugh out loud.

OFFICER DAVID HINE SAVES THE LIFE OF A YOUNG GIRL.

And in the subheading:

CONSIDERED A HERO.

Deenya groaned at the unfairness of it all. That case was hers, and she almost cracked it. But, thanks to Officer Hine for duping her, she lost out big on this one. She gasped and looked around the pumpkin patch in frustration. Her feet were freezing, and wisps of fog came out of her mouth in huffs. She wanted to toss the newspaper on the ground and stomp on David's stupid face, but the patch owners probably didn't want her littering, and they didn't deserve it anyway.

"Deenya?"

Her mom Elena called and came over with a cart full of pumpkins. Deenya's eyebrow raised in question instantly. *Now what?* She hoped that her mom wasn't expecting her to carve all these pumpkins. Unfortunately, she had been given the boot by Chief Vaughn, her dad, and superior. Well, not exactly the boot, but he didn't want her coming to the station for at least a week. So with Halloween in the next two days, she decided to head to a party with two of her friends. Tucking the newspaper under her arm, she ran over to help. The older woman smiled and thumped one of the pumpkins.

"Which one do you want? Do you want them all or just one... or two?"

"Mom, are you serious?"

Surveying the cart, Deenya picked out the smallest one and another that was easier to carry. Elena gently sat the pumpkins on the ground, and with a hand on her hips, she gestured towards the pumpkins in her daughter's arms with a frown.

"But you know your father wanted us to get the biggest one."

"Well, Dad isn't the one that has to carry these big lugs back to the car and get them into the house, is he?"

Elena giggled silently as Deenya went to the owners and paid for the pumpkin. All the while cursing David the whole way back to the car. Thanks to him, she was sure that she would be doing desk work for the rest of her life once she returned to work. And was convinced she probably wouldn't be able to work on high-profile cases again. As usual, her mom wanted to enjoy the experience of having her daughter drive her around and quickly got into the passenger side. This fueled Deenya's annoyance even more, and she sighed while putting the pumpkin in the backseat.

"Where to now?" Deenya asked, getting into the car and hooking her seatbelt.

"Well, I have to go pick up my medicine from the pharmacy," Elena replied with a sweet smile. "Then I have to get the beef for the stew tonight."

"Yeah, Yeah."

Deenya sped out of the parking lot. She would head to the pharmacy first. For some reason, she thought she'd need medicine for migraine in a couple of days.

The next morning Deenya got up earlier than usual. She went to work on carving the pumpkin that Elena had left at her place. She did mediocre at best because she wasn't really in the mood to try her best. Besides, this was the one thing Chief Vaughn couldn't judge her on. After the pumpkin carving, she placed it on the table by the front door and pulled out the Halloween decorations from an old box in the closet. After decorating was finished, she took a shower and combed her hair.

Deenya glanced at the sticky notes she had plastered on the mirror. They reminded her of why she chose to stick it out with the police force, although some of the guys in the force looked down on her. Her thoughts drifted to that rainy Halloween night she first joined the force.

Chief Vaughn wasn't keen on having her in the same department as him. She was the only girl on the team, and the guys made sure she knew it. Officer Aiden Mack was the only cop on the force that was nice to her. Of course, other women were working there, but they were assigned to other teams, not her own. Then there was David Hine. At first, he was nice to her, and they even shared an intimate relationship, but it was all a ruse.

David did his best work behind her back. He made sure to steal the cases right out from under her nose, making the team think it was because she was incompetent. There was no way someone could be that dense and a police officer. Deenya let the thoughts drop. Every harsh word they said was written on the little notes. They reminded her to show the boys in blue exactly what she could do.

"Deenya, are you home?"

Deenya smiled at that familiar voice. It was her friend Charlotte. Charlotte's footsteps drew closer as Deenya pulled her hair in a ponytail.

"Char," she screamed at her friend, who stood in the doorway. "I was just about to come and see you!"

"Yeah, well, I couldn't wait that long." Charlotte retorted before pulling her into a deep embrace.

Deenya welcomed the hug. She wanted to cry but couldn't. A year had passed since she joined the force, and felt like she hadn't done anything to prove herself. Charlotte could sense her foreboding sadness and reply instantly.

"I wouldn't worry too much about the force. You know your father is hard on you because he loves you."

"I don't see it that way," Deenya said with a sniff. "I wanted to prove to the men that I could do it on my own and didn't need their help. Maybe I should have stuck to teaching like Mom wanted."

"But being a police officer was your dream. You wanted to succeed in a field that was dominated by men. So why would you give that up now?"

Charlotte was right. Deenya wanted to succeed where no other women had. She didn't know about other places, but the force here was male-dominated. She wanted to be the first woman to conquer it all.

"I'm sorry, Char," Deenya sighed. "I needed that pep talk from you."

Charlotte took the time to admire the ghost placed on the banister, and Deenya laughed at the frown on her friend's face.

"Well, at least you're still in the mood to celebrate Halloween," Charlotte noted.

"Yeah, well. I can't let Officer Hine ruin all my fun."

Charlotte's gaze swept past her. "Umm. You might want to hold that thought for now."

Deenya followed her friend's gaze. Officer Mack was making his way up her driveway. He had a basket full of Halloween goodies and smiled when Deenya opened the door before having the chance to knock.

"Aiden," she gasped, surprise flooding her features. "What are you doing here?"

"The chief wants to see you," he announced, handing the basket to her. "Hello, Charlotte."

"Hi, Aiden," Charlotte replied with a full-blown smile. "How's work going?"

"The same old, same old. Had a new case come in." He then looked at Deenya and nodded. "Shall we go?"

Deenya didn't respond. She didn't want to see her dad or the faces of the officers, who would just laugh at her for getting her case swiped away. But she was a professional; if anything, she had nothing to be ashamed of. So she'd march right in there and show them that they couldn't intimidate her, not for even a second.

* * *

Deenya scowled and brushed past Officer Tate as he congratulated Officer Hine. Apparently, dear old dad was giving her a chance to take on another case. He wasn't mad that her case was stolen by Officer Hine. He was mad at the fact that Deenya chose to go at everything alone. So here she was again, in the spirit of 'teamwork'.

Deenya shuffled past another group of officers that blocked the aisles. "She thought that she could solve it on her own."

Deenya shot an evil glare at the male officer. He shrugged. But she held her head high and went back to the rooms to change into her uniform. She was greeted by Officer Mack again after she was done.

"You okay?" he asked, looking a little concerned.

Then he moved to straighten the collar of her shirt, but she moved away from him. She went to her desk and sat down. Officer Mack followed and placed a pile of paperwork on her desk. Deenya swallowed a lump that was forming in her throat as Mack walked away. She couldn't believe them. However, she'd show them by solving a big case without their help. They would have no choice but to look up to her.

Officer Hine sauntered over to her with a smirk on his face. Deenya ignored him and pretended to be going over one of the files. But he still knocked lightly on her desk.

"No hard feelings, yeah?" he asked with a grin and smoothed back his short dark hair.

Deenya glared daggers at him. His clear green eyes sparkled with confidence and amusement.

"You stole that case from me," she said through clenched teeth.

"Come on Deenya," he grumbled like a child. "You insisted on solving it alone, although your father insisted I partner with you."

Deenya turned her chair away from him. "You know that I work alone," she hissed, bitterly. "I don't need a partner."

"Which is why I discussed it with the Chief, and he said that I had free reign to do what I want."

David came around her desk and stood in front of her.

"Without my information, you wouldn't know where to look!" she screamed.

David looked to the other officers and grinned when they glanced in their direction. Then he grabbed a chair from another desk and pulled it close to her.

"Don't make a scene," he whispered. "If you're so bent out of shape, take it up with the Chief."

Deenya was about to protest, but she closed her mouth. She was not going to whine to her Dad like some scared little girl. In here, she wasn't his daughter anyway. She was just an officer like everyone else. But then again, out of here, she wasn't his daughter either.

"I tell you what," David started. "I'll make it up to you. I'll buy you a cup of coffee; how's that?"

Deenya ignored him and turned back to her desk, gazing at the stack of papers dropped off by Aiden. Then, she opened a file containing a drug bust from a few days ago. She pretended to concentrate on the file as David eyed her with curiosity.

"Go away, David. I'm not in the mood," she groaned, finally showing her annoyance. But before he could reply, Chief Vaughn appeared around the corner.

"Officer Hine." A deep scowl was present on his face as he motioned for David to join him in his office.

"Yes sir," David replied and then gave Deenya's shoulder a gentle squeeze before he went to join the chief.

Deenya sighed as she thought about how David was nothing but a snake in the grass. Like an idiot, she gave him all her leads, only for him to use the information she gathered to his own benefit. It wasn't the first time he got the credit for her work. She glanced at the others as they talked and shared ideas with one another.

Ever since arriving at the precinct, she'd focused only on one person, herself. She didn't care to make friends and didn't need anyone. Deenya didn't know it then, but her way of thinking was costing her big time. She was friendless, partnerless, and no one in the station respected her.

"Wait, just you wait," she whispered. "I'm going to show you all what I'm capable of."

"You might want to put that on pause for the moment," Officer Mack said from behind before placing his cell phone in front of her. "Remember the case involving the cult the Lights of Davern? It seems like they're back to posting videos online again."

Deenya watched the video with amusement. Hensley, the leader of this particular cult, stood at the front of the room.

"Oh great Davern, guide us and take us through this perilous journey of cleansing our minds, bodies, and souls."

She gave each of the girls in the cult a goblet of liquid. Deenya knew a little bit of information on the Lights of Davern. The Lights of Davern claimed they were responsible for keeping Covenstown safe from harm. They couldn't do that if their minds, bodies, and souls weren't clear, which Deenya thought was a load of crap. She watched as Hensley used a single white candle to light all the others in the room. Then she walked slowly back to the altar, her golden locks trailed in waves behind her. Once she was back to her place in the center, Hensley opened the book to complete the so-called ritual.

"Davern, our honorable and noble sister, give us your strength as we finish your work and keep our citizens safe."

The girls repeated the words and stared down into their goblets. Then, they each glanced at her, awaiting the signal. Hensley held up her own goblet and came up front so the others could see.

"My sisters," she addressed. "As the Lights of Davern, we have a duty to protect our people and honor Lady Davern by continuing her work."

"Yes, sister," the youngest witch replied.

"Let us drink and be one with Lady Davern," another one added.

With a sigh, Hensley cupped the goblet with both hands and drank the liquid without letting up until the glass was empty. Deenya wanted to laugh at the ridiculousness of the whole Lights of Davern thing. The cult in question hadn't committed any crimes, but that didn't make them innocent. Deenya watched as Hensley closed her eyes as the liquid supposedly invigorated her from head to toe.

Deenya leaned in closer as gasps were heard around the room at the emergence of a new member. The woman was dressed in a long blue gown. A golden crown sat on her head with a blue crystal jewel in the center. Dark brown hair with ice-blue streaks fell down to her waist. Golden bands were around her arms and wrists.

"L-L-Lady Davern," Hensley said in shock.

"Davern?" Officer Mack echoed. "Isn't she the true leader of this little club?"

"Could be," Deenya answered, frowning at the girls' reaction to the lady.

The one, the girl called Davern, stood before the coven of witches. She produced a silver staff in her hand; her crest stood at the top of the staff. Officer Mack gasped.

"Did you see that?" he asked with a surprised tone. "How in the hell did she do that?"

"Special effects," Deenya speculated, suppressing her own shock. "Remember, they are trying to get people to sign off on their little club."

"My sisters," she said in a melodic voice. "I'm glad to see you here."

"As we are happy to see you, Lady Davern," one of the girls stated, watching her.

"What brings you here, my lady?" Hensley asked.

Davern's brow creased with worry. "I'm afraid that something evil is on the horizon, my sisters. I have foreseen the second coming of my brother Lord Gidon."

The video ended after that. Deenya clicked the page in hopes of finding more on this Gidon they were talking about, but there were no more videos. So she handed the phone off to Officer Mack and rummaged through the files. There had to be something of use here.

"Gidon?" Officer Mack repeated. "Isn't he the leader of the Umbrage Advocates?"

The Umbrage Advocates were a rival cult to the Lights of Davern. Deenya didn't know what bad blood existed between Davern and Gidon, but she'd never heard of a sibling rivalry going this bad.

"Do we have anything on them?" she asked, hoping they would have something to give her a good start.

"Not on the Lights of Davern, but we do on the Umbrage Advocates." Mack handed her a file. "According to this, Zenon is the current leader of the group. No one knows what happened to Gidon."

"But didn't Davern say something about Gidon's return?" Deenya questioned, quickly taking the file.

Upon opening it, she saw a man that looked like he belonged in a horror movie instead of society. He was dressed in a dark robe, nails painted black, and his skin was pale. His eyes were soulless. He had dark hair that hung down to his shoulders, and some covered his face. Deenya shivered and instantly closed the file. She didn't want to see this man's eerie face for another minute.

"As a matter of fact," Officer Mack started, ignoring her question. "We have a tail on Zenon now as we speak."

Deenya bolted from her chair, grabbing her coat. Officer Mack ran after her. She didn't hear him, or better yet, she chose to ignore him. If she could crack this case involving the Lights of Davern and Umbrage Advocates, then there would be nothing anyone could say or do to her. She would probably be the lead in the next investigation. There was no way in hell she would let David steal this case from her.

* * *

It was actually a dumb idea. Deenya had no clue where to find this informant. She cursed herself for acting so rashly. Currently, she was sitting in her car outside the den of the Umbrage Advocates. But she didn't think she'd find anything going to where the Lights of Davern were located. Besides, the Umbrage Advocates committed crimes on a daily basis. The only problem was the police didn't have the evidence to prove it.

She noticed two of the members standing outside, their faces covered by the hoods on their black cloaks. It would be suicide to try for a frontal assault. So her best option was to wait. However, after some time, she got out of the car and crept slowly through the grass. The shadows of the night concealed her presence. Deenya could hear some of the members chanting on the inside as she crept closer. Most of them had run-ins with the police but got away scot-free. If they found out a cop was watching the place, they would kill her on sight. She had to do this carefully.

Across from the den, Deenya noticed a small bar. It might be best to head in that direction, so she hurried to the bar. She was glad she had made the wise decision to take off her uniform before arriving here. She pulled her hair free from the ponytail and concealed her face as best as she could.

Once inside, Deenya grabbed a table in the back and watched the door as some of the customers made their way inside. This bar housed some customers that were just as weird as the Umbrage Advocates. Deenya ruffled her hair a bit more. She tried to make sure she fit into the category with all these weirdos. As she felt satisfied with her appearance, she realized she had forgotten to arm herself. Under her breath, she released a line of curses. The gun was in the glove compartment, but she couldn't just walk out and go get it.

A man walked into the bar at that moment. His unruly dark hair was all over the place on his head. Deenya watched him carefully. He was dressed in dirty jeans and a tank top. If she didn't know any better, she'd guess that this man led a rough life or something. Deenya laughed to herself as Elena's words came back to her.

Never judge a book by its cover...

The man ordered a beer, but instead of drinking, he just stared at it. Deenya watched the man for a few more minutes before deciding to make her move. From the way the bartender and some of the customers greeted him, he was a regular there. Perhaps he could tell her something about the cult. She didn't get the chance though. Zenon, the man from the picture and the leader of the Umbrage Advocates appeared. So Deenya went back to her seat and watched the conversation play out. She swallowed nervously and tried to think of a way to take him down if she had to. She was pretty sure his goons would come running if she revealed herself. Then they would escape and she would never get another chance like this again.

"Patience, Deenya," she muttered. "Patience. You'll get the chance to nail this bastard when the time is right. Let's just observe him for now."

"You look lost, friend."

She heard Zenon say as he took a seat beside the stranger at the bar. The man glanced at him, but he didn't say anything. Zenon pulled his stool closer to the man and grinned. "Can I interest you with an offer?"

The man gave him an odd look and shrugged. "Sorry, man, I'm happily married. I don't want no hookups."

Deenya snickered. She wondered what kind of bar the man thought it was. There was no way he thought that Zenon was in that kind of business, did he? Zenon growled.

"I'm not talking about that kind of deal but a deal that can grant you absolute power."

Deenya moved closer as the man sighed and tried to ignore Zenon. From the look on Zenon's face, she could tell he was annoyed with this man. Deenya gasped in awe at the ring Zenon flashed. The man had the same reaction she did. He whistled and stared at the midnight-colored jewel. That brought a smile to Zenon's face.

"The Umbrage Advocates can help guide you towards the path of Lord Gidon."

"Who's Lord Gidon?" the man asked, finally taking a sip of the beer.

Deenya craned her neck to hear Zenon's answer but growled in frustration. Of all the times to be loudmouths. The crowd grew bigger, and the chatter was coming from different directions. But, luckily, Zenon chose not to answer the man's question for now. The crowd became a little silent again, but Deenya still had to strain to hear their entire conversation.

"First things first," he said. "I'm Zenon, the leader of the Umbrage Advocates."

The man stared at Zenon's hand and frowned at his perfectly polished black fingernails.

"Lane Wilson," he introduced himself and continued with his inquiry.

His next question was one that Deenya had been wondering ever since they popped up on the police's radar. "What are the Umbrage Advocates?"

"Come with me, and I shall explain everything," Zenon replied. "I'll introduce you to my brothers."

Deenya looked down at her table as Zenon got off the stool and motioned for Lane to follow. Then the man finished his beer hastily and stood. After leaving a few bills on the bar, the men disappeared out the door. Deenya hurried to leave; there was no way in hell she was going to lose them.

***

Surprise, surprise. Deenya lost them after some time. She had circled around the Umbrage Advocates' den for hours, but the two men never returned there. The next night she was back at the station, sitting behind her desk and doodling on her notepad. From what she learned so far, the Umbrage Advocates were recruiting new members. Although this Gidon had never been seen by the public eye, his presence was still strong. The Zenon guy talked as if the man was still around somewhere, but from what she gathered from the Lights of Davern, he was no longer around. What did the second coming of Gidon mean exactly? Did he skip town? Was he in a hospital somewhere and in a coma, possibly to wake up soon?

Deenya ran a hand through her hair. This was one tough egg to crack. She was lost in her thoughts when Officer Mack burst into the room and ran to her desk. She scowled at him. Did he really have to scare her like that?

"Officer Vaughn, there's been a murder."

Deenya perked up at the news. Perhaps the man from last night got himself killed. She stood up and grabbed her coat off the back of the chair. She made sure her gun was with her this time. Of course, she was in uniform this time.

"Where?" she asked.

"About a few blocks from here."

"Alright, I'm going."

"Hold it, Officer Vaughn."

Deenya stopped in her tracks. Chief Vaughn appeared in her line of sight, scowling and folding his arms. The tension in the room grew so thick around her that it was suffocating. She wouldn't let him see her in a vulnerable state. She held her head high and looked him straight in the eyes. Of course, David stood beside him with a grin on his face. Deenya rolled her eyes. Why was she not surprised?

"Chief, let me handle this," she stated, trying not to sound annoyed.

"Like you handled the last case or the cases before that?" he yelled, his voice booming off the wall around them. "Every time you get a case, you pass everything over to Officer Hine or someone else. You never finish the work yourself."

Deenya's eyes widened at the accusation. She was under the impression that he gave her another chance because he knew about David using her leads to solve the cases for himself. She had no idea that this was what he truly thought of her. Her lips thinned in annoyance. She never passed her cases to anyone else. If anything, she wanted to solve them on her own.

Deenya glanced at David with a pleading look in her eyes. "David," she whispered.

"Chief Vaughn's right; I don't want to keep handling your cases for you," David said with a stolid expression.

"You lying son of a-"

"That's enough, officer," Chief Vaughn snapped. "You will not be handling this case."

He held the file out to David and Officer Mack. Deenya's anger began to rise to the surface. She clenched her jaw shut and glared at David. Before she knew what she was doing, she snatched the file out of his grasp. She didn't even care if she gave him a paper cut.

"Officer Vaughn."

Deenya glared at Chief Vaughn. "I'm not sitting this one out, and I don't care what you say, father."

"Deenya, this is not your call," Chief Vaughn said, his expression softening a little. He held out his hand for the file. "Give me the file now."

Deenya looked at his hand. Her father's hands that used to hold and protect her as a kid. They were now used to man the police force, and she was a big girl now, but she wished like hell he cared more about her than his career. A hand gripped her arm tightly. David pleaded with her, his grip tightening, but it wouldn't work this time. Deenya turned her back to them, ignoring Chief Vaughn and David as they called after her. She wasn't about to lose another case, not to David, not to anyone. She would solve this one all by herself.

* * *

"Maybe the beasts are back."

Deenya questioned the locals at a diner not too far from where the body was found. It wasn't Lane from last night, after all. The patrons in the diner gasped at the old man's statement. He sat in a rocking chair in the rear of the place. He had a faraway look in his eyes. An old woman she assumed was his wife went over to the man and stood by him with a strange look in her eyes.

"Beasts?" Deenya enquired, scribbling on her notepad.

"They are called the Gayevois, and they laid waste to Covenstown a long time ago," the old man uttered in a weak voice. "These beasts were the talk of the town. They preyed on innocence and stole children from their beds in the dead of night. But, then, the white witch Davern sealed the beasts away in the woods to protect us from their harmful ways."

Deenya didn't believe in these supernatural creatures, but Davern was in their crosshairs again, and instead of being a cult leader, she was now a white witch.

"Since Gidon almost brought the Gayevois to extinction, the leader of these beasts imprisoned him in an icy tomb and made the mayor at the time swear not to let anyone else come into their domain, or they'd be killed on sight." A patron of the diner added.

Deenya didn't know what to make of this story. She didn't believe it, but Gidon was back in their crosshairs again too. She assumed they would tell her that Gidon was a witch too or a male witch called a warlock, wasn't he?

"Could you tell me more about Gidon?" she questioned. "Where is he now?"

"It's just as the man said," another patron pointed out. "He's sealed in the woods in an icy tomb."

"Yeah, yeah, and could you tell me about him before he was sealed in this 'icy' tomb?"

The old man was quick to speak up. "Gidon Dalfon is the older brother of Lady Davern. Where Lady Davern fights for the good of humanity, Gidon stands for all that is evil. He's the true leader of the Umbrage Advocates and the most powerful warlock of ancient times. His power was a force to be reckoned with."

Deenya scribbled on her notepad. "So, are he and Davern having some kind of sibling rivalry? Are they trying to see how many nutcases they can recruit to their cause and what... the loser has to buy the other ice cream?"

"This is not something to joke about, officer!" The old man's wife exclaimed. "Lady Davern and Lord Gidon are real."

"I know they're real," Deenya said, sarcasm dripping from her voice. "I just have a hard time believing that they are a powerful witch and warlock, as you guys claim."

The server came from around the bar and got in Deenya's face before shoving her slightly. Deenya scowled. They really believed in all this stuff, didn't they?

"My parents are no liars," he said. "The murder that took place the other night happened because that man went too far out. No one is to go into the woods at night. The Gayevois will get you. I even saw one a time or two."

"Yeah." Deenya placed her notebook back into her pocket. "That's all the questions for now. If you think of anything else, just give me a call."

She held out her card to the server and his parents, but they didn't take it. Deenya sighed and placed it on the table. The man that was sitting there took the card and crushed it in his palm. Deenya left the diner with their glares on her back. She went to the houses around but got the same response as the people from the diner. Creatures, Gayevois, Davern, and Gidon.

"The mayor had a plaque made to warn the locals before they venture into the woods. It was placed on a marker so no one can miss it." A passing couple told her when she questioned them. "The Gayevois are dangerous."

Deenya headed back to her car with more questions than answers. She climbed into the car and started the engine.

"Gayevois, how cute," she muttered.

She drove to the woods in question and parked her car outside the entrance. She climbed out and stood there. A couple of teens were standing at the entrance as well. Each one daring the other to go in.

"Excuse me," she called. "You guys aren't allowed out here."

"You believe in the legend?" one of the teens asked.

"No," she accepted without hesitation. "It's just an old legend. A legend to scare the locals and to keep people from going into the woods."

"No, officer, the legend is very real," a teen girl protested. She shivered and pointed towards the entrance. "I've seen Lady Davern walking around in the woods at night."

"Lady Davern?" Deenya wanted to laugh. Of course, she would be walking in the woods. She had to give some truth to the legend. After all, she was interested in recruiting followers to her 'noble' cause, and what better way than to pretend you're everything that the legend says you are.

"Lady Davern is just an insane cult leader along with Gidon and the Gayevois," she assured. "They are just a myth. It's all for entertainment purposes."

The teenagers smiled. "If you say so, officer. I bet you won't go in there."

Deenya smirked. "I will, and it's for my job," she explained, pulling out her card. "If you have any information I can actually use, give me a call. Now get out of here and go home to your parents."

The teens took her card and bid her farewell. She waited for them to drive away, then turned to read the plaque.

So there was some truth to the old man's story after all. Well, at least the part about the plaque being constructed by the mayor.

All in all, she still believed it was just some old ghost story. So without any worry, Deenya went back to her car and grabbed a flashlight. She stopped at the entrance, and with a deep sigh, turned on her flashlight.

Time to prove all of you wrong.

However, she didn't get the chance to enter as her phone rang. It was Charlotte. Deenya was so wrapped up in this case that she forgot about the Halloween party. Well, the party would have to wait. She was onto something big here. After sending a text to Charlotte about working overtime and a quick apology, she entered the woods. The deeper she entered the woods, the foggier it became. Deenya squinted. She was sure it wasn't foggy before she went in.

"It's nothing," she mumbled, shining her light on the trees in front of her.

As she shined it on a nearby tree, a shadow danced in front of her. Trees swayed in the wind. Deenya trembled, but she told herself it was just the cold. She whipped her flashlight back and forth, hoping nothing would jump out at her like it did in some of the horror movies she had watched.

"Nothing to fear but fear itself," she murmured.

Deenya pulled her gun from its holster and aimed it in front of her. If these beasts were real and they so much as darted in her direction, she was going to blow them away. But she scowled after a minute. What was she thinking? They weren't real. A chill ran through her, and the fog disappeared.

A blanket of endless darkness awaited her that not even her flashlight could cut through. It was impossible. It was just her imagination. It had to be. She walked around with her gun at the ready. She was not going to let anything catch her off guard.

A blood trail led to a clearing behind an odd-shaped tree. Deenya paused at the bloodstain. She pulled out her cell phone but placed it back in her pocket. No, she didn't need backup. If she called for help now, Chief Vaughn would probably suspend her for disobeying his orders.

"Calm down, Deenya." She tried to convince herself. "It's just the trees casting shadows everywhere."

Suddenly, a growl sounded to her right. She quickly shined the flashlight in the direction of the growl, and with her hands trembling, she pointed her gun.

"Who's out there?" she shouted in a high-pitched voice.

Loud footsteps came in her direction. Deenya moved away slowly. Whatever it was, it made the whole ground shake. She ran and hid behind a tree. Sweat beaded on her forehead as she peeped out. A breath caught in her throat. A large beast with glowing yellow eyes watched her from a distance. Deenya was petrified. A squeak was the only sound she could muster in the wake of her fear. She had never seen anything like it before. The beast growled. She couldn't move as it stalked towards her.

"Move," her mind screamed at her. *"Run!"*

Deenya forced her arm above her head and let off a warning shot.

The beast froze but not for long. It roared and charged at her. Deenya ran. She dodged through the array of trees as heavy footsteps came from behind her. She didn't have time to react as another beast came at her from her left side.

It rammed into her with such force that it sent her careening into a nearby tree. Before she could collect herself, one of the beasts got on top of her and clawed with endless fury. Deenya screamed. Each slash burned her skin. If it kept this up, she was going to die.

Mustering all the strength she had left, she brought her gun to its head and fired off a shot. The beast's scream of agony made her ears bleed. However, she got to her feet and ran as fast as she could. Two more beasts came down the path at her. She looked back at the one she shot, but he was already on his feet and coming for her again.

"You've got to be kidding me!" she shrieked.

Guns didn't even work on these creatures. Deenya made the mistake of looking back to see if they were still behind her when she no longer heard their footsteps. She tumbled down a cliff and into an embankment below. She screamed as she rolled until she landed inside an underground cavern.

Deenya groaned and rolled onto her back. She caught a glimpse of the beast's yellow eyes through the opening, along with its massive body. Lying perfectly still, she hoped they had thought she died from the fall and would not pursue her any further. After a few minutes of waiting, it moved away. Deenya breathed a sigh of relief and sat up slowly. She should find a way out of here. They would probably make their way down here to check and see if she really died. A chill went through her again. Deenya searched blindly for her flashlight and gun, but they were lost in the fall.

"Great," she muttered.

She searched for her cell phone, but it was lost too. Deenya tried to stand, but her leg ached. It was probably broken. How in the hell was she going to get out of here? She reached around in her pockets again and found her trusty lighter. Surprisingly, it didn't get lost when she fell. With trembling hands, she lit the lighter and held it up to inspect the cave.

There was nothing special about it. No markings from an ancient species or anything, just ice. No, that wasn't weird at all.

Deenya gasped as she inspected the snow-covered cave. This wasn't real. It hadn't snowed, and it was fall here, so how were snow and ice still down here? It never snowed around Halloween in this town. She gathered some of the snow in her hands and crushed it.

"Impossible," she noted.

She stood slowly, ignoring the pain in her leg. Her eyes landed on a large block of ice a little further in the cave. Deenya limped toward it. She touched it and frowned. It looked as if someone or something was inside. Deenya squeaked as she leaned in for a closer look. A man's lifeless white eyes stared out at nothingness. His face was contorted into an anguished expression. She jumped back when the eyes seemed to move.

"Cavemen don't exist," she screamed. "No, this isn't real. None of this is real!"

Suddenly, the cave shook. Deenya gasped as the lighter went out. She tried to get it working again, and when she did, she gazed wide-eyed in shock. The ice encasing the caveman began to chip away and shatter. Deenya winced. The pain in her leg got worse. She fell to the ground. She never took her eyes off the block of ice as it melted away, and the caveman was revealed.

His hair was as white as snow and streaked with ice-blue highlights. He yanked the chains that bound his hands and feet until they gave way. Deenya watched in horror as the caveman stepped out of the ice in all his naked glory. His hair fell to his waist. He stared down at her with eyes that were now a vivid blue.

She couldn't believe it. No, she wouldn't believe it and fainted as the caveman watched her with a curious look in his eyes.

Deenya awoke in a hospital room. It was the next morning. Everything she experienced felt like a dream, better yet, a nightmare. She sat up to see the old man from the diner, along with Chief Vaughn, David, Officer Mack, and Elena, watching her.

"Deenya," Elena said, pulling her into a hug, "you're alright."

"Mom," she mumbled. "Dad. What happened?"

"You were found outside the woods," Chief Vaughn revealed softly. "Luckily, some local teens found you and called the police."

"Don't ever go off on your own again," David said, placing his hand over hers. "You know I worry about you."

Deenya pulled her hand from his grasp. *Worried, my foot!* Chief Vaughn didn't stick around after learning that she was going to make a full recovery. He told David to meet him back at the station and left.

David, of course, ready to kiss up to the Chief, left the minute he did. Deenya wondered what the old man was doing here. She watched him. From the look in his eyes, he wanted to speak to her alone.

"Mom," she spoke in a raspy voice. "Can you get me something to drink? I'm thirsty."

"Sure, hon," Elena answered, placing a kiss on her forehead. "I'll be back in a bit."

Deenya smiled as her mom left the room. When she was alone, the old man walked over to her bedside.

"Now," he said. "Do you believe in all that the locals and I tried to tell you?"

Deenya nodded. "But who is going to believe me?"

Tina Diarrhea

Since their freshman year started, Tina had been arriving at school early, knowing Jason Marman took the bus and always arrived at eight-thirty. It was only a quarter after eight when Tina threw her overstuffed backpack to the floor in front of her locker and started twisting the dial on her locker door. Her head moved to one side as the metal on her headphones pulled at a few strands of hairs and *'White Wedding' blared in the earpiece.*

Tina jumped, and her headphones slipped off, but got caught halfway to the floor in her frizzy curls. Someone had slapped her hard on the back. Then, before she could catch her breath and turn, she heard a voice.

"You know Halloween is still a week away. Why do you look like that Diarrhea?"

It was Jason Marman.

Tina had her hand on her hip, and one toe pointed toward him, ready to lay it all out. Jason Marman had been calling her Tina Diarrhea for as long as she could remember. Even though she had never had diarrhea at school, her name only barely rhymed with it, and they'd both officially been in high school for a full month. Hadn't she suffered enough? How immature could he be to keep her ridiculous nickname going for the next four years?

"Eat a dick, Braceface," Tina threw back.

But Jason was too quick, a master at bullying and teasing since kindergarten.

"At least one day my braces will come off, but you'll always look like Diarrhea," he said with a ridiculous, wet smile. It almost didn't matter what he said anymore, his high-pitched screeching voice mocked you no matter what.

Tina felt her face getting hot and her lungs filling with anxious pressure, making her want to scream. But instead, all she could do was spin one hand and flip him off. "How do I look li--"

But it was too late. Principal Stewart was steps away and had definitely not missed Tina's flying middle finger.

"Excuse me, Miss. Do you mind telling me what has you breaking school rules first thing this morning?"

"He started it. He won't leave me alone." Normally Tina wasn't such a tattletale, but she was determined to not get in trouble at her new school. Not yet, anyway.

"What's this?" Principal Stewart asked Jason. Her mauve pencil skirt stayed straight and barely moved as she turned to him.

Jason Marman put his head down and didn't talk back. Tina would have given anything to have the power to make him do that.

"Are you harassing this young woman? You know we have a zero tolerance for bullying here, young man. Both of you, come with me."

"Thanks for throwing me under the bus," Jason Marman mumbled from the side of his mouth as he and Tina walked behind Principal Stewart.

"I'd love to throw you under a bus anytime." Tina wanted to say, but they were entering the quiet atmosphere of the Principal's office. *'Beast Of Burden' queued up in Tina's mind.*

"I see here you've both joined us from Northcrest. So you two know each other. Is that correct?"

"Yes ma'am."

Jason Marman was laying it on thick. Tina had never heard him be so polite in his pathetic life. But she was thankful he'd answered first before she said something snarky like, *"Unfortunately, yes. We've been in the same class since kindergarten, and the murder fantasies have gone on for just as long."*

"Well then, I believe this has gone on long enough. You two are going to work together on a project of healing for me. You've heard that song on the radio, 'Heal the World, make it a better place?'" The Principal sang the melody of the title with a wide-eyed grin.

Tina tried to not to laugh but desperately hoped she wouldn't sing the entire song. When she looked over at Jason she could tell he was thinking the same, but trying really hard to not look disrespectful and get himself into more trouble.

"I'd like a presentation that you'll both present to the freshman class at the next assembly. It will serve to both welcome our new students and inform them of our bullying policy. We need to be sure everyone feels welcome, don't we Miss Jeneaux?" The principal's drawn-on eyebrows were raised and pointed.

Tina nodded back to her, wordlessly.

"And Mr. Marman, I trust going forward, you will treat Miss Jeneaux and all our other female students with respect for the remainder of your time here and onward in life.

"Yes ma'am."

Tina and Jason both got up from their chairs and walked together to the office doors. Jason opened and held the door for Tina on the way out.

"We can work at my place if you want. I have the album at home and a whole set of encyclopedias," Jason suggested, and Tina gave a single nod with her eyes closed.

"After dinner?" Jason asked.

Tina nodded again. It was the best she could do since she couldn't believe that she actually agreed to spend after-school time with Jason Marman at his actual house.

* * *

Tina dragged her feet all the way home. She knew she was delaying the inevitable, but it felt like her only method of protest. Being in high school was what she had been looking forward to for nearly two years. She was sure that it was going to be perfect. She'd get lost in the crowd of so many students and never have to look at any of her Northcrest classmates ever again. She'd never have to be Tina Diarrhea ever again.

After a quick bowl of stew her grandmother had left for her on the stove, Tina threw some extra cassettes into her shoulder bag for her long, sad walk to Jason Marmans's house. She made sure to collect all of her toughest reinforcements: Heart, Cyndi Lauper, maybe even Wham! In case things got really bad.

At the end of Jason Marman's driveway, Tina let out a quiet, stew-laden burp. She hated Jason Marman even more as she licked her lips. She didn't have time for more stew or dessert because of their stupid project, which was all his fault in the first place, anyway.

Tina knocked on the door, and instantly Jason came to the screen to push it open. She wordlessly stepped inside, noting her step over the threshold. There was no turning back now. She was officially at Jason Marman's home––his dwelling, his centre of dickhead operations, the mother ship, his lair.

The hallway was quiet and smelled of dinner. Potatoes and gravy.

"Which way did you come?" Jason asked. The question threw Tina off guard for a second––was Jason Marman making small talk?

"Umm..." Tina struggled with the lace on her sneaker. "Down Main and up your street."

"You should take the shorter path to get back home."

"Where's that?" Tina asked, trying to sound normal as she tugged off her shoe without untying it.

"Through the back. The forest connects out there and then to George Street. Right by your place," Jason answered, matter-of-factly.

It wasn't particularly strange that Jason Marman knew where she lived––it was a small town. But something about him talking about how to get to her house made her want to lose her stew all over his glossy floors.

"This way to the basement," Jason pointed, stepping towards a wooden bannister.

"The basement?" Tina's eyes widened.

"Where we keep the encyclopedias." Jason was already stepping downstairs.

"Oh, okay," Tina grumbled while trying to discreetly look ahead of Jason and see what she was getting herself into.

She followed him down the polished wooden stairs with a green runner down the centre. About halfway, a voice startled Tina, and she almost tumbled into Jason's back but grabbed the handrail in time.

"You kids want cocoa?" A woman's voice called.

Jason stopped and turned his neck slowly around to Tina. "Cocoa?"

Tina looked into Jason's eyes. Something about how he was looking at her without blinking made her freeze. She was waiting for him to say something about how cocoa looks like diarrhea, but he never did. All Tina could do was shake her head.

"No, mom!" He yelled and they continued down the stairs.

Inside her head, part of the lyrics from *'Wake Me Up Before You Go-Go'* started playing. It gave her an uneasy feeling.

Tina was grateful it wasn't your average creepy basement and there was a grownup in earshot. Actually, she'd never been more thankful for that in her entire life. This was basically another floor of the house-- completely furnished and classy. The walls were covered in wood panelling, and the dark brown carpet still bounced as if it were new. Along one whole side was a shelving unit made especially for vinyl records. On the other was a fairly large television with a new VCR below and couches around it, making the seating for probably twenty or more people.

Tina fixated on the wall of albums.

"They're mostly my dad's," Jason remarked, seeing her gazing at the shelves.

Tina kept her hands by her side as she approached the collection. She took her time looking through them, squinting at the thin, colourful spines. She knew many of the bands but had never seen their actual records. It's like she could hear snippets of each song as she looked through.

> *Don't you want somebody to love?*
>
> *Billie Jean.*
>
> *What's love got to do with it?*
>
> *You really got me.*
>
> *Take me to the river.*
>
> *I guess that's why they call it the blues.*

"Hey, Diarrhea, you wanna get started?"

That's all Tina needed to snap right back to reality. It was like one of the records had been scratched as the needle lifted. Tina took a breath and kept her mouth shut tight as she joined Jason on the boat-sized sofas, very sure not to sit anywhere near him. She could kill him for calling her that, but it could prolong the entire project if she wasn't a team player.

"I thought we could start by listening to the song. I have the cassette here." Jason pressed the chunky button of a small grey boom box on the coffee table, and 'Heal the World' by Michael Jackson started playing.

The melody filled the basement

"I think this might take longer than we thought," Jason noted, pulling the lyrics sheet from the album sheath.

"No!" Tina screamed, much louder than she'd meant to. Apparently, her mouth was also rebelling against the idea of being anywhere near Jason Marman for any longer than she had to be.

"Whoa, chick. Chill out," Jason said, rather calmly. "Probably just one more day so we can go over our presentation after our report is done."

"Since when are you good at school?" Tina asked, her eyes squinted in contempt.

Jason got up to move the needle back on the record player so they could hear the song again. "I've always been good at this stuff. It's easy. But it's not like I'm gonna go around telling everyone I'm smart. Then I'd be a nerd."

"You are a nerd," Tina jeered. She couldn't resist the chance to tease Jason Marman.

"Cheap shot," Jason shot back with a sly smile.

Tina smirked but wouldn't give him the satisfaction of a full grin.

When they'd done all they could do for one day, Tina packed up her notes and made her way upstairs. Jason hovered as Tina slipped on her green high-tops and adjusted her headphones.

"The path is made; you can't get lost. Just follow where the leaves are all packed down."

"I think I can handle it," Tina scoffed while slinging on her backpack.

Proud of herself for surviving the worst, Tina left Jason's house through the back as he suggested. She pushed the play button on her Walkman, and soon 'Barracuda' by Heart filled her ears.

It was dusk as Tina walked towards the break in the trees. Before she went in, she took a quick look back at the house where Jason was signalling her to keep going. Even though she was walking into a dark forest at night, she took a deep breath of relief.

She'd been in knots all day about having to work with Jason. Stupid Principal Stewart had no idea what she'd put Tina through, having to work with the bully who had been tormenting her for years, calling her Tina Diarrhea and making everyone else call her that too. And the more she'd protest, tell them to shut up, even pray for their deaths, the more they just laughed and did it more.

Tina kicked the dead leaves at the thought and started making her way home.

A little further down the path, Tina was beginning to see where it began to turn, and she'd be out on George Street. The street lights made it lighter there, but it somehow made Tina feel nervous for the first time. Maybe it wasn't so smart to cut through the woods. Jason may have been trying to be helpful, but he wasn't a girl. Bad things happen to girls in the dark. The music in her headphones was supposed to give her a boost but she decided to turn the volume down to hear the sounds around her. 'Barracuda' might not have been the best choice for a trek through the woods.

The leaves continued to rustle and crunch as she walked, but she also heard something or some*one* else. She really wanted to look behind her but was scared to let whoever it was, know that she was actually afraid. So she bent down to re-tie her shoelace, hoping the person would pass her. But as she finished tying, no one passed her, and the rustling leaves had stopped. The next song on her mix tape started to playing 'No Quarter' and it seemed as if her music was sending her a warning.

Tina stood to brush off her one knee before she got going again but was quickly stopped by someone standing in her path. When Tina's nerves settled, her eyes landed on a woman, middle-aged with a stern but pretty face. She was taller than Tina, wearing brown hiking boots and a red plaid jacket. She looked like someone who was actually not afraid of being in the woods.

"Girl in the woods at this time of night. You really should be going."

Tina heard the warning, but she still felt like she should bring her headphones down to answer. "I'm fine, thank you," Tina answered politely, swallowing the urge to sass back, "I *am* going," she smiled and the woman stepped out of her way. After that Tina hurried down the rest of the path to where it curved towards downtown.

***

Out of habit, the next day, Tina got to school at eight-fifteen to avoid Jason. At her locker, as she was taking out her stuff, a girl's voice called her name, and she turned around a little bit startled.

It was Fanny Johnson and Kathy Miller––popular girls from Northcrest.

"Good morning, Tina Diarrhea. How was your date with Jason Marman yesterday?"

Tina had always found it odd that Fanny could get away with being such a brat when her name was Fanny, of all things. But she was blonde and pretty, so everyone ignored the easy joke.

"It wasn't a date. We're working on a school project."

"Oh, well, that's not what we heard. Jason's telling everyone how cute you are and how you're coming over to his house again." Fanny mocked. "Maybe there'll be one more couples costume for Halloween."

"Ya, you could be Diarrhea and Barf Bag," Kathy chimed in.

Fanny and Kathy walked away laughing, and Tina did her best to look unaffected, going back to loading her backpack with the textbooks she needed for the first period.

"Hey, cool walkman," said a voice, this time belonging to a boy.

Tina looked down and beside her backpack, were a pair of black hi-tops. She rose slowly from the floor, careful to avoid her locker door. She'd learned that lesson the hard way. As she stood she pulled the orange sponges of her headphones back from her ears to look at the boy in front of her.

"Thanks," Tina said, quickly adding a smile once she had a good look at how cute he was.

"What are you listening to?" he asked, as he blindly twisted the padlock on the locker two down from Tina's.

"Ugh, the new one by Scandal."

The boy raised his eyebrows over his dark sunglasses and gave a smirk. "So...are you *The Warrior*?"

Tina managed to give a cool laugh, but she also felt a blush coming on and quickly turned back to her locker. Then she heard him close his locker back up.

"Well, see ya."

Tina turned around to say the same, but he was already walking away and getting lost in the morning crowd. She stood there for a minute staring at all the people, for some reason hoping he'd have to come back for something, but the hallway was a violent swarm of buzzing teenagers. Then before it was too late, Jason Marman's pointed head and skinny face appeared from the crowd and caught her eye. She couldn't help but roll her eyes and try to crawl into her locker to avoid him.

"Good morning, Lady Tina," Jason greeted her in a horribly bad British accent.

"Glad you've finally learned my name, Duffus," Tina answered back.

"I've always known it. I just like bugging you." He leaned against the lockers and watched Tina fuss with her books in her locker. "My house again tonight?"

"Ummm," Tina paused and fiddled with her lock. "Did you say something to Fanny about the project we're doing?"

"I barely talk to Fanny. She's not cool like you." Jason pushed his shoulder up and away, then started walking into the crowd.

"After dinner!" He shouted over the people. "Take the woods," he added while giving Tina a wink before getting sucked downstream.

Tina nodded back but turned quickly, feeling another blush coming on. What was wrong with her this morning?

For the rest of the day, she felt like she was on high alert, looking over her shoulder for either Jason Marman or Fanny Miller to pop out and annoy her like a defective jack-in-the-box. She also kept an extra eye out for the black hi-tops guy. But the day passed without another incident from any of them. But now it was her turn to go to Jason's house again, hopefully for the last time because of this stupid project.

At the edge of the street, Tina brushed a low-hanging branch away from the space over the path. It was still perfect light out at five-thirty, but the forest seemed even darker than it had the other night when Tina walked home. As she came around the curve that led to Jason's house, she saw someone ahead of her. *Better ahead than behind*, she thought, but she was still conscious of her rustling feet in the leaves.

The person stopped and then looked back at Tina. Tina stopped too, unsure of what to do. She decided she wanted to look brave, not frozen like a deer in headlights so she kept walking. When she was closer, the woman spoke to her again.

"Thought I warned you," the woman said.

"I'm fine, thank you," Tina replied with a polite smile as she walked past her.

"That boy. He's trouble," the woman called from behind.

So Jason probably had a bad reputation with everyone. But curiosity made Tina stop and turn. "What kind of trouble?"

The woman walked towards Tina and began to walk with her. "Just see him out here a lot. Playing with things he knows nothing about. These are special woods. Was a wedding here once too."

Tina took a few more steps in the leaves before she stopped to ask her question. "A wedding? In a crummy forest next to downtown?"

The woman didn't stop.

"It was a much bigger forest fifty years ago."

Tina and the woman continued to walk together down the path.

"So what's Jason--or, I mean, 'the boy'--have to do with any of that?" Tina asked hesitantly.

"Can't really say, but you gotta get yourself ahead of all this. Protect yourself."

It took everything in Tina's power not to scrunch her face and scream, *"What the hell are you talking about, crazy lady?"* But she kept her cool as they approached the break in the trees.

"Well, okay. I'll do that," Tina decided to say as she waved to the woman and pushed her way through the straggling branches to get to Jason's backyard.

* * *

"So I met your neighbour," Tina said, letting the announcement hang in the air between them. She hoped Jason would add his two cents about the woman and her creepy forest-witch energy.

"What neighbour?" Jason asked confused.

"There's a woman that likes to walk around in the woods. She was there the other day too. She's seen you around she told me," Tina pointed out, hoping to throw Jason off guard and get him to spill what he was up to.

"Hmm. That's weird. I never usually see anyone else there. That's why I like it."

Something about how he said it made Tina pause. She thought back to what the woman said and couldn't help but think that Jason was in the woods doing something worse than she could imagine. Tina decided she'd avoid the woods for her walk home from now on.

Back down in the basement, Jason spread out his notes while Tina took her binder from her knapsack. The basement seemed darker, and the house seemed quieter than the other day.

"Are your parents home?" Tina asked, trying to sound casual.

"No, my mom's out getting more Halloween candy. Me and my dad ate it all," Jason said, smiling and obviously very proud of himself.

Tina returned a small smile but her thoughts were still on woods, Jason and that lady.

"So, where did we leave off?" Jason asked, breaking her thoughts, looking energized and ready.

Tina tried to match his enthusiasm. He wasn't going to win the battle of maturity here. Tina handed Jason a stack of her notes from the library. "Here's a list of charities we should mention. UNICEF is probably the biggest one."

Jason took the paper but barely glanced at it as he leaned back on the couch. "Hey, that reminds me. Are you going out trick-or-treating?"

"Are you serious?" Tina gave him her best and most disgusted face scrunch.

"C'mon! My friends and I got these outrageous masks, so nobody will know how old we are."

"I think people can see you're all more than four feet tall," Tina said, tapping her pencil on her binder, hoping Jason would get the hint and get back to work.

"Who cares? I bet they'll still give us candy. We got some candy last year. Why don't you come? We'll find you a mask too."

"No, I'm good. Can we get started now, please?" Tina growled, taping her page with her pen.

"Geez, ok. I knew you were a geek, but who knew you were such a *bitch* now?"

It was all Tina had been waiting for--for the real Jason Marman to rear his head.

Tina thought of the Vincent Price laugh at the end of Michael Jackson's 'Thriller.'

"Well, I've always known you're a piece of shit, Marman, so no surprises there. Suck on that list. I'm outta here."

"It was just a joke, Diarrhea. C'mon! We have to do this together. I can't have detention, or my parents will kill me." Jason's voice cracked as he pleaded. His voice was reaching even higher than usual levels.

"I'd rather have detention for the rest of my life than be around you for another minute!" Tina took her time making her point and then got back to packing up her things.

"Please, Tina. I'm sorry, ok?"

But Tina didn't even bother to answer back. Instead, she stomped away with her backpack bouncing into her tailbone as she marched upstairs, raising her middle finger behind her.

Jason got the hint and didn't follow her, but in her rage, Tina forgot that she had decided to avoid the forest on the way home. By the time she realised she should have left Jason's through the front door, taking the long way through downtown, she was already past the opening in the trees and couldn't be bothered to go back. It didn't matter--she wouldn't be coming back to Jason Marman's house ever again.

* * *

"Did I see you coming out of the woods last night?" the boy in the black hi-tops asked. Their paths crossed again the next day at school.

"Oh, I was on my way home," Tina said while heaving her math textbook into her locker, letting it fall with a thud.

"You walk through the woods at night to get home?"

"It's no big deal. There's nothing weird in there. I think it's too close to downtown for there to be any big animals or anything," Tina answered as she shrugged. She wasn't about to admit that she basically jogged the entire path through the forest, with a little help from Madonna's 'Into the Groove'.

"I'm Chuck Rounds, by the way."

"Tina," Tina introduced herself, with her best smile and head tilt.

"Just Tina?" Chuck asked.

"Just Tina." She gave a sharp nod as she answered.

Chuck walked away smiling too, and Tina let her head fall back on her locker door and the familiar melody of Alannah Myles's 'Black Velvet' seductively filled her ear.

Unfortunately, the moment didn't last long as a loud *click* startled her out of her daydream and made her jump. Her walkman was alerting her to turn the tape over to side B. She pulled the walkman from her pocket and pressed *eject*, but the walkman door stayed closed. Tina shut her eyes and took a deep breath. She knew what that meant. With a long fingernail, she wedged her finger in to open the tape deck, pulling the cassette out as gently as possible, especially as the glossy brown ribbon began to pour out afterwards.

"Sucks to be you," someone called as they walked by and caught a glimpse of her struggles.

Tina didn't look up. She was too busy mourning over her favourite mix tape and having to go without it until she had time to roll it all up. She gathered the ribbon and turned to her locker to find a suitable replacement for her walk to homeroom. Her usual favourites were there, lined up from Alanna Miles to Zeppelin, plus one extra that she didn't remember having. It was a recordable tape with a white label where someone wrote *For the Woods*.

Distracted by the cassette, Tina missed the usual drop in temperature she'd feel when Jason Marman was near.

"Look, I'm sorry I called you a bitch," Jason said sincerely, but inevitably he startled her all over again in the process.

Tina kept facing the darkness of her locker, not allowing him to see her react, giving him more fuel for teasing her again..

"And you're sorry too, right?" Jason probed, bending around to look Tina in the face.

"No. I'm not sorry, Jason. We're in high school and you keep calling me Tina Diarrhea."

"That's just a--," Jason stopped.

Tina turned to him and raised an eyebrow. "It's not a joke to me, don't you get it? I want a fresh start."

"Ok. No more...Tina Diarrhea. Last one!" Jason had his hands up in defence. He left one hand up as he emphasised his point. "I swear."

Tina couldn't help herself. Jason was actually being charming, and if she ignored the braces and the fact that he had the face of her childhood tormentor, maybe he wouldn't be so bad.

Jason moved to the side and brushed his blond bangs from his freckled face.

"Look, I know you don't want to come trick-or-treating, but what about coming over and watching scary movies? I'm having some people over afterwards to watch some primo horror movies. This guy I met can get the R-rated stuff, and he said he'll bring some over."

"I don't know. I'm not really into horror movies," Tina said, shrugging and looking away from his earnest attempts to make more eye contact with her.

"But its Halloween, Dia–– I mean, Tina." Jason bit his lip.

Tina let out a sigh. "I'll think about it."

'You Better Be Good To Me' by Tina Turner played loudly in her head.

At home, it was pretty clear that if she stayed, she'd be in charge of handing out candy all night. But the only thing she had to do was go to stupid Jason Marman's party. The only consolation was that this time they wouldn't be alone, and there were cheesy movies to watch.

Like usual, Tina grabbed some good tapes from her bag, including the stretched-out one she hadn't fixed yet. At the bottom of her backpack was the mysterious mixtape, *For the Woods*. Tina thought back to earlier in the day and wondered just how Chuck had managed to slip it by her, but she was impressed. And a mixtape? That had to mean something.

She popped the tape in her walkman and called to her grandmother, "Going out." There was already one little cowboy hobbling up their driveway with his pillowcase open for candy.

At the entrance to the forest, Tina stretched her wire headphones over her bushy curls and pressed play. The first song was 'Forest by The Cure' and then 'Hungry Like a Wolf' by Duran Duran Played.

The songs were pretty obvious choices, but the cheesiness was making Tina smile as she walked, and they'd help pass the time on the way to Jason's. She could see the opening in the trees. As she walked up to the break and around the house to Jason's front door, more and more, she wondered at how that guy snuck past her and slipped a tape into her locker without her seeing. She couldn't remember him anywhere near her locker shelf that morning. And then she realised. The only person who was near her open locker was--*no, it couldn't be.*

Flashes of the morning came back to her, and she remembered how her head was down when Jason came up to her. He could have easily slipped it past her. *Would he?*

Men at Work's 'It's A Mistake' came to mind instantly.

Tina stopped suddenly, and a wave of nausea lapped around her stomach. Any time she complained about Jason, people would always say, *"He's only teasing you because he likes you. That's how boys are."* Tina closed her eyes tight, trying to right her vision, trying to will herself not to vomit.

She looked up the long driveway to the log cabin-style house but couldn't will her legs to get going. And then, she realised that her legs knew better--better than her weak boundaries, better than her desire to be desired. Better than the deep-rooted hatred that desperately hoped this might put an end to her being Tina Diarrhea forever.

She realised her frozen legs were right: In what world would she really have walked two miles *voluntarily* to see a boy who had made her life miserable the last fifteen years?

And with that, a warm tingle began in her toes and worked its way up to thaw her legs. Taking a small step back and one last look, she turned around and started back home, slow at first, then a full jog. It felt good to run and feel the cool air rush into her lungs; the wind burned her throat, and she felt it like a fitting punishment for being such an idiot.

As she pushed harder down the path, she cursed Jason Marman for somehow tricking her into seeing even the slightest of human qualities. She couldn't believe she fell for his games. Even though she wasn't much of a runner, Tina pushed harder and kept going until she was flat on her back.

It took her a few seconds to realise she had fallen.

"You okay?" a voice called.

Tina moved her neck slowly to look around, but the forest was already too dim to see clearly. It was a woman's, which gave Tina some comfort as she stood and took her time to dust off the backs of her legs and shake the twigs from her hair.

Down the path, the trees overhead were thin, and it was just light enough for Tina to see a figure standing on the path. Tina squinted first at the figure who she couldn't be totally sure was the same woman from the other day. When she looked again, the figure silently put out an arm to the side, pointing to the left. Tina looked over to where the forest looked much lighter as if the sunlight were beaming through the trees at night.

Her curiosity was getting the better of her as she took a few steps to see where the figure had gone or where the light was coming from. But as she got closer, Tina could see there wasn't anyone on the path. She turned around and around and stepped just off the path through some thin branches. And then she was in the firelight.

The orange and red leaves lit up like a blazing blanket over the forest floor. In the middle of the clearing were two people: a woman in a white dress and a man in a suit, standing around a small fire. It was kind of boring as costumes go, but to each his own, she thought.

As Tina looked on, she realised she'd been holding her breath. She carefully released it without a sound when the screeching started––low at first and then increasingly louder and higher pitched. Tina's brow furrowed. It sounded like a car's tires grasping for the asphalt. The squeal continued to grow louder and Tina covered her ears, looking at the people near the fire––they hadn't moved.

"Look out!" Tina shouted ineffectively. She couldn't scream louder than the piercing noise that was now everywhere. She had to get closer to warn them that something was coming; she didn't know what, but it was getting closer.

As she reached the couple and stood on the opposite side of the fire, she froze. Just behind the two people were two separate lights, like orbs like––like *headlights*, beaming through the trees, getting brighter, getting bigger...

"Look out!" Tina tried again, flailing her arms.

Then the car burst through the trees, and Tina barely had time to jump out of its path. Branches snapped, and the car flew into the firelight over the two people standing there.

"No!" Tina screamed and ran towards where they had been standing.

Smoke filled the space around her from the fire being blown out. But, it settled quickly and Tina could see the people weren't there, and neither was the car. Smoke was weaving upwards from the fire pit as the coals sizzled and went cold.

What the hell?

Tina spun around and looked to see if she'd misjudged her slide down the side of the hill. This was where they were, around the fire, she was sure of it. And then the car–– Tina spun around in the space that was completely dark, without a trace of the fire.

In the dark, Tina began to truly doubt what she had seen. But before she gave up on her own senses, she decided to try to get back on the path. Maybe she could retrace her steps and get re-oriented. The dark forest floor was an obstacle course of roots and branches, even in good lighting so she shuffled her feet along the ground to keep contact and stay upright.

When she thought she had her bearings near the top of the hill, she turned to go back the way she came but she got stopped mid-step. Something had a hold of her. Tina put her hands out to push their face away, but all she felt was bulbous, boil-ridden skin.

"Tina...Tina!"

Tina struggled to get out of their arms by flailing her arms and kicking into the person't shins, but she knew her canvas hi-tops would barely make a dent.

"Tina, it's me! Take a pill!"

Tina stopped struggling, and as the creature let her go, she took several stumbling steps back. "What are you? How do you know me?"

"Oh my god, it's just me." The creature pulled at its head and removed its face. It was just a mask. Underneath it was Jason.

"Ugh, you stupid son of a––" Tina rushed forward and pushed him, two-handed and hard, in the chest.

He stumbled back. "It's just a mask; I wanted to scare you when you got to my house, but you were so late, and I came to see if you were on your way. Then I heard you screaming out here."

"As much as I hate you right now, we have to get to your house," Tina said. "I need to figure out what I just saw."

"What's going on? Are you being for real, or are you just trying to get me back?"

Jason led the rest of the way down the path towards the break in the trees that led to his backyard. He stopped suddenly in the middle of the path.

"What the hell?" Jason's hands were outstretched, feeling along the tall shrubbery for the break that led to his yard but it wasn't there, the area was full of brush with no easy way through.

"Jason? Where's the hole?" Tina's voice was shrill and full of panic as she realised Jason might be behind everything she just saw and was trying to scare her even more.

"I don't know. I can't find it. I can't even see where the path breaks off––from where I wore it down."

"Jason, this isn't funny. I need to get out!" Tina felt her neck and cheeks instantly get hot.

"I'm not being funny, Diarrhea." Jason's voice was reaching high octaves now.

"Don't call me that!" she spat out readily in a build-up of plenty of frustration.

"Okay, ok, sorry, I'm just so confused." Tina could just faintly see Jason press his hands to his temples. "Where is it, *damnit*?" Jason's voice was shaking, and Tina realised he wasn't joking around. There really was something strange going on, and he really couldn't find the way out.

"Oh, God! Jason, stop this, ok? I saw some really crazy stuff back there and I really need to get out of here." Tina was bouncing in her shoes as she talked. She was beyond anxious and felt like the trees of the forest were getting denser and pushing in on her.

Jason continued to move his hands along the branches of the trees, looking for a break. "What kind of crazy stuff?"

Tina crouched down, taking deep breaths and tried to explain. "There was this couple... around a fire, like a ceremony... then a car... I think..." she trailed off and took a moment to remember.. "It came through the trees, and t-they all... disappeared." Tina almost choked on the last word, worried it would give Jason Marman more to tease her about until infinity.

Jason was pacing as if he could think their way out. "Did you say a ceremony?"

Tina gave up her squat and sat right down on the ground, "Ya, like a weird forest wedding or something."

Jason sighed and then continued to pace, singling his monster mask at his side.

"Why, Jason? What the crap is going on?"

Jason stopped and scratched his head. "It's… it's just there is a legend about this forest." Jason smirked at Tina. "I thought you knew about it. That's why I told you to take the woods. I thought it might scare you, but like a joke."

Tina huffed, glad she'd stopped herself from going to Jason's house but disappointed in herself for letting her guard down to think that Jason Marman might have grown up.

"Ok, I'll bite. What's the legend?" Tina asked finally.

Jason put down his arms and turned to her. "Just that the two people died here on Halloween night. They were this couple that was out on Halloween, dressed like a bride and groom. A black cat ran in front of their car."

Tina cocked her head to the side in disbelief. "Halloween? Black cats? Sounds like a legend to me."

"Apparently, they swerved, and their car hit a tree on the edge of the forest, but they say they survived long enough to get out of the car and die side by side on the forest floor."

"And why would they do that?" Tina crossed her arms.

"Nobody knows," Jason said with a shrug. "But now there have been a handful of sightings. People say they see the couple walking in the woods holding hands, searching for their baby."

"They had a baby with them?" Somehow that fact made the story seem more plausible.

"It's just a legend, Diarrhea. Who knows?"

Tina was too tired to scold him again, but she could scoff and roll her eyes.

"Hey guys!" Tina and Jason turned to the voice.

"Fanny?" Jason said as she got close enough for them to see. She was in all white and had her face painted with whiskers and a pink nose.

"You invited me to watch horror movies, remember? Kathy couldn't make it. She has to stay home and hand out candy."

"Going to my house isn't an option right now," Jason said.

"Why not?" Fanny asked, hand on hip and her mouth gazed open over her jawbreaker.

Jason and Tina both ignored Fanny's question. Neither of them could give an answer that made any sense anyway. Jason had walked the woods a hundred times and never had a problem finding his way home.

"What if we go back?" Jason suggested to Tina.

"Back to where I saw the weird stuff? No way," Tina shrieked with wide eyes. She couldn't believe Jason would even suggest that after they'd just spent twenty minutes trying to get out in the complete other direction.

"What choice is there? We can't just hang out in the woods all night." Jason threw his hands up in the air. "Maybe there's something we have to see, or maybe we can just retrace our steps. It's pretty dark--maybe we missed something."

If there was anything more annoying than being trapped in the woods with Jason, it was being trapped in the woods with Jason and him being the voice of reason, Tina thought.

"Fine," Tina agreed with a huff.

"Where are we going?"

Tina and Jason ignored Fanny again because, just like her last question, there was no logical answer for it.

The path was darker than Tina had ever seen, but she knew they had to get over the ridge and then they would be close to where she saw the... whatever she thought she saw.

Fanny was good at keeping the conversation alive--maybe too alive at times, making Tina consider throwing on her headphones to drown her out. Jason was quiet and pensive. Tina could tell he was really thrown by not being able to find his yard.

"... that's why I decided to be a cat. It's just too classic and--" Fanny finally stopped talking, just over the ridge where all three of them stopped in their tracks.

"Is that a fire?" Jason said it so quietly that it felt like he was talking to himself.

"Well, at least we won't freeze," Fanny said cheerfully.

Jason was already on his way down the side of the path, and Fanny was right behind him. Tina stood back--she'd done this exact thing earlier, and it didn't end so well. But she certainly didn't want to stay on the cold, dark path alone, so she turned sideways and started shimmying her way towards the light.

"Hey guys. Happy Halloween. Wanna join me?"

It was Chuck.

"What are you doing here?" Tina and Jason both said at the same time, then gave each other a wordless look.

"Just hanging out, like you. This forest is a cool spot to have a spooky Halloween, don't you think?"

"Totally rad. Nice fire!" Fanny said, rubbing the sides of her arms as she got closer to the flames. Tina also came around the other side to talk to Chuck while he was taking out some things from his backpack. Jason was the only one who started to take a look around, completely ignoring Chuck.

"How'd you like the mixtape?" He asked Tina as she got closer.

Tina dragged a pointed toe in front of her shyly and smiled. "So it *was* from you. I didn't even see you put it in my locker. It's pretty cool. Thank you. So far, it's all bands I really like."

"It gets even better on the other side," Chuck said, smiling.

Before Tina could say anything else, Chuck skipped to Jason and shook his hand. "Thank you for being here, Jason. Thank you for listening."

Jason stared back, his eyebrows in a wrinkled triangle.

"Oh, come on, Jason. You know what I mean; getting all your friends together on Halloween to walk through here to your place, just like I asked."

Jason looked lost. "Like you asked?"

"Oh, nothing," Chuck said with a dismissive hand gesture. I'll still get you those R-rated movies as a thank you. And hey, while you're all here, why don't we do something really spooky?"

"Oooh, yes. I love spooky stuff," Fanny said, making her way closer to Chuck and leaving Jason standing where he was, still with a perplexed look on his face.

"Have you guys ever heard about the couple that died here on Halloween night?" Chuck asked, his face beaming in the firelight.

"Everybody knows the legend. What's the plan?" Fanny adjured, giving a soft clap at her chest.

Tina and Jason were less amused and exchanged looks across the firepit.

"Tina, you stand here," Chuck instructed and brought Tina in front of him. "Dude, you're here," Chuck said, pointing for Jason to be next to Tina.

"And me?" Fanny jumped in excitedly.

"And you are?" Chuck asked.

"Fanny," Fanny said with her most charming smile.

"Like Frances?" Chuck shot back flatly.

"Nope, just Fanny," Fanny said happily.

"Ok..." Chuck gave Tina a side-eyed look of judgement that Fanny completely ignored.

"Fanny, you have to be the witness," Chuck said, moving Fanny to the side. "I can't believe I forgot that part all these years," he whispered to himself.

"What?" Fanny chirped.

"Nevermind. This is perfect, actually. So, I'll start by saying the words for the ritual. You guys just stand and listen: Dearly Beloved. We're gathered here today to join this couple in Holy Matrimony," Chuck started.

"Ugh, what?" Tina was waving her hand up, but Chuck was ignoring her, reading from a thick book.

"I thought we were doing a seance?" Jason stepped forward to say as Chuck continued to read.

"We are. Just play along," Chuck finally acknowledged, looking at Tina and giving her a wink.

"Do you take this man to be your lawful wedded husband in sickness and in health for as long as you both shall live?"

"Um, no?" Tina shuddered. "I very much do not! What the hell are you trying to pull here?"

Chuck slammed the book closed. "Come on, just say it. I promise you'll like what happens next."

"Come on, Tina Diarrhea. Don't be such a loser like always," Fanny said, scowling. It took everything in Tina's power not to throw her arm into Fanny's throat right where she stood. She looked at Jason, who shrugged. "It's just for fun, I guess," he said.

Tina paused but eventually gave in and nodded. Then she and Jason both said their *"I dos."*

"I now pronounce you husband and wife," Chuck said, reopening the book.

As a reflex, Tina threw her arms in front of her face. "No kissing!"

"Is something supposed to happen?" Fanny whispered. Then as she kept an eye on everything, the fire lit up.

Tina and Jason turned to look too, but nothing had changed.

Fanny turned to Chuck. "This was a sucky seance. Weddings aren't spooky. They're romantic and beautiful and make everyone cry." Even Fanny had lost interest and was sounding annoyed by Chuck's empty promise.

Chuck flipped the pages of the book and started reading again but not in a language anyone could understand. Tina could only loosely relate it to Iron Butterfly's 'In-A-Gadd-Da-Vidda' or something she might expect from the mind of Freddie Mercury.

The dark and dense forest behind Chuck began to lighten and soon became bright as the two round orbs were beamed through the trees, just like Tina saw before. But, this time, there was no squeal, just the sound of an engine rumbling beyond the circle.

Two doors slammed shut, and Jason and Tina exchanged confused looks. Then looking towards the light, they saw two people approaching, a man in a suit and a woman in a white dress. Tina didn't know what to do or say.

The man was clean-cut and very handsome. He walked right up to Jason. And the woman had long black hair with beautiful face, like a porcelain doll. She caressed Chuck's face before she took her place in front of Tina.

"Holy crap," Fanny said, taking a step back and then fainting on the ground.

The next thing Tina knew, she was facing Jason, holding both his hands, but his face was changed. He was older, with darker hair like Chuck's––clean cut and handsome.

"Jason?"

But Jason said nothing. His eyes were wide, doting, as he looked at

Tina.

"Jason!" Tina shouted louder, this time grabbing his shoulders and giving him a good shake. As soon as she did, Tina noticed her own hands. Her fingers were petite and slim, her nails long and manicured. Definitely not her hands.

"Am I? Are we?" Tina whispered to herself but couldn't make sense of anything. If Jason looked like Chuck's dad, that meant she was--no. *Chuck's mom?*

Cue in Billy Idol's, "White Wedding," once again.

Tina's vision suddenly went blurred, hearing was muffled, and her stomach knotted itself. The world around her turned to a dull fog where she couldn't see or hear Fanny trying to call her name. She spun away from Jason and tried to shake her head free of what she was seeing. Tina crouched to the ground and closed her eyes tight, the white dress billowing around her. Someone else was trying to talk to her, but it was like she was underwater and couldn't hear them or answer. Tina felt a hand on her back and heard them loud and clear.

"Mom? Mom, it's me."

Tina looked back at Chuck in terror.

"Mom, I finally did it. You're back. You and dad are married. Now you can stay. Here. With me."

Tina had no words. She wanted to scream, but something stopped her. Something was telling her to go to Chuck, to thank him--to love him.

"Tina?" Jason was able to stammer out.

Tina looked up at Jason, who looked just like Chuck. But the way Jason said her name snapped her back into reality. It was all she needed to remind her of the nightmare--the nightmare of being married to Jason Marman.

She still couldn't get out any words but stood glaring at Chuck's face. She spat hard and didn't wait around to see what he did next. She gathered the dress in two handfuls and ran towards the path. She could hear them calling her, but she wouldn't turn back.

This time jogging didn't feel like it had earlier. The giant white wedding dress tight around her body and long at her ankles was one thing, but this wasn't her body. Tina could run the path easily--she'd done it several times. But Chuck's mom was a little less agile. She did her best to head towards downtown and try her luck at the forest opening onto her street.

But, suddenly, she was on her back. Then, just as quickly, someone took hold of her hand and was pulling her up.

"Let's go," said the woman. Tina recognized her voice and followed.

As they ran together, hand in hand, Tina understood it all--the woman wasn't warning her about Jason--it was Chuck the whole time; he was the boy.

Tina continued to stumble behind the woman off the path and through the trees. She eventually saw a porch light, and the woman rushed them both in through the door.

"This way," the woman called, leading Tina to a small bathroom. "Look."

Tina did as she was told and faced the mirror. At first, she thought it was a trick. It was as if she was looking at a painting, a painting of another woman's face around where her own should be.

"You're Brenda," the woman said.

Tina raised her hand but there was an unfamiliarity when she touched her face.Her own cheek was much rounder, her skin less smooth. "I'm what?"

"Brenda, that boy's mother. You have her face, I'm sure of it. He did this to you," the woman said, putting a caring hand on Tina's shoulder.

Tina started to cry. "What--what did he do to me? To us?" She gasped as she remembered that she had left Jason and Fanny with Chuck.

The woman sat on the edge of the bathtub, not looking at Tina.

"I saw it all. I heard the car first and then saw it crash into the trees. Two people were inside, and they crawled out, out into the clearing where you just were. They lay down together, holding hands. I was running towards them. Before the paramedics came, I did what I could to try to save the baby." The woman took a pause to hold back tears.

"They tried to say I was wrong, that I didn't know what I was doing, and they chased me out of the main part of town. That's why I live here now. But I got him out, and I heard later he was raised by an aunt and uncle nearby. Then, years later, a boy started coming to this spot once in a while, and then more and more often. I knew it was him. Their baby. Then he started to come more frequently. Then he started bringing books, reading strange languages and poems at night, on full moons, and on Halloween. I had a feeling about what he was trying to do, but I thought it was harmless. But then something changed. He got a hold of something different, more powerful, maybe, and so I started to keep an extra eye out. So when you started walking here, I didn't want to scare you, but I wanted you to see--to warn you of what might happen."

Tina wiped her tears on the wedding gown sleeve. The beads poked her skin. "So the legend is true," she said through sniffles.

"I suppose, yes. Some folks say Brenda was starting to show, so they were gonna elope to avoid the gossip. You know how we can be in small towns."

"So what's going to happen to me? I can't stay like this. What will my grandmother say?" Tina was talking overly quickly and finding it hard to breathe.

The woman firmly grabbed Tina by both shoulders to steady her and provide her with the best plan she could think of. "Go home and collect a few things, then you can stay here with me until we figure something out."

Tina turned one last time to the mirror, just to check. But she still looked like Brenda--cloud white, pretty, dainty even, like a ballerina. Her dark brown hair was straight and silky like Cher's and her brown eyes were soulful. She smiled at herself and marvelled at the symmetry and how naturally red her lips were. Definitely not Tina Diarrhea anymore.

"Come on," said the woman. "I'll help you find the way."

The woman led Tina back outside to a narrow path at the side of her small cottage. She ran quickly in front, and Tina followed. It wasn't far from where Tina could see streetlights and civilization. The forest opening was clear and open on Tina's street.

The woman moved to the side.

"Thank you," Tina said as she hugged the woman on her way past. Then she quickly gathered her dress again and jogged onto the asphalt.

Tina jogged through the streets, running on the road to avoid the little kids in their costumes. It was the first time she wondered how much time had passed. It seemed like nothing had changed out here, and yet she was so different. She was Brenda.

At her house, the kitchen light was on. That meant her grandmother was awake and listening to the radio with her tea. Tina knew how to sneak in and get upstairs without being heard.

She looked at her room full of things. Her posters, her boombox. Would she ever be able to come back for real?

Tina grabbed her knapsack and pulled everything out to make room. Down at the bottom was the unravelled cassette she hadn't fixed yet. Maybe it was just the last straw after everything that had happened that day, but Tina burst into tears again and dropped onto her bed. The fragile brown cassette film was a nest in her hands, and the sight of it was enough to make her cry even harder. But she didn't. She wouldn't let herself. She had to think of a way to get things back to how they were--to get back to being Tina and get Jason back to Jason--whatever it would take to not be Brenda, Chuck's mom, and married to Jason Marman.

As she went over everything again, she held the cassette and started to turn the dials that pulled the film back, sucking it in through the bottom, one twist at a time. She spun the plastic wheels with knobby teeth backwards, little by little, all the while her thoughts landing on her desperation. She thought back to her other school, where Jason used to get everyone to chant "Tina Diarrhea" out on the playground. She thought back to her teacher saying, "Just ignore him. It will make you stronger one day." Tina thought about all the friends she thought she had until Jason teased them too for being her friend. Her stomach twisted and pulled at the thought. She'd never had a real friend her entire life. Everyone had distanced themselves from her. Everyone teased her and avoided her. No one listened to her. All because of Jason. Marman.

Tina gritted her teeth and shook her head, all the while absent-mindedly reeling in the cassette film. And, just as slowly, the skin of her hands darkened. A warmth came into her hands, and she looked down. Her fingers were getting stubbier, and her nails had returned to their usual nubs.

She threw the tape to the floor and ran to her mirror. She was still Brenda. Her skin was getting darker, but still no sign of her face changing back at all.

"Yes, yes, Tina!" she whispered, not to herself but to her namesake as the inspiring chorus of "Proud Mary" cheered her on.

She ran back to the cassette on the floor and spun the wheels until all the brown streamer was tucked up into the plastic shield. Then, at last, she could feel the frizzy tickle of her curls caressing the sides of her face. The sensation led her to jump up and rush to her vanity to see her face. Her Tina face.

In the movie of her life, "We Don't Need Another Hero" would play now and she'd raise one arm in a victorious salute. She winked at her reflection, back in her regular clothes. Then, surprising even herself, Tina decided to go back to the woods and check on Jason and Fanny.

* * *

"Tina, thank god!"

Was she actually hearing that Jason Marman was happy to see her? Maybe things had corrected a little too much, she thought.

"Jason!" Tina smiled fully. She couldn't believe how happy she was to see them both, though she'd never admit it to them. Fanny was on her back, her head propped up on Jason's monster mask.

"Where's Chuck?"

"He left just after you. Something about finding the only other way to be with his parents forever."

"Oh no," Tina uttered softly.

"Why? What does that mean?" Fanny asked in a groggy voice. Clearly, they had stayed here until Fanny felt better after passing out.

"Which way did he go, Jason?" Tina commanded.

"Down the path towards my house. Why? What's going on, Tina?" Jason had to shout the last part as Tina was already sprinting down the path. Somehow, Tina knew exactly what Chuck was up to, and she knew exactly where to go. Down the path and out of the trees easily, she made her way past Jason's house and down his street. All the way to the end. All the way to the bridge over the freeway.

When she got to the bridge, she wasn't even winded but stopped dead in her tracks. There on the bridge, looking over the guardrail, was Chuck.

"No!" she called.

"I need to do it, Tina. I need to be with them. Don't stop me." Chuck faced straight ahead, looking down at the highway below, full-on oncoming traffic.

Freddy Mercury always wove his way in. "Don't Stop Me Now," was all Tina could hear before she realised she had to reply.

"I'm not going to stop you, Chuck, but I need you to look at me."

Chuck stayed stuck halfway across the bridge, staring into the lights of the oncoming traffic.

"This isn't the answer, I promise you," Tina shouted, doing her best to sound sympathetic while getting her message over the freeway noise.

"How would you know? I barely even know you," Chuck shot back.

"Because--because I know your mom," Tina said in a calm, even voice.

Chuck turned to her then, his face fallen. "What?"

"I was your mom for a few hours. I felt her. I heard her memories. I heard her hopes for you. When she looked at you, when you called me 'mom', her heart broke because she wished it was real. But she was really happy to see you. I'm sorry I ran away; I didn't know what was happening. But your mom even knew you'd be here. How do you think I found you?"

Chuck ran his full sleeve across his face under his nose. His dark hair was blowing around in the confused wind on the bridge. Then he finally turned to Tina. "Are you for real?"

Tina just smiled and tried to give Chuck all the eye contact she could muster against the bright lights on the bridge.

"And don't forget. Jason probably had a similar experience with your dad. Don't you want to find out what he felt?"

Chuck put both hands on the railing, and Tina thought she'd lost him--he was going to push himself up any second.

But he didn't. His knees buckled, and Chuck slumped to the ground. InstantlyTina ran up to him and threw her arms around him. She kissed him hard on his head, his hair flying up in her face. And just for a second, Brenda was there with them, one last time.

* * *

THE NEXT DAY

"In conclusion," Tina stated with relief as the nightmare was coming to an end, "we can begin by healing our relationships at home, in our classes, with our friends and even acquaintances. No relationship is too small. It all works toward the world being a better place."

"For you and for me," Jason said. Tina let Jason have the last word only because it was the cheesiest line of the entire presentation.

The freshman class didn't seem to understand the presentation was over. Because it took a few seconds for them to begin their polite clap so that Tina and Jason could shake Principal Stewart's hand and leave the stage.

Backstage, Tina and Jason flew down the back steps and skipped into the hallway, both releasing sighs of relief.

"Thank goodness that's over," Jason said with a huge exhale.

"Ya, that sucked. I never want to do that again," Tina said, nodding in agreement.

"*OOoooooooh*," two teasing voices hollered. Fanny and Kathy found them in the hall and couldn't resist.

"Tina and Jason sitting in a tree," Fanny started.

"F-A-I-N-T-I-N-G," Jason mocked back.

"I didn't faint, Marman. I just had low blood sugar and thought I saw--nevermind. You two are gross." Fanny said defensively.

"I don't think so, *Fainting Fanny!*" Jason shrieked in laughter at his new mark.

Tina rolled her eyes and then found herself humming the first bars of Billy Joel's "Honesty."

Jason really hadn't learned his lesson at all. But she did learn something about bullies: when they point fingers, you have a choice about whether or not you look.

Purple Moon

I have walked with humanity for a long time and watched as they grew from a small tribe of hunters and gatherers to the first harvesters of a planted crop. From biting an apple, they learnt how to grow them. This important step moved them from being at the mercy of nature to having a measure of self-determination.

One ability of humanity that has always amazed me was that no matter how dark the times or what age they encountered, there were always stories being told. Be it around the fire inside a cave keeping the horrors of the night at bay or those same dark shadows being banished forever by lights powered by the fiery energies of the atom—people had always told stories.

Since the first papyrus was created, I have documented my journey with humankind. And now, sitting here, reminiscing in my secret library, I find myself recalling the night I heard for the first time some of the humanities most important stories and how they related to a war that almost ended the world.

1816 – Geneva

The rain outside seemed to double with intensity, and a single, mighty fork of lightning illuminated the heavy clouds above. A rare event had heralded the storm; a Purple Moon that threw its weird light across the landscape around us, firing conversations about how peoples of the prehistoric past gathered around campfires and created tales about their world. This led to a strange little competition that would echo throughout the ages.

I sat in a dark room lit only by some candles and a roaring blaze in the fireplace. Along the far wall, a group of other shadowy figures were also just enjoying the night and the fire.

"I still cannot believe there were really ice giants!" exclaimed Lord Byron.

I smiled at the poet. "I was there, and your grandfather swore black and blue that he and those shipwrecked with him had seen giants walking around Patagonia. Just so you know, one of Captain Cook's officers also claimed to see the same thing a few years later."

Proving he had studied the world of his famous grandfather, Byron pointed out—"I believe the French voyager Louis-Antoine, Comte de Bougainville claimed he'd seen the bones of these Patagonian giants, but believed they were just the remains of elephants."

I had only recently met this strange group of friends and found them witty and warm. The oppressive weather would typically sour most holidays, but this party had decided to use the brooding atmosphere to their great advantage. The poet Lord Byron was the one who suggested each should come up with a horror story they would later recount while the weather howled outside.

The first night a young physician, Dr John William Polidori, had told an amusing story about a vampire. Then, having failed night after night to tell her tale, the very pregnant Claire Clairmont had finally begged our forgiveness and permanently abstained, claiming she had just been unable to think of anything worth retelling. And to cover her absence, I had agreed last night to pass on some of the true stories of horror I carry with me from the past. Some had become legendary tales or even stories from mythology, while others were known only to me. One was about watching the siege of Troy and how I had helped encourage Odysseus to enter the battle. Another was about watching early humans harness fire for the first time.

When someone pointed out this meant I was claiming to be both Prometheus and Palamedes, it was Byron who moved the conversation forward. "Storytellers should never be called on to tell the truth because the truth is stranger than fiction." The poet looked like he'd been struck over the head and began furiously scribbling.

Tonight we got onto the idea of dangerous giants living in remote areas as we had just heard a story by Miss Godwin, the stepsister of Claire, who had taken something from everyone's stories, including mine, and came up with a tale that would still be told centuries in the future.

"It was on a dreary night of November that I beheld my man completed…"

It was a hell of a start to a tale.

On this astonishing holiday, Byron, Godwin—or Shelley as she would become known—and the others had created not only the first vampire story but Frankenstein, The Modern Prometheus. Of course, these tales would be duplicated, plagiarised, serialised, and reinvented hundreds of times. I personally like to think Shelley had been inspired to create and name her creature after me and that I had more than a little to do with Polidori's vampire creation as well.

That was all some time ago. More importantly for our tale today, this was not the only time I encountered the effects of a Purple Moon. My long journey with humanity since it ran from my garden meant there were very few horrors or dark secrets in the world that had any hold on me. Yet, no matter how many times I entered the darkened rooms inside the Bar of Endless Sorrows, there was always something sipping a drink in its depths to remind me there were some things in the world that really do go bump in the night.

As I walked through what should have been my kitchen door and into the dark interior of the pub, I heard the familiar buzz from my pocket, alerting me my cell phone had lost its signal. There was no coverage inside the Bar of Endless Sorrows as it sat between here and there, ostensibly which meant it was nowhere.

Now, I'm not that concerned about the pubs' patrons because you expect the weirdest of the weird in the world's oldest arcane watering hole, so you're generally prepared for them. I also used to do a lot of drinking back in the days when I found myself with no purpose and looking for some way to ease the endless boredom resulting from an unending idle life. So, at one time or another, I got drunk or into a brawl with just about every creature and monster.

If you're meant to enter the Bar of Endless Sorrows, then the spell on the front door will find you. It's one of the oldest and strongest arcane magic I know, as the pub, in one form or another, has been running since the first fruit was crushed and fermented into something with a little more punch than apple juice. Why? Well, it's a universal truth that after food and sex, the next thing on the list is always, *always*, finding something to drink.

This day I'd been summoned to the bar by the one person guaranteed to get me through the door. As always, Akan was behind the counter, today polishing a martini glass. The Mayan demon of alcohol then placed it on a shelf behind him containing receptacles of various shapes and sizes, before turning and grabbing a champagne flute to work on it with his cloth. His tattooed face, with its various piercings of gold and turquoise jewellery, was reflected in the crystal.

With a nod of welcome, he greeted me, "Amun."

"Akan, how's life?"

The man's face split into a huge grin, revealing sharp teeth filed to a point. "Life's good, buddy. Every day I get a little closer to getting out of this damn bar."

Originally, Akan had been bound to the bar for going on a bender with his best mate, Cacoch. They caused so much damage that they were banned from the Sorrow for a thousand years. Being an alcohol deity, albeit a minor one, Akan begged to change this ruling and was sentenced to serve in the bar for the exact same time. I knew his sentence ended some time ago, but Akan had found himself a home, also purpose and was in no rush to leave, so I was willing to play along. As I said earlier, it's hard to describe the tyranny of unending life and the boredom that it can create. You need a purpose, and this Mayan drinking god had found his place in the world.

"How is Cacoch?"

Akan's face dropped. "Not well at all. He discovered heroin."

That wasn't good. A deity was impervious to most mundane things, but opium was a northern hemisphere drug and only recently introduced into South America. "Is he getting help?"

"Nope, he claims he's got it handled."

It was hard to read a face with that many piercings and tattoos, but I caught that Akan really did not want to discuss his best friend's fate, so I dropped it.

"I'm here to…"

Before I could finish, the demon nodded his head towards the back "...they're waiting for you upstairs."

Now, the rules of the normal world don't mean much inside the Sorrow. Not only does the door just find you whenever you need it, but the rooms inside were set out to ensure that any creature entering its sanctuary has a safe place to go.

Those with an aversion to the sun had rooms further in the back to ensure a stray spear of sunlight couldn't strike them when the door opened, while those with a more aquatic nature could enjoy the pool room. Yes, it was literally a pool, split in two, one part for the freshwater tolerant and the other half for sea-going folk.

I'd been inside the bar more times than I can recall, but I could count the number of times I'd been upstairs on one hand. Whereas downstairs was for everyone, the rooms upstairs were considered almost hallowed ground. There were the meeting rooms where so many of the treaties and laws that governed our lives in this modern human-controlled world were debated and formalised. Whatever the reason for my summons, being sent upstairs was a bad, bad sign.

I moved deeper into the bar, walking through swirling clouds of heavily scented smoke. Many of the tables were occupied; I even recognized a few. Some of the denizens of these dark alcoves nodded a friendly greeting, but many more gave me a suspicious look or showed outright hostility. If you live long enough, your list of friends will be dwarfed by your list of enemies.

As mentioned, the upper rooms of the bar were something of a sanctuary and not every fool and imp was allowed to wander about up there, so to stop those foolhardy enough to try was one of the more unusual bouncers--a large granite golem called Francis. Before you say anything, the golem had chosen the name for himself, so if you have an issue, take it up with Francis personally--I dare you.

Topping Francis's rough stone head was a Detroit Tigers baseball cap. Legend used to say you destroyed a golem by wiping away the first letter of the name etched into their head. Francis partly wore the cap, so no one had access to the sigil underneath. I never had the heart to point out that as the word was chiseled into his granite forehead. Someone would need a jackhammer to remove it.

The other reason for the cap? Francis simply loved his 80s crime shows and watched them continuously. Hill Street Blues, Hart to Hart, The Equalizer--and especially Magnum PI, who wore just such a cap.

As I approached the stairs, I could see Francis was watching what looked like Cagney and Lacy on a tiny portable TV. His great stone face was illuminated in the screen's dull light, and he looked up when I moved into his vision. A big goofy grin started to spread across his face.

"Amun, how are you?"

I had uncovered Francis nearly one thousand years ago, buried under a mountain slide. Due to the enormous weight above, the golem had been trapped--and had been slowly chewing its way free. I helped dig him out and then suggested him a job at the bar, where he'd been working ever since.

"I'm good, Francis. How they treating you?"

"Oh, cannot complain. I have my shows, and I don't really need much else."

"Good to hear. Ok, if I head up?"

"Sure. They've been waiting for you. Everyone else arrived hours ago."

"Well, ok then. Talk to you later."

Francis didn't respond, as his attention was firmly back on his TV.

I'll admit I was not expecting to meet the denizens of the main meeting room when I finally reached the top of the stairs and peeked inside. I'd never seen so many of the council in one place before, outside of some royal wedding. Of course, over the years, I had dealt with all of them at one point or another—and often many of them at the same time—but never had I faced the entire council at once.

As always, the pack leader of the world's werewolf clans sat near the head of the table, and directly opposite was King Oberon of the fay. Another dozen individuals represented the lesser group of djinn and creatures that filled most fairy tales.

"Wow, the *concilium maficut aliud monstrum*, and all to talk to me?"

"Don't call us that, Amun; it's degrading, unworthy of you and quite frankly, a poor joke," Oberon groaned.

"Where's your dog?" Lycaon asked with contempt. Now, this wasn't the Greek Lycaon, considered the first werewolf king; both just happened to share the name. However, this one was a mutt compared to the original, and he carried a real hatred for my long-time partner.

"Lycaon, good to see you. Vulk gave me a note to pass on if you were here," I pretended to get something from my pocket. Then with deliberate slowness, I unfolded the invisible piece of paper and announced, "He says he's sorry he can't be here as he's got a date with your wife." There was a long history between Vulk and Lycaon, with the pack leader causing us no end of trouble over the years, so I was happy to buy into their feud and shame the werewolf in front of his peers.

You find your fun where you can.

"One day, Amun, we'll meet outside the umbrella of sanctuary..." The werewolf growled in a fury, gesturing about at the Bar of Endless Sorrows.

"Pup, I've seen your worst, and I'm still here. How about I make a threat this time? Keep interfering with me and mine, and you'll see me at my worst."

For a second, the colour drained from the werewolf's face, only to be replaced with the blood-red flush of pure rage. One day soon, I would have to deal with the pack leader, and it was going to be a bloody, brutal fight.

"Look, I don't want to be here. You folks asked for this meeting, and I have just enough goodwill and curiosity to discover what the entire council wants of me."

"Not the entire council," Lycaon snarled.

"Enough."

Everyone stopped when the dragon king spoke. Known by Dracorex in the West, the king of all celestial dragons and various other eastern deities was short on humour, long on memory and did not brook fools easily. In fact, he was known to eat them. Vulk had the theory that his grumpiness came from the fact his name translated into English as 'Long Wang'.

"Mr Galaes, if you would be so kind, please sit and allow us to explain why we invited you here."

When the dragon king asks you to sit, shut up and listen... you sit, shut up and listen.

"The world's in serious shit." That was from a female leprechaun called Baloobas. She seemed part of Oberon's retinue, and rumour has it, his illegitimate daughter.

"Ok, well, that's got my interest peaked."

"Crass and accurate," Dracorex agreed. "Halloween is approaching, and we have a rare celestial occurrence coming."

"Yes, I know the bars' part. Those affected by the full moon can find sanctuary inside because of its ability to sit between locations and so never be under the influence of the satellite's effects."

"True, but what's occurring this Halloween is something far more dangerous. You've heard of blood moons and blue moons, correct? Well, in a month, we have a rare Purple Moon."

I tried not to laugh; I really did. But a stupid name and the solemn look on everyone's faces made that near impossible. Still, I managed to hold it together.

"This will be a full moon on Halloween, but also our diviners have warned us something terrible is going to happen that night, which will cause the moon to be a stronger, deeper shade--thus, a Purple Moon."

"Look, I know what a Purple Moon is. The last one I recall, the colour was caused by the enormous amount of material pumped into the atmosphere by the Tambora explosion; so yes, I understand it could seem like a Purple Moon is a herald of terrible times. I just doubt it's the cause, more the result."

"Tragically, this is not the case. What you likely do not know is the efforts we have gone through to keep the following information secret. When the heavens align, as they will on the 31st of October, then all magic will cease during its effect."

"I'm not sure what that means?" I asked, genuinely baffled.

"It means that a celestial convergence is about to occur that will block every type of magic—including protection, binding and glamours, for all those under its direct effect."

"What, all spells? You mean even..."

"All spells. Do you think Krakatoa erupted in 1883 and caused its Purple Moon? No, that was a brief disruption of the holding spell on an evil, so old that no one seems to recall its name. The thing nearly escaped its prison and would have laid waste to the world. It was only an effort from the entire council that ensured the creature was forced back into its subterranean prison."

I was there in 1816 with Lord Byron when Shelley told her first version of Frankenstein during that brutal, unending storm. I had seen the Purple Moon earlier, and we had no idea at the time the weather was being formed by all the material ejected from the Mount Tambora eruption. I also saw a Purple Moon after Krakatoa. In fact, I recall hearing the explosion as I was visiting Queensland at the time in Northern Australia.

"I had no idea. I mean, I knew something other than the eruption had occurred. But the loss of all magic?—well, that's more than a little frightening."

"Many of the past's darkest creatures are hidden away in places that, so far, have never fallen under the shadow of such an event, but this one is different. All magic will be gone until the event is over. All protective spells, all wards, warnings and all glamours, meaning even those who have been walking around in full view of humanity for years, their true faces will be exposed for everyone to see. I kid you not when I say the effects of this event could be catastrophic."

"Alright, well, this all sounds terrible. Not sure what it's got to do with me, though?"

"Vassago." For the first time, I noticed Rowne sitting at the back of the room. The knowledge demon had been a pain in my neck for a long time. We were not so much friends, it's that we'd just known each other for so long that it was nice to occasionally see a familiar face through all these centuries. We helped each other on occasion and been a hindrance to each other more than once. I liked Rowne, but I didn't trust a single bone in his body.

"And what does Vassago have to do with me?" I asked the demon.

"She's the one who worked out where the Purple Moon's effect will be most devastating, but she'll only tell you."

Vassago was another demon and a good friend of Rowne's. I guessed that made sense, as a knowledge demon and a demon of lost things would have something to talk about. Honestly, both were from the lower-orders and not that bad, considering some of the true monsters I've dealt with over the years. I once thought there may have been more to their relationship, but honestly, I do believe they're just friends. Plus, I've always known Rowne's hunger is far more specific than that.

"Still not sure what it's got to do with me?"

"Honestly…"

"That would be nice." I cut in, reminding Rowne of our history. He gave me a little knowing smile, then continued. "...I don't think she trusts these guys." I watched how that piece of knowledge landed amongst the council. A few looked peeved, but most had their heads so far up their arses they failed to pick up they'd just been disrespected.

The demon then stepped forward and handed me a note. *It takes a carpenter to build Halloween.* At the bottom was Vassago's symbol, the four-pointed star of a compass. I folded the paper and put it in my pocket.

"You're asking me to go talk to Vassago, get what she has and then lead the charge to try and stop the end of days."

"I understand what we are asking, but I am also aware you're not as aloof as you make out to be... and I believe every single one of us sitting here has suffered your strange idea of justice at one point or another." That Long Wang... he never says much, but when he does, he gets right to the point.

"Fine."

"You'll have the full support of the council," the dragon king promised.

"Whatever that's worth," Rowne cuts in. Now that was interesting. I wasn't aware there was a rift between the council and the knowledge demon. That was something to investigate later, as you never know what could be useful in the future.

I exited the pub through a different door than the one I'd entered. This one just happened to place me right next to my car. The pub knows all. I pulled the phone from my pocket and swiped it open. I then turned off the audio recorder I had running the entire time I'd been inside. Again, you never know when evidence of such a conversation could be important.

Then I pulled up the phone's contacts and rang Vulk.

"You're alive," he answered on the first ring. "I was starting to wonder, dealing with those assholes."

"We have a job; can you meet me at Vassago's?"

There was a pause for a moment before Vulk said, "Sure, be there in twenty minutes." Then I heard some muffled voice in the background, but Vulk's voice covered it all. "Make that an hour."

"Fine." I hung up. The old wolf really was a dog when it came to women.

An hour later, Vulk's V8 Ford Cobra roared up to the front of a large house with a manicured garden. The werewolf jumped out, all showered and smiling. I didn't need to ask what had put the smile on his face as she slid across from the passenger's seat and leaned out the driver's side window.

"Meet you at home, sweetie."

"Cool." Then he turned to me. "Do you mind if I get a lift with you after we're done?" Vulk asked with terrible puppy dog eyes. "She wants to go buy some things for my place. Apparently, I need stuff like plates and glasses."

The wife of Lycaon pulled away, and I turned towards the house, shaking my head. "You really are asking for trouble."

"Me? I'm a sweetheart. Is it my fault trouble seems to just find me?"

Together we walked through the garden up to the front door as I explained what our mission was. None of it seemed to faze the werewolf. I supposed it wasn't exactly the strangest mission I'd asked him to join me on over the years.

As we approached the house, it became clear something was wrong. The front door was open, and there were no lights on inside.

"Well, that's not good," Vulk needlessly voiced. He then took a long sniff. His sense of smell was far superior to mine, even in human form. I watched his face for the result.

"Blood."

"Shit."

Together we ran through the door, ready for anything, and searched the house. In the library was the body of Vassago. Vulk started sniffing around the room, looking for a scent to find who'd killed the demon, while I concentrated on the body. Often a murder victim can help lead to their killer, sometimes by the way they were killed or how the body was positioned. Everything has a reason.

"Nothing," Vulk stated after a few minutes.

"Same here," I admitted.

"Actually, when I said nothing, I meant to say we're not alone," Vulk added, turning towards the doorway. Standing there was Rowne.

"We didn't do this," Vulk remarked, raising his hands in fake surrender.

"I figured." The knowledge demon fake-smiled. "I've been following you since the bar."

"Any idea where she would have hidden the map?"

"What did the note say?" Rowne asked, ignoring Vulk's remark. I really didn't need to read it again, but I took the note out and handed it over to the demon.

It takes a carpenter to build Halloween.

"Well, that's not terribly helpful," Vulk said, reading the note over the shoulder of the knowledge demon. "Is it Jaysus?" he asked, mimicking a southern accent.

We both looked at him.

"What? He was a carpenter, wasn't he?"

"Search the room," I ordered. "There's likely a reason the body was in here."

As the others searched the dead demon's desk and furniture, I concentrated on the bookshelves. There were hundreds of books, all ordered in some strange filing system that likely had made sense to Vassago. Next, was a bookshelf full of DVDs and videotapes.

Looking through the titles, I found what we were looking for. I pulled the video off the shelf and ran my thumb over the pencilled four-pointed star on its spine. I then held it up. "Got it."

"What's that?" Vulk took the videotape from my hand and pulled the cassette out of its clamshell cover. The large black oblong cassette had the words HALLOWEEN emblazoned on the small sticker between the two plastic windows showing the magnetic tape inside. Vulk then put the cassette back in its cover and opened the clamshell flat. He then reached behind its clear plastic sheet and pulled the movie's printed title sheet from underneath. He inspected the back in case something was written there.

"Nothing... do you think there might be a message with invisible ink on there? Hey, maybe there's something on the video?"

"You think?" Rowne scowled, snatching the tape from the werewolf. "Where the hell are we going to find a VHS player to watch the damn thing?"

I announced, "I know a place!"

The centre of the city was undergoing urban renewal, which most metropolises went through when they got to a certain age. The old, rotting and often dangerous interior was in the process of being pulled down, and new glass towers with shiny new apartments, new businesses and new restaurants were appearing in their place. Yet every city kept that one street or suburb where bulldozers never reached. Here, not so much the lifeblood, but the darkest part of a city's soul could be found.

Our two cars pulled onto a dilapidated street filled with shattered windows and broken doors, making every building resemble a toothless face. But, inside, even the worst of these existed denizens of the city's underworld, and right in the middle of all this decay was a store.

The *OPEN 24 HOURS* neon sign occasionally flickered, reflecting in the grimy window with 'Civic Classic Movies' painted in large block letters across the glass. The store looked old and rundown but if you asked anyone who'd ever lived in the area, they'd be unable to tell you a time it had not been there.

Vulk and I jumped out of my car. Rowne also pulled up, parking behind us and seemed to slither out from behind his wheel.

"This it?" The demon exclaimed looking doubtful. However, before I could answer, he held up a single finger towards us and answered his ringing phone. "What? But it's there! ...You're kidding. Right... right... I'm on my way." He then ended the call and moved back to his car. "I'll be back. Someone's stolen Vassago's body."

"What? Who'd do that?" Vulk asked.

"Dammit. Here... take this." I took a piece of paper from my pocket, tore off a corner and wrote on one side the address we would be heading to afterwards. I handed the address to the demon. "We'll be heading here next."

Rowne took the note, thanked me, jumped in his car and pulled away.

"Who'd steal the body?" Vulk wondered to himself before turning to me. "Maybe we should go with him? Maybe it was the killer."

I ignored the Old Dog and stepped into the video store. Vulk followed and soon forgot all about the demon when he saw the store's inventory. He didn't seem to be able to help himself as he began picking up videos before putting them back and moving on. I could not tell if he was doing so with a modicum of reverence or disgust.

From the back room, a blind man with dark sunglasses and a bone-white complexion made his way to the front counter.

Vulk took a sniff, lifted his hand and pointed one thick finger at the chest of the man. "I think you should stop right there, my friend." The threat in those words was as heavy as an anvil.

The werewolf gave me a non-too-subtle nod of the head as a warning but never took his eyes off the blind man before him.

I placed my hand on my friend's shoulder. "It's ok." I stepped into the space between the two men and made our introductions. "Vulk, I'd like you to meet Cheyenne… Cheyenne, Vulk." The two men didn't move. "Cheyenne here knows more about movies than anyone alive… or dead."

"Cheyenne?" Vulk asked, looking at the not-at-all Native American standing before him.

"A name I gave myself. I always name myself after Morricone characters."

"Well, Cheyenne, you can call me Harmonica," Vulk said, turning his pointed finger into an offered handshake.

Cheyenne smiled at the shared joke and took the hand warmly. "Any friends of Amun's…."

I didn't answer that one.

Before morphing into a video store, Civic Classic Movies had been a record shop, and before that, it sold books and manuscripts. In one form or another, The Civic Classic Movies store had been around since the city first outgrew the small farming village that had once occupied the same spot. It had seen empires rise and fall and once been ignored by Roman centurions the way the local Police force still walked by, blissfully unaware of its existence. This store would still be here long after the buildings around it had crumbled to dust and humanity was dancing amongst the stars. It was just one of those places that almost every large, important city had.

You could say the Civic Classic Movies store was immortal, and so was its current manager, as long as he stayed out of the sun and away from garlic. In many ways, it reminded me of the Bar of Eternal Sorrows, except this was far more of a local entity.

"So, what brings you to my store today, gentlemen?" The Blind Vampire's voice halted my train of thought.

"I was hoping to use one of your machines." I held up the videotape as an explanation.

"Halloween," Cheyenne said, taking the cassette from my hand and inspecting it curiously. "Hey. This is an original VHS with *the* white stripe. Released by MEDIA for a home sale, not a rental. These things are worth a lot of money. You looking to sell it?"

"How much?" Vulk asked within a heartbeat. Some people never change I guess.

"It's not for sale." I snatched the tape from his hand. "Do you have a machine that will play it?"

Cheyenne held out his hand.

I looked at him, not moving.

He kept his hand in place, palm open. Finally, with a defeated sigh, I placed the video in it.

The vampire pushed his fingers into the side tabs on the cassette, opening the hinged flap that protected the physical tape when it was being transported. Cheyenne looked at the tape with a professional eye, making sure it wasn't compromised before putting it in one of his machines. He then used a coin from his pocket to move the two sprocket wheels to ensure the tape was still tight.

"Everything seems good. Let's see what we have here."

Cheyenne walked to the front counter and stepped behind. There was a video player that he slipped the tape into and then picked up the machine's remote. Then, stepping back out, he looked up at a blank TV screen that sat above the desk and hit play.

Instantly the screen flickered to life—first with a blue screen accompanied by an audible hiss. This was quickly replaced by an FBI warning not to duplicate the following movie or there would be serious consequences.

"I read in the newspaper the other day that some guy was arrested by the police for an old warrant when they ran his name. It turns out he hadn't returned a video tape fifteen years ago, and there was a warrant issued for felony embezzlement."

Cheyenne gave Vulk a look like that sort of pain was all too real.

The tiny bell above the front door rang as a huge figure in a trench coat stepped inside, his features hidden under a cap. Bizarrely, this was the second Detroit Tigers Cap I'd seen today.

The figure placed a plastic bag filled with videos on the table and grunted, "Hi, Cecil."

"Cecil?" Vulk grinned.

"His real name." I winked at him.

"Good timing as always, Mike." The video store manager sighed. "Sorry buddy, cannot talk shop right now, just helping these two gentlemen."

Vulk took a step back and, again, started to bristle as he saw who was standing under the hat.

"Settle, this is Mike. He's just a customer."

"What the hell is this place?" Vulk growled.

"It's a video store... for folks like us..." Cecil tried to smile while concealing his fangs.

"There are not many places where we can go—and you can only watch so much TV these days. It's terrible." Mike held up his clawed, reptilian-scaled hands to Vulk as a peace offering, and the werewolf slapped him on the back and stepped out of his way.

"Got some new tapes I found at a garage sale in the western section, Mike," Cecil called out, then apologised when he saw our faces. "Sorry."

With Mike perusing the western section, Cecil pointed his remote back towards the front desk and hit play. The video machine started up, and the steady hissing and blue warning appeared on the screen again.

However, a new screen suddenly replaced the FBI notice with a bunch of international warnings. This only lasted for a few seconds before the screen went blank, and some tinny 80s music and what was likely considered good computer graphics at the time began flashing with a bunch of lights and stars forming the word MEDIA.

Vulk looked at me to see if any of this meant anything. I shrugged my shoulders. Though it had previously mentioned the FBI and Interpol, none of that meant anything to me specifically.

The distributor's logo faded into a dark window, and the video store filled with the iconic rhythmic piano theme of the John Carpenter-directed classic. Across the dark screen appeared the words 'Compass International Pictures', and underneath was a symbol combining the first letters of these words--two C's back-to-back with the 'I' running between them to create something of a pole with the C's creating a circle at the top.

"Pause if you could, Cecil."

"Cheyenne." The vampire prompted.

"Settle down, Cec," Vulk piped in with his signature wink.

Cecil lifted the remote and hit the pause button, freezing the picture of a grinning Jack-O-Lantern with the lead actor's name that was starring in the film next to it.

"You think Donald Pleasance is our guy?" Vulk asked looking between me and the paused image.

I gave him the evil eye. "Take it back a few seconds, could you?"

Cecil lifted the remote again and rewound the tape, then hit play.

"... and pause."

Pressing the pause button, Cecil froze the image on that weird symbol again. "That means something to you?"

"Yes." I looked at the symbol again. "If you add something to that icon, it could very well be the Rod of Asclepius."

"The what?" Vulk asked, scratching his head.

"The Rod of Asclepius," Mike said from behind the video stacks. "It's the symbol of doctors and hospitals everywhere. You know, the rod with a serpent wrapped around it that you see on ambulances?"

We all turned and looked at Mike. "It was wielded by the Greek god Asclepius–the son of Apollo and a known healer."

We all continued staring at the creature.

"What..." he finally blurted. "I have a lot of time on my hands and pretty decent internet coverage in my sewer."

"Well, that explains the smell," Vulk commented, with a raised hand of apology. "No offence meant; I just have a strong sense of smell."

A light seemed to go off in the werewolf's head. "Wait... serpent? Were you this Asclepius?"

"No," I admitted, "though that's the kind of thinking that will solve this. I'm thinking this message was indeed meant for me. Without some serious prompting, I'd be the only one to associate myself with that symbol."

"Interesting," Cecil added, looking from the video to me. "Ok. So, what's the message then?"

"Let me think for a minute." I stepped away from the group and started running all the conversations I'd ever had with Vassago through my head and what the demon had stood for. Standing around, scratching my chin in deep thought, a tiny bell brought everyone's attention to the front door. Inside stepped one man, who moved to the side and kept the door open while a dozen more entered. They're of all shapes and sizes and tooth count. All sported some form of jewellery with the same symbol, a fiery sun with an eye in the middle.

Most wore their demonic shapes, while others had the faces of angels.

"Hand over the map," one demon demanded.

"You the leader of this snappy rabble?" I asked.

"Map," ordered a man who was possibly the single most beautiful creature I'd ever seen. By his accent, he sounded like a Principality, one of the lowest casts of angels.

"I thought you guys were the mortal enemies of demons?"

"We're all on the side of Kaos!" A voice from the back said with that fervent tone that only comes from the highly devout or highly susceptible. "Only by returning to what was can the path be found."

"Not this again," Vulk said, rolling his eyes and flexing his giant fists.

"Again?" Cecil asked with furrowed eyebrows.

"Yeah, every decade or so--or during some ominous celestial event—someone gets the idea that their place in life isn't what it should be and the only way to right the greatest wrong known to history was to try and start a war between the humans and everyone else."

"The last time was just a year ago," I added, "we had to deal with a wacky Cockatrice on a holy mission to save us all from this plague of humans…"

"And what happened?" Cecil asked. No one noticed the video store clerk had been slowly moving to stand behind my shoulder.

"Well, the world's still here, and no one is suffering from an influx of the drug Trick-or-Treat, so the same as every other time, I guess…"

"Those others were not of the true faith," the leader of the group shouted. "Not like us."

"We'll see about that." Mike removed his hat and his oversized raincoat. Beneath was a huge reptilian creature with the features of a man. I thought I recognized that face.

"Typhon?"

Mike's slitted eyes moved to my face. "I recognized you straight away, Amun, but now may not be the time for a reunion."

"Good point." I agreed. "Vulk..."

Next to me, the large shaggy features of Vulk melted into the enormous shaggy features of Vulk the werewolf.

"We knew the dog was here," the leader sneered. The group then parted, and for the first time, I saw the vehicle outside. It was a flatbed truck with several figures standing on the back.

Before I could ask, 'is that a harpoon gun?' a huge projectile exploded into the room, trailing a wire cable, which hit Vulk in the stomach. The werewolf barely made an audible grunt before the winch on the truck hauled both werewolf and harpoon out the door.

I could not say what happened next as I was moving to get out that door as quickly as possible, and there were a handful of assholes in my way. Now, I don't have the strength of Vulk in full werewolf form, and I never considered myself a great fighter, but living for a long time and surviving more battles than anyone that's ever lived, I've learnt a few tricks.

From my pockets flew several nasties that I always carried with me. None of them were lethal, but some were annoying enough to give pause to those around me. Holy water, silver powder and iron filings, to name a few, glittered in the air. All were toxic to various sprites, nymphs and demons.

As a few figures in front of me began to gasp or clutch at the burns on their faces where these elements struck them, I started to throw fists and kicks at anything within striking distance. I felt something's face break under one punch while kicking something else in the shins with my heavy boots brought a satisfying shriek of pain.

I wasn't in this fight alone, though; I caught a glimpse of Cecil with a shiny rapier in his hand. The blade was flicking in and out of the gathered crowd at a near-impossible speed, and the steel blade was carrying a more crimson hue in no time.

It was the creature known as Mike, however, that proved a real asset.

He just charged into the group before us and began swinging. Powerful clawed hands and anvil-sized fists tore into flesh and armour alike. There were small blades and even what looked like a blowgun dart sticking out of his green, scaly skin, not that he seemed to notice any of them.

I caught sight of Mike grabbing a demon with both hands, and, with phenomenal strength, he pulled both arms off the creature. Then he moved to a second figure and beat him with the limbs from the first, until he was a red pulp on the floor.

Kicking one creature's knee with a loud crack, then pivoting the blow into a spinning elbow to another's nose, I slipped past the last of the demons and found myself outside, my heaving lungs pulling in the cool night air. Vulk was on the road before me, struggling weakly to pull the old-style whale harpoon out of his guts. Blood and viscera were everywhere.

At the back of the truck, three figures rushed to reload their cannon, but I wasn't going to give them that opportunity. With a single bound, I leapt onto the truck and kicked out at the nearest creature. It was only a glancing blow, but it proved enough as the beast pitched backwards, losing balance and then fell off the truck. The following screams told me it had fallen within arm's reach of the wounded Vulk.

Whenever you enter a battle, there are a few golden rules; try not to do what your enemy expects, and always strive to do the unexpected. Yes, they sound like the same thing, but there is a subtle difference.

These goons had been warned about Vulk and came prepared, well so had I. Ever since I got a call to visit the council, I'd figured there was far more going on than any of them admitted. I pulled the handgun that was hidden under my jacket from its shoulder holster and fired. The first bullet took the rearmost figure in the temple, sending the beast spinning in a spray of blood and sweat off the truck. I next turned on the last creature and fired twice. Both bullets struck the demon, first shot hit the guts and the second in its knee. The creature's body went limp, and its limbs flopped about.

Turning and covering the front of the video store, when no new targets appeared, I leapt over and inspected the truck's winch. The spear was attached to a steel cable, not a rope, so there'd be no cutting it. I searched the truck and eventually found the bolt cutters our attackers had likely brought with them for the same reason. With the tool in hand, I jumped off the truck and stood behind Vulk, who was busy feeding on the creature I'd kicked to him.

"Settle, buddy, this is going to hurt a little, but it needs to be done."

I strained on the bolt cutters, and they eventually cut through the cable with a loud snap. Next, I tore a shirt off one of the dead creatures and, carefully pushing Vulk forward, wrapped the cloth around the head of the harpoon until it was nice and tight. Vulk grunted and growled with pain as I worked, but not once did he move. I had learnt some time ago that a small sliver of my friend remained inside when he changed, and rarely would he do anything to hurt me. Causing him this much pain, though, was one of those times when he could have let his animal nature get the best of him and snapped at me.

Once the cloth was nice and tight, I took a good grip and apologized, "Sorry, Vulk, this part is really going to hurt, but I have to do this." With that, I put my foot on the werewolf's body and began hauling backwards with all my might.

Vulk screamed and wriggled, and at first, my efforts had no effect. I dropped my gun and put both hands on the shaft, trying to yank it free. I soon broke the surface tension created by the blood and other body fluids that were keeping the weapon in place. Once I had some momentum, I could not afford to stop, so I pulled, yanked and began walking backwards, slipping a little on the blood and guts all over the road. The harpoon finally pulled free, and then I kept pulling to remove as much cable as possible. I'd been worried the attachment of the cable to the shaft might be an issue, but the wound the harpoon had made was so horrendous that the knot just pulled straight through Vulk.

With the harpoon free, I threw the shaft away and, retrieving my handgun, ran back inside. Vulk would have to look after himself for a minute.

The battle had destroyed the video store while I was away. Cecil was near the back wall, his rapier gone, and he was struggling to keep two of the creatures at arm's length. I lifted my gun and fired twice, the second bullet catching one of the creatures in the shoulder and sending him pinwheeling away. The vampire took that chance and charged forward with incredible speed. Before the other creature knew what was happening, Cecil had his jaws wrapped around his throat.

Things had been rougher for Mike. His right arm hung at an unnatural angle, and he was covered in blood. He had one creature by the neck and was simply trying to squeeze the life out of the beast with his good hand.

As I walked through the room, I fired into the most healthy-looking bodies on the ground. Experience had taught me when you were stuck in such a tight space with a lot of bodies, for sure someone was going to be foxing and hoping to put a knife between your shoulders as you walked past. When those on the ground heard what I was doing, two of them leapt up and tried to run out of the store. But I shouldered one into the Romcom section and shot the second in the foot. He fell headfirst through the open front door, and the blood-curdling scream that followed suggested he fell into the clutches of Vulk. A little feeding would have the werewolf back on his feet in no time.

"Keep at least one of them alive," I yelled. "We may need to ask them something later."

Once the area was clear, I contacted the council, and they had a team of cleaners outside the store in no time. Soon the bodies were gone, and they brought in a few blood-drinking Draugars to take care of what was splattered everywhere. Those undead creatures began lapping and licking every surface that had any blood.

"That's disgusting," Mike shuddered, looking greener than before, if that was possible. He then moved through the store and found his discarded cap and coat.

The fight had done nothing to help clear my brain, and thinking maybe taking my mind off the issue would help, I began picking up video tapes from the floor and piling them into one of the cleaner spots in one corner. Soon we had an impressive multi-coloured wall reaching almost to the ceiling.

"So, you're the serpent on the staff?" Cecil asked as he pushed a broom past me.

"Not exactly. I just think the icon with the serpent missing might symbolise the staff of Asclepius and the absent snake, a sign this message was for me."

"You don't think you're overthinking it?" Mike asked, dropping another pile of videos onto our wall. It had taken a while to remove all the barbs and weapons from his skin, and already I could see some of the more superficial wounds were healing.

The lizard man had a point. Maybe I was overthinking this?

"Ok, let's start at the beginning. I think that's the staff of Asclepius, and it's leaving a clear message that only I would understand."

"Well, what is the staff of Ass-phinctus?" Vulk asked as he limped into the room. Never underestimate the healing factor of a werewolf. As long as nothing vital was destroyed and they get to feed, they can overcome just about any wound.

"The staff of ASK-LE-FUS is from Greek mythology. It was carried about by the Greek god Asclepius…"

"…yeah, but what is the actual staff?"

Before I answered, Mike, stepped in. "Well, funnily enough, there's some evidence that the snake is actually one of the serpents from the story of Moses."

"You saying the Bible's real now?" Cecil asked sceptically.

"No, I'm saying that the story used something that was real in it. There's an odd little copepod around Africa and the Mediterranean that is a host to a parasite that causes serious health problems with the locals."

"What the fuck is a Copepod?" Vulk frowned at the new term, and I turned to Mike expectantly, urging him to continue.

"Think tiny shrimp. They host these things that are more like worms that burrow into your skin when in adult form. When the female is ready to lay its eggs, they cause this intense burning sensation, and to relieve it, people go and stick their hands in a river or a creek. When the female worm senses the water, it releases its eggs, and now you have a whole new generation swimming through the water, looking for a new host. That burning sensation is the possible reason why this thing might have ended up in the Bible," Mike explained.

"Those worm things are called *Dracunculus medinensis*," Vulk proudly announced. We all gave him a look, and he held up his phone with a grin. "I googled it."

"May I?" I asked, holding out my hand for the phone.

Vulk handed it over, and I began scrolling down the information.

"I know where our next destination is."

We were all on a plane owned by the Arabian Knights, don't ask, but I will say that the 60s cartoon on the Banana Splits was based on something very real and very nasty. It was great being in tight with the council. Mike was along for the ride.

"I haven't been out of my sewer in years, and I expect to eat some great food and get a new batch of videos. It'll also be nice to see the old lands again." He sat in a large chair, looking out the plane's window.

"You lived in Arabia?" Vulk was curious where Mike had been.

"Hey, it's the Mediterranean. That's close enough."

"So why are we headed to the island of Isola Tiberina?"

"Well, Tiber Island was where the temple of Asclepius was located– but if that doesn't work out, we're heading to the Aeolian Islands," I explained.

"Aioli Islands?" Vulk pondered.

"It's where the cyclops lived," Mike explained.

"Well, if we believe that message was for my eyes only..."

"Yes?" Vulk prompted.

"And that the symbol on the video was the staff of Asclepius..."

"Right?"

"... and the serpent on the staff is actually this tiny little worm thing called Dracula..."

"*Dracunculus medinensis.*" Vulk interjected proudly. "I'm with you so far."

"Well, the scientific name for the entire weird group of copepods that they live off is called Cyclopes."

"You're kidding me?" Vulk said, catching up.

"Then that suggests we need to be at one of these two locations."

"I understand your thinking so far, but why?"

Mike got it instantly. "The Aeolian Islands are where the Cyclopes lived in mythology, and Tiber Island is where people worshipped Asclepius..."

"... and either could hold a long-lost entrance to Hades... also there's one last thing that seems important. Chaos was the god those clowns back in the video store were sporting around their necks."

"The sun and eye symbol?" Mike offered.

"The very one and Chaos was also one of the primordial gods, the ones who brought forth all the latter gods like the Titans and Olympians."

"They were real?" Vulk questioned with wide eyes.

"Everything's real in one shape or another," Mike answered knowingly. "There were certainly real entities, maybe just not how they were remembered in the stories."

"Right, well, what's so special about this primordial dude then?" Vulk looked between me and Mike waiting for the answer.

"Actually, Chaos was female, and she had a brother. You might know him as Tartarus?"

"As in the hell where the Titans were imprisoned?" Vulk said, surprising us again. "What? I've read a book. But how can Tartarus be a place and a man?"

At Vulk's quizzical look, I explained. "The Greek gods can get complicated. But yes, they are one and the same. Tartarus was the god of its own location, the deep dark subterranean prison where the Titans were imprisoned."

"And on Halloween, when all glamours are out of commission from the effects of the Purple Moon, anything locked up in Tartarus for all these years will be released?" Mike asked in horror.

"Correct... maybe. Normally things have to be under the direct influence of the Purple Moon—and being buried away in a deep hole under the very bowels of Hades, the spells of the normally impervious Tartarus would hold. But under this special event..."

"Then anything and anyone trapped inside the actual Tartarus is likely going to be set free on the world." Mike completed my sentence.

"Who could that be?" Vulk mused.

"Who knows, the Titans? ... oh, holy crap."

"What?" Mike blurted seeing my expression.

"In mythology, the Cyclopes were also held inside Tartarus. I was positive we were headed to the right location," I explained. "That's why we need to get off this plane."

"What?" Mike asked, confused at my sudden turnaround.

"We need to head back to the Endless Sorrows."

"We need to do what? Why?" Vulk shouted, confused.

"Because I've been a fool."

We got the plane to land in Malta, and I took the lads onto one of the older streets where the Knights of Malta used to be housed. It's a cheat, but the quickest way back home was through the Bar of Endless Sorrows. I found a door that looked like it had been hanging since the time of the crusades and walked through. Mike and Vulk followed, and we stepped back into the bar, but something felt different. The mood inside was tense.

Akan was on station as always, but he didn't offer me the ceremonial 'The usual Amun?' welcome he'd been giving me since I first met him. There were more warning signs as we moved deeper into the bar, past hard stares and whispering heads nodding into each other's ears.

Francis the golem was standing at his station as always, but he looked the worse for wear. He had a broken ear, and his Detroit Tigers cap was missing. "What happened to you?"

The friendly smile was also gone; instead, what remained was the reason he'd been chosen as a bouncer. He threw a punch at my chin that was so fast that it could easily have taken my head off if it had connected. Thank gawd for Mike. Our friendly neighbourhood monster caught the fist in a hand almost the same size as the golems, but he didn't do anything more than stop the punch.

As Francis and Mike stood there, hand to hand, a familiar voice came out of the darkened pub cubicles from behind us.

"I'm going to kill you."

"Well, If I'm going to die, I'd like to know why first?" I said, turning to face Rowne.

"Because you're a murderer." The demon said, slipping out of his booth and walking towards us.

"I most certainly am, but not recently."

"What do you know?" Vulk asked threateningly, turning on the demon.

"You're wanted for the murder of a council member," Rowne stated.

"Who?" The three of us asked in unison.

"You killed Lycaon after murdering my friend Vassago."

"I did? Well, this is news to me."

"You both did… why are you smiling?"

"I'm constantly amazed how predictable people can be," I explained to my companions, "Even Demons."

"What the hell does that mean?" Rowne asked, looking far less outraged than he was a minute ago.

"OH, TOKOLOSHE..."

On the shoulder of Francis, a small imp blinked into existence. From Southern Africa, Tokoloshe was a troublesome sprite that once had fun playing tricks on Zulu warriors—so that should give you an idea that it was a few zebras short of a game park.

"I did what you asked. The second Rowne left you at the video store, he called in the hit on you guys, before joining up with a few others who were following the councillor home. There was an ambush, and they killed Lycaon."

"And who was in charge?"

"Not this bozo," the imp replied and threw a thumb at Rowne. "He seemed to have organised the attack on the werewolf, but he was on his phone beforehand and after. So as far as I can tell, Rowne was under orders from someone else."

I pretended to tip my nonexistent hat to Tokoloshe, then turned on the demon. "Murder, two murders actually, and framing us? You've had a busy day, Rowne."

I could feel the mood in the bar had changed, and many were now paying real attention to the demon.

"You're going to trust the word of an imp?" Rowne asked, clearly aware he now had an audience.

"I owed him a favour." The imp answered, shrugging his shoulders in apparent disappointment at the situation he'd found himself in.

"How could you even know where to find me?"

It was my turn to have a little fun. I walked up to the demon and put my hand in his shirt pocket. Inside was the note I knew he was never going to read. "I figured you were up to something when you handed me Vassago's note during the meeting. I didn't know what you were up to exactly, but I took out a little insurance before the meeting." I gestured at the imp, who gave one hell of a bow, I have to say. "When we arrived at the video store, and you suddenly had a mysterious phone call about the missing body, I knew you were up to something, so I put Tokoloshe on your tail."

"I saw the whole thing," the imp explained. "As you thought, they'd set you up right from the very start."

"I couldn't see the picture, but I sure could feel the frame," I explained as the demon's face started to cloud over with anger and frustration.

I faced the imp. "Who was the 'they' in that conversation?"

"I couldn't be in two places at once, but I'm pretty sure it was a dragon he was talking to. They were talking in Chinese, but not a form I knew."

"That would be Proto-Sinitic," I explained. "The oldest form of Chinese. Of course, a knowledge demon would know the dragon's secret language."

Honestly, it came as no surprise the dragons were involved. The celestial Parthenon came across as aloof and serene, but they'd been looking to improve their lot for some time now. Bored of ruling their fiefdom, the dragons had always been an ambitious lot who were never that keen on sharing. They also resented the hell out of having lost their venerated position in China and having to stand on equal footing with Oberon and the western deities.

Mike could obviously see the look of concern on my face as I realised we were going to take on the dragons. With a friendly slap on my back, he said, "forget it, Jake. It's Chinatown."

A big piece of the puzzle just fell into place right there, but as I said before, I could still feel a frame but not the entire picture. We exited the bar of Eternal Sorrows into a bright sunlit day. Around us stood flowering peach trees towering over ornately placed boulders. We moved under the grand pagoda looking for someone to alert our presence.

Turns out they knew we'd arrived.

What poured through the large moon door on the far side of the garden, like a satin sheet in a strong breeze, was huge and scaly. Without a word, it hit Mike with a tremendous blow, sending the monster sailing into a peach tree with a sickening thud.

What greeted us was a young dragon. Its head was the size of a man's chest, and its long, elongated body was only a little thicker than a telephone pole. If it had been an adult dragon, we'd be dead by now.

It managed to turn with impossible speed for something so large and blocked the pagoda exit, ensuring we couldn't escape through the door we came through.

"You going to help?" I asked the imp that had been riding on Vulk's shoulder.

"That's a dragon boss." Tokoloshe shrilled.

"I don't need you to fight it; just give us a hand. You're in this too, now."

"Good point." The imp nodded and disappeared.

The dragon was just about on me when Mike stepped between us. No longer wearing his huge overcoat, I could see the enormous muscles of his back and arms rippling underneath snake-like scales covering his entire body. As the dragon charged closer, Mike struck out with a tremendous punch, catching the creature under its chin and sending it pinwheeling into the far garden wall.

Dragons are tough, but they're still physical creatures. I heard something break under the impact. Sadly, it proved not to be the beast's jaw. Stunned, the dragon began shaking its great toothy head, whiskers and barbels whipping around like the coat of a wet dog drying itself.

From behind me, a werewolf leapt onto the dragon and started tearing into its neck. The thick scales of the serpent here were great protection and had evolved to withstand the bite of a rival—so they were plenty tough enough to withstand a werewolf attack... but that was never the point.

Vulk was the distraction. Mike also jumped into the fray, holding that mighty head in place while the imp appeared, a tiny assegai in hand, and drove the Zulu stabbing spear deep into the dragon's right eye. Tokoloshe then disappeared before the wounded creature could take its revenge.

The dragon screamed in anguish and rage, its thrashing forced Vulk to lose his grip, and he slid off the animal and ass first into an ornamental bush.

"STOP!" the king yelled.

The young dragon's blood was up, and he wasn't listening. He tried to strike out again when something much larger and far brighter snaked between us. Dragons, as they get older, get larger, far more armoured, and much more colourful. They're the kings of our plane of existence.

No longer in human form, Long Wang stood before us in all his glory.

"Explain yourself," the dragon king demanded. Though he seemed to talk in a whisper, the words seemed to vibrate through my head.

"I..."

"Not you." Long Wang growled at me, then turned on the smaller dragon. "Explain..."

It took me a beat to realise who he was talking to. As the younger dragon went to speak, Long Wang whispered menacingly, "just be aware... your punishment may depend almost solely on what you say next."

The dragon baulked at this and went silent and pensive before finally explaining. "These outsiders infiltrated..." the young dragon never got to finish its sentence as the great tail of Dracorex came around and slapped its face.

"Do you think you can lie... to me?" This time Long Wang's face moved in close to the stunned youngling, his face barbels flicking and rolling about his great head like seaweed caught in a strong tide.

"You now have none of my sympathies nor any of my patience. If the next thing is not the truth, I will simply bite your head off and move on to my next problem."

If it was possible for a dragon to have all the colour in their face drain away, I'm sure that's what I just witnessed as the young dragon opened its mouth, then slowly closed it as though biting down on its own lie. The dragon then explained, "There is a growing movement amongst all the clans that began last year. The world today has become stagnant and conservative, especially for the young. Old gods seem to just hang around and do nothing but live off their former glory. For the rest of us, the normal attrition of war and politics no longer works. Centuries roll by, and we, the younger generation, just sit and rot in the ground like un-gathered crops. Then an idea found us... talked to us. It explained that we needed to take our future into our own hands... that we needed to go back to the past, to a time when the next generation replaced their parents through nefarious acts."

"Nefarious?" Long Wang asked as Mike walked over and began whispering in my ear.

"We decided to start a war amongst the gods and shatter the council's stronghold on us. For too long, we have been crushed under their heel; well, now we'll forge a new future for the new gods."

"Eat him," I said to Long Wang coldly.

"What?" both dragons said in unison.

"He's lying, and you said if he lied, you'd bite his head off, so do it. We don't have time for this shit."

"I'm not..."

"You're lying, and I know what's going on. Kill him, and let's go. We still have work to do. I dealt with these idiots and this issue last year at Halloween. The young trying to overthrow the old, blah blah blah. This isn't the issue, and we need to call the council together and make sure no one overreacts because we've all been the victim of a terrible, murderous joke."

One enormous reptilian eye drew close to my face as Dracorex loomed over me.

"Mike..." I said.

"That's not a dragon!"

Dracorex looked like he was about to argue, but then Mike seemed to grow in size as he stood up to his full, impressive height, showing off his scaly, well-scarred body.

"Introductions are always important. My name is Typhon, son of Gaia and Tartarus—so you can understand when Amun's investigation seemed to be leading towards my father being involved, I took an interest. I was, at one time, also husband to the shape-shifting trickster called Echidna." With this name, he pointed to the young dragon with a sausage size clawed finger.

We all turned and watched as the young dragons' features began to morph. What soon stood before us still had a long, serpentine body, though this time, it far more resembled a snake. That great dragon head, however, seemed to melt before our eyes and formed the features of a beautiful woman.

"All right, you got me." She said, raising her hands. Blood and gore still oozed from one eye where the imp had stabbed her.

Dracorex swung his head close. "What was this all about, and more importantly, did you kill Guoxin?"

"Who the hell's Guoxin?" Vulk asked around his fangs, now in partial human form.

"The dragon she's been impersonating," Mike whispered, then snapped, "now please shut up."

Vulk raised his arms in surrender and stepped back, allowing the major players in this odd tale to talk. I leaned around Dracorex's head and asked the shape-shifter, "I'd also like to know how you got to Rowne?"

For a knowledge demon, he'd been surprisingly easy to outwit. Rowne would never have fallen for that little stunt with the imp if he hadn't.

"Guoxin was a little shit, and I enjoyed killing him." Echidna smiled. She then turned to me and winked with her one remaining eye. The effect just looked weird. "I have no idea what you have done to that demon in the past, but he has a real hatred for you. It didn't take much at all to get him scheming and plotting to take you down."

Let them talk. Words mean nothing to you and could end up costing them everything.

"What does this have to do with the Purple Moon?" Vulk asked. The old dog just couldn't help himself, and he sometimes did ask the right question. "Who are they trying to release?"

It was Mike who answered. "This was never about the effects of the Purple Moon. Some people just want to see the world burn and are looking for any opportunity to lite the match. Echie there, she doesn't need any excuse to do anything to upset the balance of things."

Before anyone could react, Dracorex's tail whipped around and impacted with Mike, sending the creature flying away. Instantly Echidna was on the move, trying to close the distance between us. Her body serpentined across the ground far faster than anyone could have run in the same distance.

For a moment, I considered taking a swing at the monster, but the better part of valour took control, and I managed to duck and avoid the worst of Echidna's attack. She struck out at Vulk, who was ready for the blow and kind of took the impact by lowering himself as low as possible. The monster's hit bounced like a ball hitting a rock, meaning most of its energy was lost.

Instead of paying attention to it, I decided to try and talk to the Dragon King. Above us, the sky darkened as the moon began to cross the sun.

"What are you doing? You sided with someone who murdered your own kind?"

"You don't understand," Dracorex said; the pain on his face at the betrayal was clearly visible. "She promised me we could bring my daughter back to life if I helped."

"Your daughter?" For a second, I could not recall the dragon having a daughter; then, my formidable memory brought back a name from the deep, deep past. "You mean Sagara?" Dracorex had many sons, but as far as I know, only one daughter, who'd always worked to help her father achieve and hold the dragon throne. I was unaware of her death, though having not heard of Sagara for many centuries... that could explain it.

"I have held her body in storage, pickled in the finest wines, hoping to one day bring back my heart. Echidna promised me she could find the Rod of Asclepius and revive her."

"Have you not been listening? The whole Purple Moon thing was a ruse. She's been playing everyone against everyone just for the fun of it. Even if she knew where the staff was, I doubt it could bring your daughter back to life. There's just not that sort of magic in the world anymore." I tried to convince him.

"You lie," Dracorex snarled, the look of betrayal now replaced with a father's desperate anger. "It will work."

"It won't work," I said calmly as the sun's light began to disappear completely, and the solar eclipse took full effect.

"And who's going to stop me from killing you all and finding the rod?"

"Them," I said as an oblong of light spilt across the darkening garden. The light was coming from an open door with Tokoloshe the imp standing in it. Through the door, I could see the interior of the Bar of Endless Sorrows for a moment before the opening filled with creatures of every ilk and shape—witnesses to the betrayal of the dragon king.

"Do you think even they could stop me?"

"No," said a voice that cut across the battle like a bell. "But I can."

Entering through the door were Oberon and the other council members. The king of all the fay, even in the dark, looked furious. "My old friend, I understand your grief, but surely you could see through the lies of this thing." He didn't even gesture at Echidna, who'd coiled her snake body under her in one corner of the garden to give herself maximum protection against the growing odds stacked against her.

"Any chance to bring back a child must be taken." The dragon king explained. "Any chance."

"You've been fooled by a trickster, old friend," Oberon reasoned, opening his hand in a friendly gesture. "Don't expand your mistake by making me draw my sword."

This was purely ceremonial. Oberon indeed wore a sword on his hip, which was probably a very nice, very expensive blade, but that wasn't the true threat. Oberon could bring the power of the fay to the battle, and that was something even the celestial dragon king had to be wary of.

"You would start a war?" Long Wang gasped in surprise.

"No. You would have started the war. I'm just promising to participate."

Man, that was cold. You can see why Shakespeare wrote a play about this guy.

The garden was starting to fill with more dragons, some in human form, others in their full scaly glory. It was hard to see what exactly was happening as the eclipse left everything with a deep dark purple hue. Still, it was possible to see shapes moving past any of the light filterings into the garden from a hundred tiny sources, and of course, there was the bar's door still open.

"You may win the war, but we will win this battle today." The dragon growled.

"That's certainly a possibility," Oberon agreed. His confidence suggested that he may have already thought of that and had a surprise even I was unaware of. The answer then came with a glance. Oberon looked up at the Purple Moon, then back at those in the garden. Those directly under the moon's effect had indeed changed, but Oberon, standing in the shadow of the moon gate, retained his human form.

Dracorex looked at the fay king, then turned his great head to his own.

"Enough, we submit."

There was less than a minute before the moon moved on and sunlight came back. Those from the Bar of Endless Sorrows that had an aversion to sunlight had already started to filter back through the door while the rest of us stood around and watched as the dragon king, now in human form, walked over to Echidna.

"Tell me the truth."

"Why?" Echidna smiled, raising her body to loom over Dracorex. "This is far more fun."

"There was no staff?"

"Oh, I'm sure there was at some point. No, I told you what you wanted to hear. I needed your help, well, someone's help." The monster started to laugh. "All I had to do was figure out who was desperate enough to throw all their rules out the window and believe that bullshit about the Purple Moon. Guess who fits the bill."

"I... you..." Long Wang wasn't taking this well. Maybe it was because he'd ruled his little fiefdom for centuries, so he was never really a target for the fighting that's been occurring between all the various groups living in the shadows; or maybe it was because the daughter he loved so much, to risk everything for, had just been taken away again.

The dragon seemed to expand before our eyes as he rose to his imperial greatness. One great clawed hand reached down and grabbed Echidna, who struggled and tried to bite at one of the huge fingers holding her.

"As it was just told to me by a wise man, some of us just exist to see the world burn..." he said and started to raise the struggling monster to his face. I thought to get a closer look and maybe make eye contact with his tormentor. I was wrong. "...well, the world is just a better place if we remove those thorns from our side."

It was all happening in slow motion. The dragon opened his mouth, huge teeth catching the returning sunlight.

"You wouldn't dare," Echidna yelled, but the dragon king was no longer listening to her. I thought about stepping in, I really did, but Mike's powerful hand clasped my shoulder and held me in place. "This has been coming for some time."

"Typhonnnnn," Echidna screamed as she closed in on the dragon's maw that opened wider and wider. Her long snake-like body wrapped around Long Wang's arm as though it could strangle it or maybe break a bone and help her escape. None of that happened.

Her one-time husband watched as the dragon placed Echidna in his mouth, roughly from the chest down. The trickster went into a thrashing frenzy, her body writhing and her tail flicking around violently as she tried to break the dragon's grip and slip away.

With uncaring slowness Long Wang bit down, his teeth puncturing the monster's skin with a strange pop as her armoured scales gave away under the dragon's bite. Her muffled scream of terror was horrible as it was now backed by real pain.

Blood and fluids began running down the dragon's mouth and hand, but he never stopped until he bit right through Echidna's body. As he pulled the torso away, it continued wriggling the way a gecko's detached tail does to attract a predator and allow its owner to escape.

Worse, when Long Wang opened his mouth, the upper torso of Echidna was still visible, and the monster was still very much alive. Her pleas were weak, but she continued to cry out for Mike to help. Finally, with this gruesome sight, he turned away.

Long Wang moved the body around his mouth with his enormous tongue until what was left of Echidna was between his teeth again, and then the dragon bit down. This time there was no playing with his food. This was the coup-de-grace, and Echidna's life ended with a crunch.

The dragon then swallowed, and I thought he was about to drop the rest of the monster's body—but no. He placed the snake part of Echidna's wriggling body into his mouth and continued to feed until she was completely gone. The lesson was not missed by anyone, especially Oberon, who had watched the entire affair with a stone-cold face. I'd known the fairy king for some time, and I had noticed the way his eyes had opened at the sight of Long Wang biting Echidna in half. One day these two monarchs were going to come to blows, but right now, the dragon had taken a psychological advantage in their cold war.

However, that was a problem for the future. Today, now, it looked like everything was returning to the status quo. Long Wang and his dragons returned to their human forms and started filtering out of the garden. Whoever was left from the Bar began re-entering its doorway. Oberon was the last to leave. He gave the three of us a little nod, then held eye contact with me for long enough to convey the message that once my work was done here, I should seek him out for a conversation.

I was more than happy to talk to the fay king—who I believe had set most of tonight's events in motion. Who gave Echidna the idea to use me as a distraction–and what was her end goal? Simply screwing around with the pompous dragon king sounds like fun on paper, but we just saw the consequences if you get it wrong.

No, something else happened here tonight. I think it was Oberon who fired the first shot of the upcoming war. And though it looked like that shot missed its target, the fairy king just gathered some valuable intel about the strength and mindset of his opponent.

Everyone had been played tonight—including me, and I wasn't

happy about it.

"Let's get drunk," Vulk said, putting his arms around the shoulders of Mike and myself.

"I could certainly use one," Mike agreed.

"You coming?" I asked Tokoloshe, who was still in the doorway, keeping it open for us. "You certainly earned one or three."

"Sure," The imp said. "If you make mine a Umqombothi."

I smiled at the thought of the little imp drinking a flagon of the traditional Zulu beer. Sure, the future was looking bleak, but tonight there was peace, and I had some good friends to get a drink with—and in the end, what more could you want?

Author's notes:

"It was on a dreary night of November that I beheld my man completed" - or those who know Shelley, this was the original line the author wrote, it was later changed to "It was on a dreary night of November that I beheld the accomplishment of my toils." As this was supposed to be the reading of basically her first draft I thought the original line was more appropriate.

As much as you can say any mythological creature was real, the ones highlighted in this story were all real.

The Moon, of course, never turns purple, blue, red or any other colour. When light reflected off the Moon passes through the earth's atmosphere, it becomes obstructed by various particles in the air... the more particles, the deeper the colour. This is why 'Purple Moons' are so rare. The amount of material required to create one normally is caused by an enormous volcanic eruption.

There was indeed a Purple Moon in 1815, created by the vast amount of material injected into the atmosphere by the devastating Mount Tambora eruption in Indonesia. This created what was known as the Year without summer in 1816...

...and yes, there are reports people in central Queensland had heard about the Krakatoa eruption.

The wacky weather caused by this eruption likely caused the monster storms lashing Europe, leading to that famous holiday where Shelley created 'Frankenstein' and John Polidori 'The Vampyre'... there is no report that I can find where Amun was the basis of either...

Lord Byron's grandfather was Commodore John Byron, who was captaining the *HMS Dolphin* on a circumnavigation of the globe and returned with the report of giants living in Patagonia—a story backed up by Captain Charles Clerke—the man who took over from Captain Cook after the explorer's death in Hawaii. It's often reported that Clerke, who was part of the *Dolphin* voyage—made up his report as a joke--but I'm not sure how a young career officer gained anything by making false reports to the admiralty back then.

The French voyager Louis-Antoine, Comte de Bougainville–one of the leading French officers from the Seven Years War (fought mostly in Canada) later explored the Southern Oceans and indeed saw the bones of giants. These were likely fossils from mastodons, mammoths and giant sloths.

Dracunculus medinensis, or the Guinea worm, is indeed a parasitic worm that burrows into human skin and creates a burning sensation to force its host to find water when it's ready to lay eggs. It's also the source for one theory behind the Rod of Asclepius, and great news, they're also likely going to be the first parasites that will be completely extinct thanks to modern medical efforts to eradicate the worm.

...and yes, the copepods that host the Guinea worms are called Cyclopes.

Finally... I have no idea if 'some guy' was ever arrested for overdue video rental fees... but I do know a lady was. Kayla Michelle Finley was arrested and charged when police noticed she had an active warrant from a video rental she had not returned in 2005.

Mirror Mirror Minotaur

CHAPTER 1

>>The Beast<<

The Minotaur Princess, Kiretana, rushed into the atrium room in the center of the Minotaur Heir's labyrinth prison, where he spent most of his time. "Tauran, the witch found her!" The princess looked around in dismay as he struggled to his feet.

Lowing in pain, he told her, *'She is in the labyrinth somewhere.'*

"What did you do?" Kiretana demanded with her hand on her hip, and head tipped in judgment, her expression accusing with her lips pressed together in a twisted scowl.

'What did I do?! I don't know. I smiled at her because I was happy, and she attacked me,' he mooed in the language of his beast, remembering how his One crouched in terror, then punched and kicked him before throwing him across the room. His clawed hand cupped his bullness gently. It would be bruised for days.

"With your smile, she probably thought you were going to eat her." Snorting, Kiretana laughed in a very un-princess-like way, then gasped when they heard the stone door moving. "I'll try to find her. Keep Mother busy."

She sprinted in the direction where she could smell the terrified female, grinning to herself because she was happy his Daisy was a fighter. A strong and compassionate queen was just what the kingdom needed after her mother's cruel reign. She followed the scent back and forth as she listened to the murmurs of her mother and her brother's bellowed denials. After a few turns around the circling corridors she was shocked to find herself at the crevasse that led to her room. Quickly, she squeezed through the gap and tumbled out to find her father and a wizard talking in her bedroom.

"Who are you?" she demanded, halting the discussion between them.

"I am Oren Oleander. I came about your mother's petition, but find what she wants to be done abhorrent. It cannot be accomplished without erasing your brother's mind completely." The wizard bowed to her. "Princess Kiretana, if you are seeking your brother's soul-half. I sent her to the home of my mother's family. She will be safe there until the autumn equinox."

"Can you send me to join..." Kiretana started to ask as her mother, and another wizard rushed in.

"Where is she? Where is that common cow?" Queen Dejanira shrieked as she glared at Oren. "Wizard Oleander, what are you doing with my family? You refused my request."

"Queen Dejanira, the thing you are requesting is too dangerous."

"More dangerous than my son losing himself to his beast as my husband did? I do not think so. Tauran may choose from the royal stable; there are many heifers of high status families in his harem." She glanced at the guards and her warlock. "Seize them."

The king bellowed and lowered his head, pulling his daughter behind his bulk as the queen's warlock pointed a wand at them. ***"Sominatosa minotaurus!"***

"Stop!" Oren shouted as the two minotaurs collapsed unconscious, then Dejanira shattered a potion bottle at the warlock's feet and Oren yelped in surprise. Within a second, he was engulfed in flames. A few moments later, only a pile of ash remained.

"Seal him in a bottle," Dejanira ordered, "And toss it in the sea."

"Yes, my queen." The warlock scooped up the ashes, putting them in a blue glass bottle, and retreated as two burly minotaur guards hefted the king.

"Put my husband in with our son," the queen ordered.

"And what about the princess?" A third asked as he picked up Kiretana gently.

"Put her in the harem. If she doesn't choose a mate from among the royal lords by the summer solstice, she can join her father and brother." Dejanira hissed, then turned around the room. She opened a secret drawer and pulled out one of Tauran's sketchbooks, flipping through the pages until she found several of the common cow's human face. She tore the pages out. "Show these to the guards. Find this girl and bring her to me. She is in the palace somewhere."

<<@Daisy@>>

Citadel of Thorns, Mountains of Despair

The giant King of the Minotaurs threw me into the mirror, but instead of breaking, I went through it like a splash of cold water before landing on the floor and sliding into a wall. The mirror showed the room I was just expelled from as I heard the wizard call out.

"Don't worry, Princess. I can send the Prince later. Happy honeymoon."

I thrashed in the bed as the nightmare continued.

My frantic search for a way to escape from this place had failed. My fate to be the next princess killed and eaten by the homicidal Minotaur heir was sealed as I looked out the window at the thorn-briar-covered building and tower.

"Noooo!"

Waking as I screamed the word in my dream aloud, I sat up in a bed. It wasn't a nightmare; it was a memory. I had fallen asleep curled in front of a fireplace downstairs. I had no idea how I had gotten into this room or the bed. In the corner, a small stove offered warmth. I was wearing a nightgown. My tattered skirt, shirt, and waist cincher were on the chair.

"Hello?"

The cold phantom caress, which had haunted me for moons, touched my cheek like it was trying to wipe my tears. I swatted at it. "Don't touch me!" Hissing through clenched teeth, I pressed my warm palm over my tear-wet cheeks as I looked around. "I hate it when you touch me. I hate you!"

Dawn lightened the sky beyond the window. I climbed up on the dresser again and peeked out. Every window in the tower was so high, like the bottom part had been blocked with stone bricks. Thorny vines the size of my pinky finger covered the bedroom window. It took several hard yanks, but it opened, and I was greeted with a gust of bitterly frigid, thin air. I could only see other mountains around my prison. They looked higher and more barren than the White Mountains of home. Reaching out, I tried to clear the vines, but the woody stems wouldn't budge, and the thorns tore at my skin, leaving burning pricks and bleeding scratches. Finally, I pushed the window closed.

Desperate to escape, I jumped down, deciding to search the tower and citadel again. I hoped I missed a way to escape in my panic yesterday. Carefully, I crept down the stairs, wondering who put me in bed.

"Hello?"

There were no footprints in the dust beyond mine, as I went up and down the stairs during my panicked search for escape. I went from window to window again, trying to find one that wasn't blocked by vines while going down the spiral stairs from the tower. Only a few opened inward; most seemed to be sealed shut. There were two landings with small sitting areas. Everything was so dusty, making me sneeze over and over. This whole place needed a good cleaning. Only my frantic footprints made last night were on the floors. I found my way back to the bottom floor. The wizard called this place the Citadel of Thorns, but as far as I could tell, it was laid out just like the lighthouses on the Stone Coast. Geal had taken me to see the one on the edge of the harbor.

Geal... The thought of the mate-lost Selkie male, who was always so kind to me, made my heart ache. I realized the day he left me on the plains at Lady Emula's Inn that he loved me, but Selkies can't live away from the sea, or it hurts them. I should have kissed him, I should have run after him, but I stood there like a fool.

Stopping at the door of the entry hall, I peeked cautiously at the mirror. I had heard of magic mirrors, but had never seen one. Honestly, I thought they were just another tale told to taunt uneducated Shifters like me who didn't know about witches. I mean, people who talked to their own reflections were vain, right? And walking into a mirror would mean bumps and bruises, at least, or a body full of cuts and shards of glass, at worst, but I tumbled through it like falling into a pool. There were so many things I was still learning. The world of dangers and monsters claimed to exist beyond the fences by my clan was real.

Here I was, almost a year after I was bitten, after I was changed, and I could still hear the mantras in their voices. I broke all the rules of my clan. I passed the fences alone, after dusk, in the moonlight, and I was bitten by a monster. I expected to be punished by my clan, not exiled to be killed like my cousin Rosie. The keepers had pushed me out of the hole in the fence into the meadow with the wildflowers that doomed me and cast me out of the clan, or herd as it was. Keeper Emmie told me to go south and find the monster who bit me. When the fever came, I didn't die. Tauran's bite turned me into a shifter, one of the infected of the Evolution Plague. I didn't want to have a human; I liked being a cow.

Behind a set of musty draperies that hung from floor to ceiling, I discovered a tall window which was actually a door. It was unlocked, so I rushed out into the frigid air and dappled sunlight of a giant cage. The half-roof was glass, and the walls were wrought iron bars wrapped in thick vines. The thorn-covered vines were the size of my thigh, growing and dividing as they climbed up and over the entire house and tower. Some had knots and gnarled places like they had been cut. I went into the kitchen, found a dusty knife in a drawer, and started to rush back out, but then I noticed it. Sitting on a pristine tray was an apple with a bowl of oats and milk. It was still warm and steaming.

"Who's here?" I yelled. Only my bare footprints were on the floor.

"Where are you?!" Only my panted breaths answered.

Terrified, I ran outside again and tried hacking through the vines, but it was impossible with a small paring knife. Finally, I went back into the kitchen and cautiously ate the cold meal before going back to the mirror.

Standing in front of the tall mirror where the door should be, I looked at the slide marks on the dirty floor. When I looked at the mirror, I saw only my reflection and not the lavish room I had been thrown from. The first thing I had to do was make sure Prince Tauran couldn't come through the mirror and eat me. I didn't want to be a princess; I liked being a maid.

"He's not going to eat me. I'll kill him first." I promised myself aloud, "I am going to get back to Geal somehow."

I picked up a chair and smashed it into the mirror with every bit of strength I and my beast possessed. The glass fractured like a spider's web and fell to the floor. It didn't sound like any glass breaking that I had ever heard. It sounded like a scream. Startled, I stumbled back against the wall and stared at it. I held my breath with my hand over my heart, half expecting blood to leak from the ornate frame. Nothing happened, so I went in search of a broom.

In the dusty, unused kitchen, there was a straw broom behind the cold box and a dustpan. Going back to the foyer, I was shocked. The shattered mirror wasn't lying in a pile; it was back in the frame. The spider web of lines glowed as they melted the pieces back together. The mirror sounded like it was crying. My reflection was fragmented then it looked at me with tears running from my eyes.

"Why?" It sounded like it moaned a word in warbling discordance.

Running out, I slammed the door. I realized in horror that the mirror was alive somehow, and then a worse thought occurred to me— if I couldn't break the mirror, then I couldn't stop Prince Taurian from coming here and eating me like he had all the other princesses.

Panicking again, I rushed outside, seeking a way to escape. Shifting to my minotaur midform, I tested the bars shaking them as hard as possible. I rammed into them to see if they would bend or break, but the vines crept around the iron, reinforcing it. Battered, bruised, and bleeding, I laid on the winter-withered grass and wept, then my midform bellowed an enraged moo into the afternoon. I was freezing, so I decided my cow was better. Looking up at the Citadel of Thorns, I decided I'd rather sleep outside. I moved to lay as far from the door as possible. I was a White Mountain Heifer; I had been out in colder air than this every winter for most of my life.

Λ^^^^Λ

>>The Beast<<

Rolling onto his side in the darkness, Prince Tauran grunted out a curse. He was still in the entry room of the Labyrinth. His mother's warlock made him sleep. In the darkness, he could hear something breathing. Cautiously, he raised up and prepared to defend himself from what or who came into his prison, but then the dark lump on the floor near the door snored slightly.

"Father?" Tauran stumbled forward, still groggy, and knelt next to Asterion. "Father?!" Tauran shook him until he stirred and sat up.

"My son? How did I get here?" He mooed in the language of their beasts.

"I do not know. When I woke, you were here. Mother's warlock made me sleep when I refused to let them search the Labyrinth for my soul-half. She's here somewhere." He stood and relit a torch from the wall. "I need to find her; she was terrified."

Asterion caught his arm, stopping him. "She escaped into your sister's room. A warlock ally sent her to safety through a mirror."

"Safety? Where? Mother has assassins looking for her everywhere. One almost killed her before." Tauran revealed as they walked toward the center of the Labyrinth.

"How do you know this?" Asterion demanded, surprised by the revelation.

"I saw it happen. Kiretana hired a witch to find Daisy. She gave me a magic mirror. I have been watching her. A large black minotaur, a satyr, and a scarlet wolf saved her."

He stopped at an unremarkable stretch of wall, handed the torch to his father, then pulled out a stone near the top. Reaching inside, Tauran removed a bundle of cloth and a sketchbook. Unwrapping the mirror, they saw a beautiful brown-haired woman asleep in a bed. Tauran touched the mirror wishing he could brush the strand of hair off her cheek. Instead, he sighed in relief that she was safe.

Asterion watched him and declared, "She is beautiful, and she is beyond your mother's reach. But, right now, we have a more pressing matter."

"Mother finally staged the coup you feared." It wasn't a question. Both had realized in the last year that if Tauran did not mate and make queen a female Dejanira chose, she would usurp her husband and son.

"Yes, we must escape and regain the kingdom from your mother, before she starts another war or sends half our people off to the slaughter." Asterion looked down at his gnarled and clawed fist. "Your mother never loved me. I am beginning to believe she intended to steal my forefathers' kingdom all along. I discovered Dejanira used magic to bewitch me and falsely present herself as a minotaur. I wonder if our cursed states are her doing."

"Father, where is Kiretana? Was the warlock able to send her to safety too?"

"No, your mother has her. I was in her room with her when your mother attacked us. I do not know what became of Kiretana or Wizard Oleander. I am just grateful he was able to send your One away before Dejanira found her." Asterion bowed his head with a low bellow. The anger of his beast echoed off the walls.

"My king?" There was a sound from the atrium skylight. "Prince Tauran?" A whispered shout came, and they rushed toward the sound. The daughter of Master-At-Arms Angus was leaning over the opening in the darkness.

"We're here, Bovina." Asterion lowed in the language of his beast.

"My King! How can I help you?"

"What is happening in the kingdom?" Asterion demanded.

"The Queen is imprisoning all who are loyal to you, my King... and forcing all those without a midform to go to the arena. I fear she means to slaughter them. The Princess is locked in the Royal Stable; I couldn't rescue her." Bovina dropped a bundle that landed with the clink of metal. Then she began to lower a basket with a rope. "I brought you some tools and things so that you might escape..."

"Hey! You there." There was a scuffle above and the clang of swords, then two guards and Bovina fell through the skylight. She killed one before they landed.

"Bovina!"

Tauran rushed toward his childhood friend catching her before she smashed into the hard floor as the dead guard landed with a squishy thud next to his head. The second guard screamed as

Asterion impaled him on his horns and flung him into the wall. They stood staring up and listening as the second guard wheezed his last breath. No one else came as Tauran put her on her feet.

"They must have found the ladder I used to climb up." Bovina scowled. "I sent a message to my father, but I do not know how quickly he can return. My brother is leading many through the caves to the coast." She bowed her head, adding, "The Queen has several witches and a warlock supporting her."

"Then we must escape and not be recaptured. What of Wizard Oren Oleander?" Asterion mooed as he looked through the tools and in the basket.

"She burned him, had his ashes put in a bottle, and the bottle was cast into the sea. No witch may kill another." After repeating the restriction of the magic-wielding species, Bovina huffed, "She isn't even a real minotaur. I heard her bragging to her supporters that she only needed a few drops of your blood to mix with a potion to fool everyone. The witches have taken over the kingdom. What can we do against their magic, my King?"

"We escape and save our people; then we find a way to notify the Council of Magic in New Magehatten."

CHAPTER 2

<<@Daisy@>>

My pleading voice was drowned out by Suzie and Aunt Bea, who began chanting the mantras. Then, finally, the whole clan picked up the words.

"Never pass the fences.

Never forage or walk alone near the fences or in the far fields.

Never leave the longhouse before Dawn or after Dusk.

Never go out in the moonlight.

Never let the monsters bite you."

Over and over, they chanted the words as the fence was stood up and reinforced. The Keepers left. Then one by one, the clan walked away until only my mother and other aunt remained. Finally, they turned and walked away too.

"Mama... no... Aunt Bess... come back... please come back."

Pressing my forehead against the fence, I had run out of tears. My voice was harsh from begging for mercy. Not knowing what else to do, I staggered down the hill among the wildflowers which had seduced me to my doom only a few short hours earlier.

I woke with a shudder; I hated that nightmare, but it was my truth. My rebellion cursed me, and I was banished for it. The monsters were real, and I was the soul-half of one of them. I stretched my neck to yawn, then lowed in surprise. My cow was inside, more specifically in the tower bedroom, asleep on a pile of cushions in front of a small coal stove with a blanket over my back. Rapidly, I grew into my midform and stared around the room, ready to attack the first person I saw. I couldn't smell anyone else. There were no footprints on the floor but my own from my frantic search for escape. I crept down the stairs as quietly as I could. My hooves wanted to slip on the smooth marble, so I placed them down carefully with each step. Reaching the floor, I tiptoed through the sitting area past the fireplace to the glass door.

"You do not need to be afraid, Princess. No harm will come to you here," a voice startled me.

I turned, snorting in threat, but no one was behind me or by the fireplace. "Who?" my beast bellowed. No one answered.

The wide mirror above the fireplace shimmered like moonlight on the misty fog from the Stone Coast. My reflection tipped its head and smiled at me. "Hello, Princess, I'm your Mirror Mirror."

I backpedaled so quickly that I fell out of the door onto my arse in the giant cage.

"Come back so we can talk. I have so much to teach you," the voice implored as I scrambled to crab-crawl away from the building.

I only stopped when my back collided with the cold iron bars and thorny wood of the vines.

"Please, Princess, come inside. It's too cold outside for a princess," the voice insisted in velvety feminine tones.

Shifted back to my skin, shivering in the bitterly cold air as I knelt on the frost-covered grass, I shouted at the open door, "I don't want to be a princess; I liked being a maid!"

The voice continued to beg me to come in, but I wouldn't. I didn't want to be bewitched, or whatever magic mirrors did to people besides sending them to remote prisons in the mountains of Moon-knows-where. I shifted into my cow and stayed by the cage wall. Chewing dead grass when I got hungry or licking frost to slake my thirst. This place was cursed somehow. I knew it was.

Bored and hungry, my cow began cautiously chewing on one of the vines. As we nibbled, we waited to see if it would make us ill. The vine was surprisingly sweet and floral, almost like the wild mountain roses of home. The sun moved slowly along the southern horizon, and too soon, the wind began to blow as silvery clouds fled to warmer climes. I wished I could go with them.

Tired of listening to the mirror cooing and cajoling me that I should come in and act like a proper princess, my cow walked over and kicked the door shut hard enough that the glass should have shattered, but it didn't, confirming the tower was cursed. I went back to lie down in the corner of the caged atrium furthest from the door as snowflakes began to fall. I'd rather sleep outside in the freezing air of these unknown mountains than surrender to being bewitched.

/\^^^^/\

>>The Beast<<

Tauran and his father cut hand and hoof holds into the walls in a place where Tauran noticed a hole in the roof. Then Bovina stood on the prince's shoulders and chipped away at the grout holding the block while Asterion bellowed loudly to cover the noise and beat on the walls.

"Move!" Bovina shouted, jumping down as the block fell, dragging several others down with it. The hole was big enough for the two large minotaurs to escape through. They looked out of the hole as Asterion rushed toward them. Bovina grinned, then announced, "I'll slip out through Princess Kiretana's room and sneak into the harem stable. I'll get her out."

The king snorted his agreement. They only had to wait until sunset then they could begin to take back the kingdom.

While they waited, Tauran stared at Daisy grazing in a large cage next to a thorn-covered, lighthouse-shaped building in the mountains. He tipped the mirror, trying to see around her.

"Father, where did your wizard send my One?"

"To a refuge of his family, he called it the Citadel of Thorns. It is in the Mountains of Despair, in the far northeast." Asterion lay on the bed resting. "Do not fear. No one can get to her there."

Frowning, Tauran mused, "But if we cannot find Wizard Oleander, how will I get there? How will I be able to be with her again? She looks like she is imprisoned."

Asterion rolled onto his side. "Get some rest, son. We will explain everything to her once you are reunited. It will be fine; common cows are very trusting and forgiving. She will be happy to be a princess when you are reunited."

Tauran watched her lay down to go to sleep as the snow began and wondered why she didn't go inside. He knew how cold it was to sleep in the snow. She seemed afraid to sleep inside. He watched her until he dozed off.

When his father woke him next, Tauran put the mirror in its secret place with his sketchbook and climbed out of the Labyrinth. If his mother imprisoned him again, he would still have access to his mirror. They moved almost silently through the palace. Tauran was shocked to turn a corner and find his sister with Bovina; both females were covered in blood.

"What happened?" Asterion lowed quietly in the language of his beast.

"We killed the lords holding us prisoners for Mother. They were going to force themselves on us as mates." Kiretana whispered. "The rest of the princesses have escaped too. I found out something about the ones our mother sent into the Labyrinth, the females you went mad and killed. They were the daughters of her enemies on the Council."

"We tortured two of the lords. They admitted that Mother gave the princesses potions, then added a different potion to your water, my Prince." Bovina sucked in her lips like she had her whole life when she didn't want to say something, but Tauran already knew what it was.

He staggered back a step and sank down against the wall. He barely remembered killing and mauling those princesses. Dazed visions of the females who weren't his *One* trying to seduce him. He had assumed it was his beast's doing, but now he realized something much more terrible.

His father knelt before him, placing a hand on his arm, trying to sooth him in the tones of their beasts' language. *"Son, you are not the only one who loved her that she used as a weapon."*

"I'll kill her," Tauran growled more like a wolf than a bull. He looked at his clawed hands, made fists, and slammed them on the marble floor, cracking the stone. He pushed himself up, looking at his sister and childhood friend hard. *"If she kills me, you're father's heir. Take care of our people."*

"Tauran, don't be stupid. She's a witch. She can't..." Kiretana started, but Tauran shook his head.

He grunted out and mooed in the language of his beast. *"A witch without a wand is almost helpless, and Mother needs potions to do other magics. She isn't as strong as some, or she wouldn't have surrounded herself with shills. Father, you need to go with Kiretana. If Mother has your blood, she can make you obey her, and she will make you kill your children like she made you kill your father."*

"She'll do the same to you," Kiretana protested. "Come, and we'll escape."

"Mother doesn't have any of my blood. If I can catch her and her warlock unawares, I can kill him before he can make me sleep, then I can capture her for trial."

"What about the other witches?" Asterion asked in the bellow of his bull.

"Two left to run an errand for her; we saw them go. One is dead after Princess Lakenva knocked her into a fireplace. Lakenva scooped up the ashes and is going to dump them in the sea so they will be scattered. She's my brother's *One,* but the Queen and her witches refused to let her see my brother to tell him." Bovina unshouldered her bow, finishing with, "That just leaves Wizard Hemlock and the Queen. You restrain your mother, my Prince, and I'll deal with the warlock."

"Tauran, you can't. Please, Bovina, no. Mother won't hesitate to kill you both. She knows I'm too young to rule by law. She'll..." Kiretana objected, but Bovina stopped her protest with a kiss.

"My Princess, I cannot do my father's duty in his place if I am worried for you. If we die, I know you will be a great queen, regardless of who stands behind your shoulder." She rubbed her cheek against Kiretana's, then turned and walked away.

Tauran reached out and squeezed her shoulder, lowing, *"I promise to send her back to you. Keep her safe, Father."* Then, after glancing meaningfully at Asterion, Tauran followed their young female Master-At-Arms. He hoped they all survived this night.

As he caught up with Bovina, she handed him a thin chain. "This was used by my father in the Cattle Wars to keep wizards and witches from attacking minotaurs. Wear it around your neck to protect you from magic. We can bind the queen with it so she can't escape.

Λ^^^^Λ

Tauran and Bovina moved quietly to the king and queen's chambers. There was a young bull asleep in his parent's bed. Tauran recognized him as the captain of the guard's eldest son and scowled in disgust because they were the same age. His hands seized the male's neck and broke it with only a single cracking sound. His hooves only made a slight rustling on the soft rugs as he searched for his mother. There was water running in the bath. Bovina pointed at him and then toward the bathing room. Next she motioned at herself and the other rooms before she circled the bed to search the sitting room and study.

Queen Dejanira was sitting in front of her mirror, talking to it angrily, "What do you mean you can't find her? She should be at the Oleander estate. Find out where else he would have sent her."

Tauran couldn't hear the other side of the conversation or see who she was talking to, but his mother slapped her hand on the marble dressing tabletop.

"Find her, or I will take the fees I've paid you from your flesh!" Dejanira threatened.

Tauran snorted in anger, and she straightened slightly before making a slight gesture. The mirror shimmered as she stated, "I see you escaped the Labyrinth."

"Keep your hands where I can see them, Mother." Mooing his threat, Tauran stomped forward and seized the back of her neck. He picked up the wand with his other hand and snapped it in half with his teeth before flinging the pieces into the room's giant tub.

In their reflection, she looked forlorn while he looked homicidal, as she refuted him, "I only did what I thought was best for you, Tauran. Every mother only wants the best for her children."

"You drugged me with potions to make me kill the princesses sent into the Labyrinth," he accused.

"No... the potion was supposed to make them irresistible to you. I never meant for you to harm them. It was your beast, it's mad," Dejanira murmured as she turned to face him when he released her like she burned him. Looking up at her son with tearful eyes, she begged, "Please let me help you overcome your monstrous beast."

"Liar! My beast is fine. You used me to kill your political enemies' daughters. You cursed me like you cursed Father." Tauran panted for a moment, then demanded in the language of his beast, *"Would you have made me kill my One as well? Would you have trapped me like this forever?"*

"The kingdom needs more than a common cow as a queen. In time, you would have understood that and forgiven me," Dejanira insisted.

"I would never have forgiven you."

Her eyes flicked past him.

"Sominatus Minota..."

Nothing happened. The warlock started but did not finish another incantation as he fell into the pool with an arrow in the back of his head.

"Say the word, my Prince," Bovina murmured with an arrow notched and pulled.

"How dare you?!" Dejanira hissed at her, all pretense from moments before gone. Fire exploded around them, but he didn't burn.

Tauran seized her by the throat, slamming her into the mirror, and squeezed as she pulled at his hand. *Promise me you will not kill my One or any other cattle-shifter, and I will not kill you.* He loosened his grip enough for her to breathe. *Promise me with a sacred oath, by your magic, lest it be lost.*

"I... I p-p-promise," stammering, she nodded as the magical flames flickered into mundane ones and dimmed, but the rugs still burned.

I remember what your books taught me. Say the words, or join your shill, Tauran bellowed in her face with all the rage he could muster. The fire was starting to spread from the rugs to the furniture.

"I vow by my magic, my soul, my flame, that I will not kill your *One* or any cattle-shifter, lest my magic be lost," she wheezed out.

He held up a claw, then snorted in threat when she hesitated to prick her finger. She cut herself and held out her hand; a drop fell into the fire. Releasing her neck, he dragged her out of the burning room by her arm. Once clear of the flames, he pulled the chain off his neck and wrapped her hands, binding them and her magic.

"Tauran!" Bovina's brother Brangus and Princess Kiretana rushed up the hill toward the burning palace with those who escaped.

King Asterion came last; he looked at his son with pride and his mate with disgust before letting out a mighty, trumpeting bellow.

"Do it!" the queen shouted at him. "I never loved you. I killed your *One,* so I could be the queen."

Before they could stop him, Asterion seized Dejanira and threw her into the burning palace. She didn't even scream as he knelt and wept in deep, baying sounds. Kiretana cried as Tauran held her. He found he couldn't weep for the mother who turned him into a murderer. Suddenly, his bones burned like his first shift. Tauran clenched his teeth so hard he thought they might break as his body bent and contorted. His father screamed in agony while Kiretana shouted for the healers to come. Tauran staggered and collapsed, writhing on the ground near his convulsing father. Pain... the pain of shifting forms was terrible after being trapped for so long as his beast.

"Daisy!" he bellowed her name because if he was going to die, she would be his last word and thought, then everything went black.

CHAPTER 3

<<@Daisy@>>

Citadel of Thorns, Mountains of Despair

The coolness of the house below the tower crept up the stairs and under the bedroom door. Waking up on the cushions in front of the little coal stove again, I was startled. I was in my cow form with a blanket over my back, just like yesterday, the day before, and the day before that. Every time I went to sleep outside, I woke up in the tower bedroom. My cow melted into my human form as I bellowed out my frustration. There was nothing in the tower dresser or closet that fit me, and my clothes were ruined by my shift to fight off Prince Tauran, so I wrapped an age-yellowed sheet around myself, twisting and tying it into a dress of sorts.

Then, stomping over to the dresser, I shouted at my reflection, "Stop it! Leave me alone."

My raging reflection melted into disappointment. It insisted, "You're a princess. You shouldn't sleep outside like a commoner."

"But I am a commoner. As a matter of fact, I was a common cow only a year ago." Waving my hands in futility, I sat down on the end of the bed, putting my head in my hands. Then, after a few moments, I looked at my reflection looking at me. "What are you? Why are you doing this to me?"

"I'm your Mirror Mirror," it repeated, but that didn't answer my question... then it said, "I want to be your friend."

"Are you a witch? Because the last witch I befriended almost got me killed and eaten after she told me I was a princess. I'm not a princess," I insisted again.

"You wouldn't be here if you weren't a princess. The Citadel was built to keep special princesses safe."

"I. Am. Not. A. Princess." I huffed.

"I can help you become a princess," offering, the mirror smiled at me.

"I don't want to be a princess." Refuting the mirror, I begged, "Please let me go."

"No," the mirror answered primly, "And you won't go outside again either until you understand that your duty is to prepare yourself to be a queen." She turned and walked away from me, then the mirror shimmered, and my real reflection stared back at me.

Worriedly, I rushed downstairs and yanked back the long curtains to open the door, but the vines had grown over it. "No!" I screamed as I pulled and jerked as hard as I could until I was exhausted.

Sinking to my knees, I put my forehead against the glass and watched the pristine snowflakes filling in the indention where my cow had laid hours earlier, chewing the vines. There were strange furrows in the snow, as though a giant serpent had slithered into the house. My breath fogged the glass. The snow looked unsettled, then something slapped the door, and I scrambled away from it. The mirror above the mantle was empty except for my reflection and the living room, but I was certain I heard it laugh. Huffing, I went back up to the bedroom and slammed the door. I picked up the blanket that covered my cow and threw it over the mirror. Sitting on the bed, I cried.

After a while, I got up and climbed onto the marble-topped dresser to look out the only window in the bedroom. Most of it had been bricked up with stones, so only a small part remained at the top. It took three hard pulls to get the tightly framed glass open again. The cold air felt like a slap against my flesh as it gusted in. As far as I could see, the mountains and the sky were different shades of the same ashen gray. I didn't move from there until darkness crept across the clouded sky. Closing the window, I ignored my grumbling stomach and sat down on the bed again. Eventually, I fell asleep.

I didn't leave the bedroom for three days. Only shifting to my midform to chew the vines covering the window. Out of boredom, I began cleaning my room until it was as clean as Lady Orva's Inn. I missed the hard work of being a maid and having something to do to keep me busy, so I wouldn't think about what happened to Maisy and what probably happened to my father and half-brothers. After I was exiled from my clan farm, I wanted to go find them and maybe change them to be like me. But then I was told what happens to bulls and steers who weren't needed. I was grateful I had never eaten beef; I would never eat it.

After scrubbing the years of dust off the furniture, I opened them. In the dresser drawers and wardrobe were dresses too fancy for me to ever consider wearing and much too tight across my udders. The richly brocade fabric was beautiful, but I couldn't breathe after buttoning them up only halfway. While they soaked in the bathtub, I left my room in search of a sewing needle, hoping to make something that would fit or repair the clothes I had arrived in. I was tired of wearing sheets, and even the slips to go under the dresses were too small across my chest.

The dust in the kitchen made me sneeze as I opened and closed drawers. Outside, I could see the snow had melted, and the green of a late spring peeked from between the dry taupe grass of winter.

"Come in and talk to me, Princess," the mirror begged from the entry room.

"I'm not a princess!" I yelled down the hall.

"Fine... please, Mistress, come into the living room. I want to talk to you. I'm so lonely."

I finally found a small sewing kit, but no thread in a basket of odds and ends on a pantry shelf. Coming out into the kitchen, a tray with an apple and a steaming bowl of boiled grains sat on a pristine tray with hot cinnamon tea. My stomach grumbled.

"Please eat, prin... I mean, Mistress," the mirror corrected itself.

I walked into the living room and stared at the mirror until it shimmered before stating, "I need thread."

"Thread? Do you wish to learn embroidery? I know many patterns in classical designs."

"No." I shook my head. "I just need to alter the dresses I found."

"They should fit."

"They don't... I can't breathe when I wear them; I can't even fasten them up," I revealed as I looked in the drawer of a small table. I found a box with colored embroidery threads.

"Princesses don't need to breathe deeply. They don't do work. That's what servants are for," the mirror insisted primly. "The dresses are to accent your... natural assets."

"I'm not a princess... I'm a maid," snapping, I turned to go get the tray before going upstairs.

"You were chosen by a prince; you'll always be a princess. You can't change what you are going to be, Mistress," the mirror insisted. "It is your fate, your destiny, your truth until you die."

"No!" Dropping the thread box, I yanked the mirror off the wall above the mantle with violence that terrified me. Carrying the mirror into the entry room, I placed it on the floor facing the wall.

My reflection in the entry mirror asked in surprised worry, "What do you think you're doing?"

Ignoring it, I removed the mirrors from the bedroom, bathroom, and sitting area halfway up the stairs. All of them went into the entry room.

"Answer me!" Mirror Mirror shrilly demanded.

Bellowing at it irrationally, I revealed, "I am never going to be a princess. I refuse to die that way, and if you won't let me go outside, then I won't let you outside this room."

"Stop. You can't do this!"

"And you can't make me be someone that will get me killed and eaten!" Snarling, I slammed the door.

The mirror began wailing but I ignored it as I took the tray and thread box upstairs. Using the tiny embroidery scissors, I began to take out the seams and cut new pieces to sew in. I wished I had Master Vinko's skills. I still owed him for the beautiful traveling clothes. The stretched, embroidered leather of the waist cincher was impossible to sew with the tiny needles, so I saved it for my beast to wear. I wondered if Scarlet Charlotte the wolf kept my clothes. I wondered what she did to Winnie the witch. I wondered if they found Wiess Lars and saved Charlotte's grandmother.

Did the Selkie clan have a good spring fish harvest? Did Vinko and Geal return safely home?

I wondered so many things as I sewed, pricking my fingers over and over. I managed to repair my skirt, but my blouse was ruined. I cut one of the bodices off a dress; it was the only one with a faux lace-up corset that I could make loose enough to fit my udders. It took me the rest of the day and most of the next to get three dresses taken apart and sewn back together as two, and all the while, the mirror wailed.

∧^^^∧

"Please, I'm so lonely… come talk to me." The mirror cried almost like a baby until I thought I would go mad. The keening would rise and fall like the waves of the Stone Coast but was inhuman enough that it didn't break my heart.

Finally, I stuffed bits of cloth in my ears to mute it and began cleaning the entire place. The windows were covered with years of grime. The floor had to be swept multiple times, but the water still needed to be changed every few feet I mopped. The counters in the kitchen took less work because it seemed the kitchen had never been used. It took days. The furnishings in the living room were deplorable. I needed to take the cushions outside and beat them. I pushed against the doors as hard as possible but could not get them to open to drag the furniture outside, so I covered them with sheets.

I could still hear the mirror's whining over the thunder and my stuffed ears. I held a red-hot poker to the vines outside, but they would not catch fire. Nothing besides chewing them seemed to make them retreat, and I knew there was no way I could eat enough of the thicker vines to make a hole large enough to escape through. The tower window was my only hope. When the rain stopped, I squeezed out of it. Standing on the slippery wet roof, I surveyed everything. The chilling phantom caress touched my cheek for the first time in days, but I brushed it away.

The Citadel was at the top of a mountain with a sharp cliff on one side, surrounded by a wide briar of thorns around the house and tower. If I sprinted as my beast, I hoped to be able to clear it by leaping from the roof opposite the atrium. Scanning the horizon, I realized if I escaped this place, there was no way I could find my way out of these mountains without a guide. There was nothing left to do but climb back inside. While braiding an escape rope from sheets, I watched the bitterly cold rain fall on the window and ignored the calling of the cursed mirror locked in the entry room.

/\^^^^/\

>>The Beast<<

Tauran woke slowly. His whole body hurt like when he had fought off the dire wolves in the White Mountains. Reaching up, he rubbed his face with his hands. Suddenly, he jerked his hand back and looked at it. Almost weeping, he staggered to his feet. He was in the seaside villa of the Angus family, where he spent many summers as a child. He walked on unsteady human legs into the bathing room and stared at himself in a mirror. A sob shook his chest as he dropped to his knees. The curse was ended. Hearing him crying, Kiretana rushed in with Bovina.

"It's okay, brother, it's okay. You're healed." She rocked him as she hugged him.

"Father?" He spoke in human language for the first time in almost two years.

"He's still asleep." Kiretana glanced at Bovina and then announced, "I'm sorry, Mother escaped. She rose from her ashes before we could collect them. The Council of Magic in New Magehatten has been informed, and she is a wanted witch now, but... they have no way to find her because they banished her decades ago for using curses on shifters... do... do you think she will go after Daisy?"

Tauran shook his head. "I don't know. I took her oath that she would not kill her but... but that doesn't mean she won't find another way to harm her. I must get to her." He looked at Bovina. "Has anyone found the bottle holding Wizard Oleander's ashes?"

Bovina shook her head. "No, my Prince, the people are searching after every tide. Your drawings of Princess Daisy have circulated widely, and they are excited for you to bring her home. She is such a fair maiden."

"My mirror... I need the magic mirror Witch Hyacinth made. It's in the Labyrinth." Tauran started to walk out, but Kiretana giggled as she grabbed his arm.

"Big brother, maybe you should dress first. I mean there are many who wouldn't mind a naked prince walking through the kingdom, but your princess may object to you being eye-mauled by every unmated minotaur in the land."

"This is the largest garment in Brangus' closet." Holding out one of her brother's summer togas, Bovina chortled as Tauran rolled his eyes at the size. It barely fit across his chest and around his hips while riding high above his knees.

Kiretana fell on the bed laughing as Bovina coughed, then suggested, "My Prince, perhaps an undergarment would... um... or swimming brief..."

"Why? I am not going swimming." He twisted to look at himself; he seemed presentable.

"Dear brother, what Lady Bovina is trying to say so politely, is that you have a rather obvious dangling problem below the hem of your garment." Kiretana snorted in a very un-princess-like way, laughing loudly as she dug through Brangus' drawers before throwing him the undergarment. "Tuck in your bullness, or you'll never get the Stable Harem Princesses to stop chasing you."

Λ^^^^Λ

Brangus followed Tauran to the ruins of the castle. Only the Labyrinth survived the fire. He reached up and into the hole in the wall and pulled out his sketchbook and the mirror.

Brangus flipped through the pages. "She is very beautiful, my Prince. You are a lucky bull."

"No!" Tauran gasped as he looked at the mirror.

The wind was blowing her hair wildly while Daisy was standing on top of the tower. Tauran's fingertip touched her cheek, and she absentmindedly rubbed the spot with the back of her fingers. She walked around the edge, looking down, studying the area.

"What is she doing?" Brangus muttered in shock as he watched over Tauran's shoulder.

Both males held their breaths as she scrambled to get back inside when the rain started again. Resolutely, she began tearing sheets into strips, twisting them, and braiding them together. Her jaw was set in a look of fierce determination.

"My Prince, what is she doing?" Brangus asked again. "If she had fallen..."

"I believe she is trying to escape. I have to get to her. Those mountains are filled with dire wolves and bears," Tauran revealed as they hurried back toward Brangus' family home. "If she tries to traverse them alone, she'll be killed."

"But my Prince, your sister told mine... she feared and attacked you. Will she let you rescue her if she believes you are to blame for her imprisonment?"

Brangus' question caused Tauran to stop dead in his tracks as he suddenly wondered the same. Fear for her like the burning grip of dragon-fire forged chains wrapped his heart as they had once wrapped his limbs. He did not know if Brangus' concern would prove true, but it felt like a prophecy of doom. He had so much to make right with her.

"I must go to her," Tauran declared then he began to jog back to the manor of Angus.

CHAPTER 4

<<@Daisy@>>

It was the middle of the night, and the mirror was still crying and cajoling after five days. Finally, I couldn't take it anymore as I lay in bed with rags tied over my ears and around my head. The phantom fingertips touched my tears as I wept in helpless frustration. I sat up and waved my hands around my face violently, trying to get it to stop, then I stomped down the stairs.

"Stop it!" I stormed into the entry room with the poker for the coal stove in the bedroom. As I yanked the cloths from around my head, I ranted menacingly, "Shut up, or I will smash you again and throw the pieces out the window over the cliff!"

"Please don't," the mirror begged.

I watched my reflection shimmer, and she pressed her hands together.

"I just want to help you be a better princess."

Swinging the poker menacingly, I pointed it at the reflection in the mirror. "I am not going to become minotaur food."

"What are you talking about?" The mirror looked at me in confusion. I noticed the color of the edge of the mirror changed slightly; it was pale greenish, like dry moss.

"I was bitten by the Prince of the Minotaurs and changed from a cow to a shifter. Minotaurs eat cows. He killed and ate my cousins before he attacked me and left me for dead. The witch who found me told me that he had gone crazy. He killed and ate several other princesses offered to him as a mate." I panted in my exhausted fear, then vehemently argued, "I am not going to be next."

"Did he fall in love with you?" The mirror's question caught me off-guard.

"What does that matter? He's a murderer and cannibal!"

"It matters. Did he fall in love with you?" Her tone made me hesitate.

"Winnie said he did and refused to turn back from his beast... but he ate every princess offered in my place," I begrudgingly revealed. "He could have just sent them away; he didn't have to kill…"

"Ahh, that's true love," the mirror interrupted as it shimmered bright pink.

"No! It means he's a homicidal monster who can't control his beast. I don't know how I survived the first time, but I didn't fight him the second time to escape for nothing. I won't stay here and wait for him to come eat me too!" I fell on my knees, begging, "Please, Mirror Mirror, please let me go."

"I cannot. True love will cure him. Once you are together, he'll change and not just back from his beast." The mirror-me tipped her head with a sly smile as the edges of the mirror turned red. "I hear minotaurs have very fulfilling male… attributes."

"Fine, you marry him and die. I want to live!" I started to storm out, then stopped. "We're done talking… and open the damned doors. I need to clean the furniture and rugs!"

"Wait!" Mirror Mirror shouted after me. "I'll open the door if you put my mirrors back. I can't teach you if you won't talk to me."

I turned back and shook my finger at the reflection. "There's nothing to talk about. I lost everything because of him. I didn't ask to be changed. I liked my life with my clan; I was cast out because I became one of the infected." I couldn't stop the tears that came as I sobbed in exhausted grief, pressing my hands over my mouth.

The mirror shimmered a sympathetic mauve as it cooed, "It sounds like you have some resentment against your prince."

"He's not my prince." Wiping my tears, I laughed, but it wasn't a happy sound. "He's taken me away from my life twice. I lost the family I was born into when I was exiled. Then, after I built a new life, I had to flee because the minotaurs started hunting down and killing all brown heifers. Their Queen wants me dead and…"

"How?"

"How what?" I was tired and getting frustrated with it constantly interrupting and not listening, but at least it wasn't still caterwauling.

"How did you build a new life alone without your prince?" It tipped my reflection's head at me; the pale green color was back. I realized the thought that a female didn't need a male seemed to confuse it.

"I have people who care about me. They taught me how to survive, work, and live without a herd... how to do everything. I even learned to protect myself. My beast is strong, and I am the kind of cow that kicks," I proclaimed as I held up my head proudly. I crossed my arms, announcing, "No male milks me for free, and I won't become the next course in the murder bull's princess buffet."

"I see we have a lot of work to do," it muttered, mimicking my posture with one hand under my chin. The edge of the mirror was a sickly yellow-gray. "We can start tomorrow."

"The only work I have to do is finish cleaning because this place was filthy." I grounded my teeth together, waiting for it to refuse. "I'm going to bed."

"Put my mirrors back, and I will open the doors to the atrium," it bartered.

I couldn't let it see what I was working on in my room, so I bargained, "I will put the mirror above the mantle. I don't like being spied on, so I won't have one in my bedroom. It's bad enough that someone is always watching me and touching me."

"Touching you?" My reflection looked perplexed. "How?"

"It feels like ice-cold fingertips." Her look changed, so I held a desperate hope that my torment could stop. "Do you know what it is? Can you make it stop?"

"Someone is using a magical mirror to watch you. It requires a drop of your blood or your soulmate's blood, so it is probably your prince. Put me back in the living room now, please. Goodnight."

"How do I make it stop?" The mirror shimmered, and my normal reflection stared back with an aghast look. "Mirror Mirror?" It didn't answer.

Going into the living room, I saw the vines were no longer blocking this door, so I carried the large mirror in and put it back over the mantle. Opening the doors, I stood outside in the moonlight, fearing that I would never be free. All this time, the monster who changed me was the one watching me.

/\^^^^/\

>>**The Beast**<<

Tauran felt gut-sick. The sorceress from the Council of Magic had enchanted his magic mirror so he could hear Daisy, but he had not expected to hear the hatred she held for him. He watched her putting the mirror back over the mantle and then dragging herself up the stairs to her bedroom. There she lay on her side and cried until she fell asleep. Wrapping the mirror carefully, he went to see High Witch Orchid.

"Come in, Prince Tauran. Why do you look so upset?" The white-haired witch had crows-feet around her eyes.

"Can you see the exchange my One had with a magical mirror in the Citadel of Thorns?"

"Of course." Witch Orchid waved her hand over the mirror, but her pleasant smile faded instantly.

"Please help me win her back," Tauran begged, "I did not mean any of those deaths. How do I make her understand that I was cursed?"

Orchid looked at him sadly. "My Prince, that is the least of your problems. The spell holding her hostage is corrupted. It will not let her leave until she becomes a proper princess. You must rescue her immediately. I can send you to a town on the edge of the Mountains of Despair, but no closer."

"How can I rescue her if she blames me for so much? She hates me," Tauran despaired.

"Perhaps I can help you." Orchid reached into the small bag tied at her waist and pulled out a medallion. "This carries a painful curse that once belonged to a saint. A curse that will bring you to your heart's desire or cost you her trust forever. Are you willing to risk your life for your love?" She handed it to him.

Holding it in his palm, Tauran looked at the pattern. Fear and hope warred, but he tied it around his neck as his will spoke for them both, "I would do anything to save her, even be cursed again."

Λ^^^^Λ

<<@Daisy@>>

"Daisy?" Mirror Mirror's tone told me it wasn't happy that I wasn't listening to its lecture on being fashionable and following the trends other royals created. I hated wearing clothing as it was; why would I wear something with no purpose beyond how it looked to others? It seemed like a bunch of nonsense.

"Yes, M." I tried not to sound annoyed.

Having put one of the mirrors in the kitchen as part of the barter with Mirror Mirror so it would allow me to prepare meals. Usually, while I cooked, Mirror Mirror took the time to lecture me on different aspects of being a princess. I was just happy it was letting me cook my own meals after weeks of arguing about it. I was about to give up when I came into the kitchen and found a basket of ingredients instead of a boring prepared meal. It felt like a small victory but also a bribe.

"Wouldn't your friends be happy for you to be a princess?"

This again. I almost rolled my eyes. "Not if being a princess gets me killed. My friends went through a lot of trouble and expense to keep me alive. They helped me leave even though they loved me. They let me go to keep me safe."

"Tell me about your friends."

Mirror Mirror was quiet as I chopped vegetables and talked about Lady Orva and the Inn in Cave Cove, then about what I was making; a heavy vegetable broth to cook buckwheat noodles called Soba. Then, I began talking about the Selkies and how they loved salted fish and noodle soup with dinner or eggs and pickled fish for breakfast.

Interrupting, Mirror Mirror asked, "What was his name? The one you want to go back to. The Selkie you love enough that you don't want to be a princess."

Inhaling sharply, I could suddenly feel the creeping cold of being watched. The bite on my shoulder burned as I reached up to rub it. "I don't know what you're talking about," I muttered the lie. Silently, I continued to make the noodles.

"Don't you want to talk about them anymore? If you tell me his name and put a drop of your blood on the mirror, I'll show him to you," it promised in a cooing voice, but the edge of the mirror was purple. "Tell me his name, and I'll help you."

I knew it was lying, and suddenly, I was very afraid to say Geal's name. I turned away, slowly stirring the vegetables in the boiling broth, then looked at my reflection. Its eyebrow was raised at me.

"I won't say any of their names again, M. He's watching us."

"He can't hear you. Watching mirrors don't work that way." She smiled again, but the purple edges remained. "Tell me your lover's name, and I will show him to you."

My heart hurt in my chest because it was pounding so hard that I was surprised it wasn't echoing off the stone walls. "He wasn't my lover. He was my friend, and I won't let you or that mad minotaur hurt him or anyone from my village." I could see how pale I was as I threatened, "I will smash every mirror in this prison and burn everything inside. I will kill myself before I let you hurt those I love."

"No, you won't," refuting me, my reflection smirked. "You want to live too much. You're special, Princess Daisy. You were chosen by a prince who loves you. You and your minotaur prince could live happily ever after like in the fairytales if you would just surrender your willfulness and let me teach you how to be a proper princess." Suddenly, her expression became hard and cruel as the edges of the mirror glowed like embers. "You will not leave this place until I decide you are ready."

"You're delusional, Mirror Mirror, like that Witch Winnie. Love won't change that he's a murderer who killed my kin, ate several princesses, and..."

"That was just because they weren't you."

"And attacked me twice," I reminded.

"You'll learn to love him like he loves you." It talked and talked as I continued to make noodles, ignoring everything the mirror said until my soup was ready.

"Enough! You can't talk me into loving someone who ruined everything in my life twice, and you're forgetting that his mother, the queen, wants me dead." I put the vegetables in a bowl, stirred the noodles in the broth to cook them, then added both the broth and noodles to the bowl. "I am going to eat my soba in the atrium." I walked outside, closed the door behind me, and sat on the grass with my bowl in my palm. As I ate my soup, I wished I had fish or shrimp to add to it.

As I was eating, I noticed a stag again in the small meadow below the thorny briar surrounding my prison. It was the third day he had grazed there. He raised his head and looked at me, bugling.

I waved my hand to acknowledge it. "Hello."

It walked up the steep mountainside. It was the closest he had come since I first saw him a few days earlier. He stopped on the other side of the briar. He bowed his head to me, but I could smell something strange about this shifter, something wrong.

"Can you shift?"

He looked up at the sun, then shook his head.

"Are you cursed?"

He nodded.

"Me too." I watched him, then whispered, "Could you guide me out of the mountains? I can pay you."

He tipped his head, then nodded again. He extended his neck, sniffing.

"Would you like some soup? I made the noodles today." I held the bowl out between the bars as far as I could reach, ignoring the thorns becoming more prominent. Stretching his neck, he sipped the vegetable soup broth, then chewed the vegetables and noodles while I warned in a much quieter whisper, "Don't come near the vines except as your buck. The thorns don't like people. The crazy mirror that lives here is using them to hold me prisoner."

The door slammed open. "Come back inside now. Princesses shouldn't talk to strangers." The mirror's shrill demand made me cringe more than Lady Orva's ever did. "Come in."

I ignored Mirror Mirror while he looked toward the house, then he bowed like he understood, before he turned and trotted back to the meadow. I studied him curiously. He reared and hoofed one of his front legs at the setting sun. I watched in shock as he collapsed. He thrashed for several minutes, then lay very still in a human form. Slowly, he struggled to rise, and then he dug into a gray lump that I thought was a rock before he dressed. Carefully, he made his way back up the mountain, carrying something.

Standing safely beyond the thorns as they twisted tighter around the cage, he stared at me. His dark brown eyes reminded me of Geal's, but instead of brown hair, his was black. He was very handsome, but there were scars on his face and arms. They were barely visible in the quickly darkening twilight.

"Are you Princess Daisy Brown?"

"No… I mean yes… I mean… Yes, I'm Daisy, but no, I'm not a princess."

He grinned, chuckling. "Princess or not, I'm here to rescue you."

"Can you guide me out of the Mountains of Despair without the wolves or bears killing us?" I asked again in desperate hope.

"I got in, didn't I? Besides, it's my job to get you out of here," he announced as he hefted the ax he carried.

"I wouldn't…" I warned too late. As soon as the blade struck the thick vine, it knocked him away with a swat. The thorns shredded his shirt, leaving his chest bleeding.

"Run!" I yelled as a vine as thick as my thigh reared back like a snake, then slapped on the ground where he had just stood. He quickly retreated as a vine seized me around my waist.

"Daisy!" He yelled to me.

"Get back to the meadow," I shouted as it dragged me inside.

CHAPTER 5

<<@Daisy@>>

The thorny vines tightened around the atrium blocking him from view. They blocked the door once I was inside.

"Princesses shouldn't talk to strangers; they could be witches in disguise. Who was that?" Mirror Mirror demanded, its edges a hostile ember-orange.

"I didn't catch his name," I answered truthfully. "He asked if I was Princess Daisy, and I said no, I am not a princess."

My reflection rolled its eyes. "Why did you tell him to go to the meadow?"

"I figured it was safer there," I squirmed. "Will you let me go? I don't want to be a princess."

"No." Mirror Mirror shook her head at me. "I am going to have to lock you in just like Princess Persinette."

"Who?" Suddenly, I was dragged upstairs by one of the vines. "Hey! Stop it." I was roughly thrown onto the bed then the vine pulled the door shut. I ran over to it, but I couldn't open it.

"You will stay in there." The mirror called up the stairs.

"Mirror Mirror, let me out!" I shouted while beating on the door and kicking the furniture. I stripped out of the dress I had sewn for myself and grabbed the pack I made out of a tapestry, also the rope made from the braided sheets.

"I hate you, you evil mirror!" Ranting, I kicked the door a few times, then climbed up on the dresser. I pretended to sob. "I told you I don't want to be a princess. I don't want to be killed and eaten by the minotaur prince. Please, let me go."

"No," the mirror's voice admonished me from beyond the door.

I muffled loud sobs like I was lying in bed while I climbed out of the window onto the roof naked. It was a terrifying thrill because directly below the window was a steep cliff; falling would mean death. Creeping across the tower roof, I had one chance. I attached the rope to a beam and climbed down, careful not to step on any of the vines. The stag shifter stood in the meadow in the moonlight. Gingerly, I stepped along the spine of the roof, then down one side. I was on the lowest point of the roof, but it was still a further drop than I expected. I looked back at the makeshift rope tied to the beam on the tower's roof beam and then down at the ground. I had a choice, go back in and give up or jump. I heard the mirror shout my name as I shifted. So I sprinted for the edge of the roof, diving between the vines that suddenly grew upward like trees. The giant thorns of one sliced open my side, and I landed hard, rolling down the rocky incline. Battered and bruised, I clutched my side with one hand while grabbing my bag with the other. My beast staggered away from the Citadel of Thorns as Mirror Mirror shrieked my name.

"Shift so I can carry you," the stag shifter demanded as he ran up to me.

I screamed as I did, then panted, "But your chest?" I could smell the blood.

"Just a few scratches, it's fine." He scooped me up and then ran away from the nightmare of thorns and waving serpentine vines. "I can't believe you escaped by yourself, Princess."

Clutching my side, I groaned, "I'm not a princess. I'm just a common cow turned maid. Call me Daisy, Daisy Brown."

The stag-shifter stopped in the meadow and set me down as he introduced himself, "Huntsman Bert St. Hubert."

He pulled a roll of cloth and a pot of ointment from his bag and slathered it on my wound. "Do you have something besides a dress to wear? Something loose?"

"I have a slip," I murmured as I opened my pack and dug for it.

"We can wrap you in my cloak. I'll get you as far from here as I can by morning." He barely glanced at my udders as he wrapped my side. "At dawn, I'll turn back to my stag. I don't know how he will react to you. He only lets children ride on him, but he shouldn't run off and leave you."

"What... what happened to you?" The medicine numbed my side, but it still hurt as I pulled the slip over my head. The vines were starting to crawl down the mountain like serpents.

"Drink this. It will help with the pain." He wrapped his cloak around me and picked me up. "I was cursed. We need to hurry."

"Who sent you to find me?" I asked before I sniffed the medicine.

"A witch told me you were sent here by mistake. She said you didn't belong here and needed to be rescued."

"Winnie sent you to find me?" I asked, then cried out in pain as he stumbled. The vines were chasing after us, but not as quickly as he could jog.

"Uhm, yes, Winnie sent me. Drink the pain medicine; it will help you heal. I am going to have to move more quickly to get us as far from the Citadel of Thorns as I can. It won't be gentle." Bert scowled as he glanced back at my prison. "Pray we don't run into any dire wolves or bears in the darkness."

Looking over his shoulder, I was shocked to see how far the vines were spreading in the pale moonlight. "It's coming after me. If you have to, leave me and escape."

"Don't worry, Daisy. I won't let it take you back there," he promised as he strode through the dark forest with purpose. "Why didn't you just escape before?"

"Because I don't know where I am," admitting the truth, I closed my eyes. "Thank you, Bert, for guiding me out of the mountains. Thank you for helping me."

"Helping you helps me. The witch says after I rescue you, she will reverse my curse."

"I'm happy for you." I yawned, then passed out despite the pain in my side, hip, and leg.

Bert paused and looked down at her with a frown. His lips pressed together then he muttered, "I'm sorry for everything." Inhaling deeply, he continued walking until almost dawn.

/\^^^^/\

I woke, leaning against the huntsman's backpack. My hand-made tapestry bag was under my injured leg. A warm fire crackled in a stone half-ring against a cliff, and I was still wrapped in Bert's cloak. A bowl of boiled grain sat next to the fire. Cautiously, I tasted it, hesitating at first, then I began eating. Suddenly, I started giggling and crying at the same time. It had just the right amount of honey and dried fruit like I made it when I worked for Lady Orva. Mirror Mirror refused to let me have more than a single apple a day and no honey or sugar or syrup, fussing that I would get fat and that princesses should not be fat.

I looked up sharply at the crack of a stick. A giant stag with antlers that spread like a tree stood before me. I wiped my tears with the back of my hand.

"Thank you for breakfast, Bert."

He came closer and sniffed my wet cheeks, then tipped his head carefully. I got the impression he was not used to his giant antlers. He made a whining, grunting sound.

"I'm not sad... exactly... I am just happy to be away from that mirror. I don't think I realized how bad it was. It wouldn't let me eat anything sweet because princesses aren't supposed to get fat. It didn't want me to clean up the place because that's what maids are for. I told her I was a maid, I liked being a maid... and it didn't want me to alter the clothes there because princesses aren't supposed to breathe." I stopped to sob; everything from the night I was bitten poured out, and finally, I finished with, "I don't even want to be a princess. I just want to go back to my life in Cave Cove on the Stone Coast and pretend none of this ever happened. I don't know what I did to be so cursed."

Bert had laid down beside me and rubbed his cheek against the side of my head or shoulder. Tears leaked from his eyes. I had never been this close to a stag or buck. I didn't realize how much they smelled like bulls.

"I'm sorry, Bert. I know you're cursed and in a much worse way than me. I don't mean to complain. I'm grateful for your help. I promise I'll pay you for helping me."

Shaking his head, he made a deep sound in his throat, then stood and walked away. After a while, the warmth of the sun on the rocks around me lulled me to sleep. I was so tired, I began to dream almost immediately.

I stood at the door of the laundry shed, staring up at the moon as tears ran down my cheeks. I couldn't make myself step outside to hang the towels I had just washed and wrung out. The mantras of my clan shouted in my mind.

"Never go out in the moonlight," I whispered the words into crystalline clouds. It was only my third day at my new job at Lady Orva's Inn. The towels wouldn't dry if I didn't hang them in the cold night breeze, but I couldn't make myself step outside.

"Are you okay?" A male voice startled me. I recognized him from serving meals in the dining hall.

Swallowing, I admitted, "I'm afraid... I'm afraid of the moonlight and the monsters in it."

The Selkie chieftain's son stepped closer. In the light from the washing shed, I could see his concerned expression as he offered, "There aren't any monsters here, but if you want, I'll stand guard for you... I'm Geallan."

I closed my eyes. "Thank you. I'm Daisy."

"I know."

Then I took the first of many steps out to the lines in the moonlight. He talked about the Coast of Stones and how the Selkies had always lived in the caves of the cove, even before the Evolution plague. He talked to me until I finished, then walked me back to the barn.

"You're not sleeping in the Inn?" Geal asked in confusion.

"No, I like sleeping with the cows. It reminds me of the longhouse at home," I admitted, then stepped back. "I'm sorry, I won't invite you in. I'm not that kind of cow."

He chuckled. "We've heard you're the kind of cow that kicks. Don't worry... we aren't the kind of village that allows any male to harm a female. Goodnight, Daisy."

"Goodnight."

He stopped and turned back, "Where was home?"

"The White Mountains. I grew up on a farm."

He nodded. "I've been there. My father made a deal to trade salted fish for aged cheese."

"Cheese?" I couldn't remember if I had ever seen the traders come, but then I was so young I wouldn't have paid attention.

"I like cheese... see you in the morning." He went back inside the inn, and I climbed up the ladder to the hayloft to sleep.

Hours later, I woke up and added more wood to the fire. The potion was healing me much faster than normal, but I would still be injured for days, maybe a week or more. I saw Bert grazing below a tree. Quickly I checked my wounds; the deep scratches from the thorns were almost healed. I could shift. He came back when I waved. I was happily surprised when he dropped an early dandelion in my lap.

"I love these. Thank you." Taking a leaf in my mouth, I savored the green goodness. It tasted like those from the White Mountain. "I can shift, and we can start walking out."

He shook his head, staring pointedly at my side where the blood had seeped through the bandages.

"I'm fine. It's just a shallow gash. We can't stay here. There are dire wolves and cave bears, and we need to go." I stood gingerly and began stuffing my slip into my pack. "It's better for me to travel as my cow or beast because the only shoes I have are slippers."

Bert made several grumpy sounds, but I ignored him. I threw my bandage into the fire, then looped my tapestry bag around my neck. The shift into my cow hurt, but I gritted my teeth and did it. We only had a few hours until sunset, and I wanted to be as far from the Citadel of Thorns as possible. Bert made a troubled sound in his throat as my cow rolled in the dirt to clot the blood seeping from the torn open wounds. Standing, she stomped her hoof, looking down the path. Bert picked up his pack in his horns and trotted ahead. I followed as we wandered the deer paths along the curves of the mountains.

Λ^^^^Λ

The sunset was almost upon us when his stag brought us to a cave. I shifted, pulled a slip on, and began to make dinner. I had never seen a shifter with a more painful change. It seemed like the first time every time, as Bert screamed in agony. I held his head in my lap.

"Bert, what happened? Who did this to you?" I demanded as I lifted a flask of water to his lips for him to sip.

"I was cursed by my mother; she turned me into a monster and a murderer," he admitted with tears running from his eyes. "I hurt the female I loved and lost her. I thought I was going mad as my father had. After my mother was burned as a witch, we found out she had cursed both of us. We never meant to hurt anyone, but she... I don't know why she did it."

"Oh, I am so sorry." I ached for him then I remembered something about witches. "But wasn't the curse broken?"

"One curse was broken, but another began. My penitence for the harm I caused." His dark eyes held mine, expressing how sorry he was for everything he had done under the influence of the evil magic.

"That isn't fair; you were cursed, and it wasn't your fault," I said to him what was once said to me as I ran my fingers through his ebony hair. "Tell me. Sometimes it helps to talk to someone."

We stayed there for a long time. He talked quietly about how he watched his father going through periods of madness and being locked up, how he and his sister would sneak into the prison to visit him. Then how his mother ruthlessly controlled their lives, even demanding to dictate who they mated.

"I met this beautiful female with the kindest heart. She was always looking after the children of her village, and she loved wildflowers. She would pick them in the moonlight. I loved her from the first moment I saw her, but I marked her in a moment of madness, then abandoned her afterward. I didn't mean to... my beast... he just wanted her so much. I didn't know the reason I couldn't control him was because I was cursed. I regret it every day. I know she fears me, but I don't know how to make it right." Bert turned his face away and wept bitterly.

"I'll help you," I promised. "I'll help you, and I'll even go with you to talk to her before I go home."

"Why would you do that? Why would you help me?" He sat up, not looking at me. His posture spoke of shame he didn't deserve to feel. "I can't even control my shift anymore."

"I couldn't control my shift for months after I was changed. Because I was an adult, most shifters, even the ones who knew that I had just become a shifter, scorned me and mocked me when they learned I couldn't control it. I still shift unawares when afraid or angry or asleep." I patted his shoulder, then moved past him to move the simple soup I made away from the coals of the fire. Splitting it between two bowls, I held one out to him. "I've only had my human a year or so... I am not even certain what day it is. I lost track when I was being held in the Citadel of Thorns."

"It's two weeks until the summer solstice," he revealed as he sipped the soup.

"Really?" I had no idea I had been there that long. It felt like years, but it also felt like only a few weeks.

"Daisy? Are you okay? You are so pale."

"I'm... I'm fine... I need to get home as soon as I can." I was suddenly very upset that I might miss Geal's birthday.

Sipping more soup, Bert appraised me and then asked, "Who do you miss so much?"

"Everyone... my friend Geal's birthday is coming. He risked his life to get me to safety," I explained.

"Geal and Vinko are the ones who escorted you from Lady Orva's to Lady Emula's," Bert repeated what I told him.

"Yes." I looked down at my bowl, suddenly not hungry, while thinking about the minotaur who tried to kill me. "I don't think the queen seeking to kill me would look for me in the place I fled from. I hope not. I have to warn you. The minotaur prince has a magic mirror he watches me with. I can feel it when he touches the mirror." Unconsciously, my hand rubbed my cheek where I usually felt the cold brush of his fingertips. "If I tell you to put your hood up or to stay away from me, do it. It means he's watching. I don't want to risk that he might try to find you and kill you like he did my cousins. No one should die the way they did."

"I'm sorry your cousins died too." Bert bowed his head over his soup. "You're such a good cook. Get some rest. We can spend the night here. It isn't safe to travel."

Chapter 6

"Climb!"

We managed to avoid the cave bears and dire wolves for several nights and days, becoming traveling companions and friends, but our luck ran out, and three of the giant wolves found us. Now, we were climbing a cliff as the dawn approached.

Standing on a thin ledge, Bert cast a worried glance at the southeastern sky. "Daisy, I… I have to save you. Keep following the trail we were on; it will get you to the closest town in two days."

I grabbed his arm, refusing what I feared he would do. "Bert, you can't fight them off as your stag; they'll just chase you down and kill you."

He glanced back toward the glow of the rising sun, then looked into my eyes with an intensity that would have made me step back if we weren't so precariously perched.

"Daisy, I love you. I fell in love with you the first night you sang in the moonlight. I fell in love with you, watching you take care of the children in your clan, and every day I watched you while I was imprisoned. Everything I told you about my mother was true. She cursed me and drove me mad. I'm sorry for all you struggled through because of it."

He kissed me with a suddenness that shocked me, then he pulled the medallion from around his neck and kissed me again, but this time was different. This time it tingled and felt like happiness. Panting, Bert leaned back. He touched my face with his fingertip exactly the way my watcher always did.

"You're so beautiful… I am so sorry I lied to you. I just wanted you to know me without your fear and without my curse. I agreed to be cursed again just so I could know you. So we could start over. I promise I will never let any more harm come to you." He jerked his shirt off over his head and kicked off his boots and pants.

"Who are you?" I demanded in stunned worry as my mind chanted, *Don't be him. Don't be him.*

"You know who I am, my One. Don't forget. I love you more than my life." Then he jumped down, shifting into the minotaur of my nightmares.

The fiery sunrise overhead turned everything the color of blood as the giant minotaur attacked the wolves. Stuffing my clothes and slippers into the tapestry bag, I shifted into my midform. I hoisted both the packs and ran down the ledge jumping as far as I could. The ledge crumbled and fell under my weight, but I made it to a steep slope and slid down. I sprinted down the trail, but at a bellow of pain, I stopped. Tears leaked from my eyes, blurring my vision. My cow head mooed angrily, shaking back and forth, then I picked up a fallen log. Stomping back toward the battling beasts, I swung the limb like the warhammers and clubs Fergie and Lana taught me to fight with, knocking one of the dire wolves down the hill. It rolled off the cliff. Two more wolves had joined the three, and from the howls, I could hear more coming. Stamping and snorting, I stepped forward and crushed the hindquarters of the one trying to flank Tauran. His giant Minotaur ripped another one of the wolves in half. The last wolf fled. Stomping over to the one I crippled, Tauran stomped his skull, crushing it. The bull Minotaur turned toward me and snorted, then bellowed angrily in my face, but my cow minotaur mooed back just as angrily then we lifted our hoof to kick him. He backed away quickly with one clawed hand over his man parts and the other held up in surrender. We were happy that he understood we were the kind of cow that kicked as we turned to trot over the bloody stains on the path. The whole while, I scanned the woods for more wolves. I knew they would follow us if they didn't decide to just eat their companions. We would have to travel straight to the village, no more sitting by the fire and talking about our lives.

Our lives? More like my life and his lies. Stopping, I picked up his pack and slung it at his chest, then hoisted mine over one shoulder and rested the log-turned-club over the other.

"Please, Daisy. Let me explain," Tauran begged after he shifted.

My minotaur turned our head, giving him the side-eye with a warning snort. His human form was as attractive as his minotaur, but we weren't interested in being a princess. Keeping walking through the day, we set a grueling pace that Tauran was forced to shift back to his minotaur to keep up with. The whole time, he talked and talked and talked. Finding a meadow filled with wildflowers and lush grass, I stopped. I was starving and could hear Tauran's stomach growling like a bear. Dropping my log club and setting my pack by it, I shifted to my human.

"Daisy, please. I'm sorry I lied."

"I am going to graze and rest as my cow, Prince Tauran. Once we are back to civilization, I am going home to the Stone Coast, and you can go wherever lying princes go," I shouted at him before I shifted to my caramel-brown cow and began grazing.

Tauran bellowed out in wordless frustration, then he snarled at me. "Tell me the truth... would you have spoken to me or listened to me if I had come to you as myself with the truth? My own mother cursed me with a murderous madness so she could steal my father's kingdom and send our people off to slaughter for profit. My people need you after having her for a queen. They need your kind heart. This isn't just about you and me and what happened when I was cursed. Hate me forever; I'll deal with it, I deserve it, but I need you to come back for my people. I saw you taking care of those in your herd, even when you were so young. I watched you in the village and how sweet you were to everyone. You will be a great queen someday, Daisy. Everyone sees it but you." He stomped away, then shifted to his bull at the edge of the meadow closest to the forest in case something tried to attack us.

I turned my arse to him and lowered my head to the grass so he wouldn't see me weeping. I didn't want to be a queen; I liked being a commoner. As I ate, I thought about all he had said before I knew who he really was. He was right... I wouldn't have listened if I knew who he really was... I would have run away as fast as my hooves could carry me. I laid down in the grass and stared at a dandelion. Its merry yellow head bobbed in the breeze, carefree and happy. My cow lowed in quiet, mournful tones as I bent my neck toward where Tauran stood, watching me sadly and chewing a mouth of clover. He swallowed as he walked over to me. He mooed comfortingly as I laid in the grass and wept. Finally, I shifted back to my skin, and he did too. We stared at each other, surrounded by the golden warmth of sunlight and the vibrant green of the meadow.

"Would you have still bitten me and changed me if I hadn't gone into the meadow that night?"

"Yes," he answered honestly. "My beast heard you singing one night. Later, we felt your desperation when your sister died. You were begging for someone to help you. We almost went off a cliff trying to find you," Tauran admitted.

"You heard me?" I stared at him in shock.

He nodded his head. "I bellowed out to you every night after that... my mad beast was already planning to kidnap you. He... we... think you are an amazing female. I am so sorry you were left behind, but I am glad you were because my mother would have killed or cursed you." He folded his hands, begging, "Please forgive me."

"I'm trying."

He reached up to touch my cheek, hesitantly. When I didn't lean away, he tucked my hair behind my ear before tracing my cheekbone. "I love you, Daisy."

"I..." Suddenly, my throat was dry, and my heart was pounding. The tingles from his touch on my cheek shocked my senses.

"Your majesties!" A familiar voice called out. It was the minotaur who had searched for me in Lady Orva's barn.

I jumped to my feet, ready to fight or flee.

"Easy. I know him." I could hear Tauran's teeth grinding as he muttered, "Get dressed." Then he stood and walked toward the male minotaur riding a horse.

Several of the warriors with him gawked at me until Tauran snorted at them. I turned my back on them and dressed in my pants with the bodice I cut off from a dress to wear as a shirt. Putting on the slippers I took from the Citadel of Thorns, I scowled at them and decided the first thing I would buy when we got to civilization was walking boots. Sitting next to my club and pack, I reached down and picked a dandelion. Slowly eating the leaves, I tried to calm my traitorous heart.

"Those are your favorite," Tauran said from behind me, but I didn't look at him.

"I should hate them, they cursed me... like you did... but I don't. I don't hate either of you," I announced as I popped the golden blossom into my mouth, chewing it as I looked at the clouds forming. An afternoon storm was building. I needed to buy a cloak too. Standing, I started to pick up my club, then decided to leave it. It was very heavy for my human form to tote around.

"Master-At-Arms Angus brought normal horses. We'll be at the village by sunset."

I looked past Tauran and sighed, admitting, "I've never ridden a horse before."

He chuckled. "Me neither. It should be fun."

Λ^^^^Λ

An hour after sunset, we arrived at the largest of the Inns. The town sported a central square filled with several shops. It was a much larger settlement than I would have imagined for just a remote place, but Tauran explained that there was a larger tourist industry for winter skiing that ran most of the year, though few ventured as far into the Mountains of Despair as he had to find me. My derriere felt like bread that had been over-kneaded or perhaps like croissant dough after the butter had been beaten into it. I ached in places I didn't know I had muscles. Trying to get off the horse, I fell into Tauran's arms. I could feel the warmth of him through his wet clothes. Looking up into his dark brown eyes, I could see how much he wanted to kiss me again as he glanced at my lips.

"I need a hot bath," I complained as I looked down at the fancy buttons on his coat.

"Tell them when you go to the desk; I will join you in a moment," Tauran promised.

"I'm not sharing a room with you," I declared as he set me on my feet on the porch.

At my tone, he deflated slightly but responded tactfully, "And so you shouldn't, Princess. Our mating ceremony isn't until the autumn equinox."

His teasing tone made me grind my teeth. Walking into the Inn, I cringed as my forlorn slippers left wet footprints on the floor. The female cougar-shifter at the desk looked me up and down with disdain only a feline shifter could manage. I knew I looked rough in my tapestry print coat, travel sack, wet taffeta pants, and dress bodice.

"I need a room and a bath, please," I asked, pulling out my purse. The little leather bag had managed to stay with me through all my unfortunate travels. I fished out my single gold coin.

She showed her fangs a little and purred, "We don't normally rent rooms to..."

"Minotaurs?" Angus's offended voice boomed from behind me. Several people in fine clothes began gathering at the door of the ale room to watch.

"Commoners." The Clerk hissed at him slightly as he dropped a large bag of coins on the counter.

"The Prince and his betrothed Princess require separate rooms with baths. Preferably adjoining so they may dine together. And I will require rooms on either side and the ones across the hall for the royal guard." Angus held himself to his full height and glared down at the clerk.

"She doesn't look like a princess." She was right. I was soaking wet and mud-spattered, very far from Princess-looking.

"We are traveling on horseback. The Princess chose suitable riding attire to travel through Dire Wolf and Cave Bear-infested wildlands, which we have been attacked by. The Princess even killed two wolves who attacked her, so I would mind my tone, Clerk Kitty," he rebuked her as an ostrich-shifter came out from the office.

"Master-At-Arms Angus, enough." I stopped him before he got her fired. I knew what it was like to deal with difficult visitors to Lady Orva's Inn. Those in the door were murmuring, but when I looked back, the expressions of haughty judgment had been replaced by curiosity.

"But Princess, she cannot treat you..."

"I said enough. May we please have rooms and baths for our party for the night?" I asked sweetly, then added, "Has dinner service ended? What time is breakfast served?"

The bird came immediately to the counter, eyeing the bag of coins and gems. "Of course, Minotaur Princess, whatever you would require. I can prepare the east wing; no one is staying in it since the snow melted, and I will have the cooks put out a late supper of soup, bread, and cold meats and it will be brought to your rooms. Breakfast is from dawn until mid-morning. Come this way... I will show you the rooms and have my staff make the beds fresh. I am Landlord Ostri, your host. Please follow me." He bowed in the fluttering way only bird-shifters could manage.

"Master-At-Arms Angus, please ask the soldiers to come in the side door and remove their muddy boots before walking on the rugs," I begged, thinking of the maid or maids on duty, then I followed Ostri.

Landlord Ostri showed me the rooms and the in-room baths. The taps worked just like the ones in Lady Orva's laundry shed. "My Princess, may I have my laundry maid pick up your traveling garments so they may be cleaned and dried by morning?"

It felt so strange to be on this side of Inn life. "Yes, thank you." He turned to leave, but I asked, "Where can I get new boots and a cloak? I lost mine at the last Inn where I stayed."

"I will write the shop names down for you, Princess." He bowed as he backed out.

Looking around the room, I sighed as my eyes landed on the bed. I was so tired.

No… bathe, eat, then sleep. I chastised myself as I stripped out of my wet clothing while the tub filled.

There was a knock, so I wrapped a towel around myself to open the door for my food, but Tauran was standing there. He gasped, seeing me, but I slammed the door before opening it slightly to peek out.

"Yes?"

"I… I came to see if you needed anything or if we could have dinner together." Tauran tried to keep eye contact, but his eyes kept glancing down at where I clutched the towel at my cleavage.

The third time, I grabbed his chin, forcing him to look into my eyes. "Goodnight, Prince Tauran."

Closing the door, I shook my head, then went and got in the tub. A maid brought my meal and took my wet clothes. As I ate, I felt someone was watching me. It made me angry that he would start doing that again after I told him how creepy it felt. Turning out all the lights, I climbed into bed and covered my head. I would deal with him in the morning and he was going to learn the hard way that I could kick with more than my hooves.

Chapter 7

>> The Beast<<

He hung his head as the door slammed in his face, then rubbed his jaw where she held his chin. It still tingled.

"Stop standing outside her door like a lovesick calf and have a meal, Prince Tauran." Angus laughed heartily.

Going into the largest community room at the end of the hall, they sat and ate with several warriors he knew; then, they played mancala. It felt like when he was a young bull before he was cursed. It felt good to be with them, without the fear of losing control of his beast and killing them. His old friends were amazed when he told them how she fought the wolves.

"I'll have to get her a warhammer for a wedding gift to keep you in line, my Prince," Angus teased.

"Please don't. I can still feel where she hoofed me in my bullness," Tauran whined, and they all laughed louder.

Eventually, the tired warriors went to bed, leaving only the Prince and Master-At-Arms.

"I am so sorry I left her behind," Angus apologized.

"It was actually the best thing that could have happened." Tauran yawned and stretched, then revealed, "I fear if you had brought her home for her change, mother would have cursed or killed her." A tear leaked down his cheek. "My own mother turned me into a monster and a murderer." He reached up to rub the strange coldness like a dew-wet spiderweb on his cheek. "She hated me, and she hated my One before she even met her. I still just want to know why?"

"I can't help you with that, lad. I can only say, love your One with all your heart and all your beast." Angus understood part of his struggle. "Finding Bovina and Brangus's mother was the best moment of my life, even if she did hate me for a decade or two. Eventually, she gave me two fine calves. When we went back to her village, her best friend was still there and accused me of killing and eating her. I made so many mistakes with my One because I was being bull-headed. Don't do what I did. Listen to her, earn her trust, and she'll love you like no other could." Standing wearily, Angus patted Tauran's shoulder and then went to his room.

/\^^^^/\

<<@Daisy@>>

I woke up feeling suffocated under the blankets. I took a cold bath in the water I hadn't drained and then dressed in my clean traveling clothes. The place where I had cut the skirt off and left a ruffle on the bodice was ironed and starched stiff to match the sleeve poufs. Going out to the laundry shed, I found a young bear-shifter doing the laundry.

"Excuse me, did you clean and dry clothes last night?"

The juvenile female bowed deeply. "Yes, Princess, and this morning all the ladies are asking for their clothes to be altered like yours. You've caused quite a trend."

"I didn't mean to. I just cut up some dresses to make decent traveling garments." Rolling my eyes, I held out a half copper coin. "This is for you. Thank you for doing my clothes last night. I truly appreciate it. It was only a few months ago that I was a maid too."

"But you're a princess!"

"I hate being a princess; I liked being a maid much better." I left her with the coin and went into the dining room. I ate uncomfortably while two large minotaur guards stood nearby. They were trying to be unobtrusive, but their size made them hard to miss.

"Princess."

"I'm not a princess, Master-At-Arms Angus. I wasn't a princess when I hid from you in Cave Cove on the Stone Coast, and I am not a princess now," I announced as I held up my head.

"You were the heifer at Lady Orva's Inn," Angus said as he raised an eyebrow.

"Yes." I stood up to leave because I couldn't bear to sit at the table with him. "Lady Orva told me what happened during the Cattle Wars. She told me what your kind did to her best friend Blu. How everyone fought, but she survived and was spared because she had a midform like me. Blu was taken from her husband and friends and eaten."

"Princess, it wasn't…"

"You yourself said a reward wasn't enough to make up for what was done before. I heard you telling another minotaur that. It's what happened to Blu, and I am still not certain it won't happen to me. They still grieve for her, you know? I don't want them to grieve for me. I'm going home. I don't want to be your queen." I felt the cold touch of being watched. "Where is Tauran?"

"He may be sleeping in; he was up very late," Angus admitted, "We were..."

"Oh, I know what he was doing. I could feel him. Excuse me." I went to his room and kicked open the door instead of knocking politely. The maid in the hall just stared at me in shock as I bellowed, "Tauran!"

He sat up suddenly, then rolled out of bed, staggering to his feet gloriously naked. For a moment, I forgot why I came to yell at him. We stared at each other, then I glanced away and saw a mirror on the table.

I stomped over and picked it up, yelling as I waved it at him, "I was in the next room! You did not have to watch me all night to make certain I was safe!"

"I didn't," he stammered.

"Evidently, you did! And I felt it." I threw the mirror at him as I snarled, "I am going to get a pair of boots and a cloak, and then I am going home. Find someone else to be Queen of the Minotaurs."

Slamming his door, I started to leave the Inn.

"Princess Daisy?"

Taking a deep breath, I turned and smiled at the Innkeeper. "Lord Ostri, how are you this morning?"

"I have the list of shops... is there a problem?" He looked very worried; it only took one disgruntled Royal to ruin an Inn.

"No. Your Inn and your staff are wonderful. Thank you for the list of shops." I tried to sound gracious, then I turned and stomped out, walking away from the Inn.

I was so sick of the lies, sick of being treated like I was something I was not. I looked up at the gray sky, knowing it was going to start raining again. Looking at the list of shops, I found one selling cloaks and coats first. An older white-haired woman who smelled like a Llama was sewing buttons onto a garment made of gray and brown spotted fur.

"Can I be helping ye, dearie?"

Remembering Master Vinko and his kindness, my heart ached for my friends on the Coast of Stones. "Yes, ma'am. Please, I need a cloak or coat for traveling in this weather."

"Ahh, came to the mountains without a cloak, did ye? Aye, those travel company witches all tell people about the views and such and never about the mornin' mists and afternoon showers." She waved at the racks with a judgmental air. "You should have looked into it before you came."

"I was sent here against my will, and I am leaving to go home today, but I was raised in the White Mountains and know how unpredictable weather can be in the late spring." I hoped I sounded more sensible than resentful, but I felt offended by the suggestion that I would have come unprepared.

I tried on and then hung up many things, but I couldn't find a coat to fit around my udders. The cloaks were all too short in the back and front but long on the sides and completely useless for keeping one's legs warm and dry. I scowled, thinking it must be this year's fashions, as I remembered the lectures Mirror Mirror gave me about how a princess should always wear the latest style. Then I saw someone walking by in almost my exact outfit. I wondered what they would think if they knew I had picked these things just to have something to wear so I wouldn't be escaping a crazed mirror in a thorn-covered tower naked. There was a shift, and I glanced at the mirror; my reflection stared back at me. Looking through the last rack, I kept looking toward the mirror, but my reflection did everything I did. Shaking my head at myself, I decided my time in the Citadel of Thorns made me paranoid.

"Excuse me, ma'am. Do you have any long cloaks?"

The shopkeeper raised an eyebrow, asking, "You don't like the fashionable ones from the royal courts?"

"I'm not a foolish princess or prince." I tried not to sound resentful.

"I have this one which was traded if you don't mind wearing something someone else wore."

There was a slight edge to her tone that I assumed was because the shopkeeper thought I was trying to cheat her. "I will pay full price for something sensible," I reassured her. "I need something for my long journey home."

The shopkeeper waved me onto a dressing pedestal. "And where is home, dearie?"

"The Coast of Stones, ma'am." I stood very still as the shopkeeper placed the soft gray fur over my shoulders and began buttoning it. It was very tight, so tight I couldn't raise my arms, there were only mitts for my hands, and I doubted I could do more than hop to walk.

"I don't think this fits..." I wheezed, trying to take a deep breath.

"Now, dearie, let meh put the hood up. It changes the whole look." The shopkeeper flipped the hood up, and I felt myself falling as magic shimmered around me.

I yelped in surprise, but the sound came out as a hoarse bark. Struggling, I couldn't get free of the constricting cloak. The shopkeeper began laughing in a surprisingly young-sounding voice.

"It's a perfect fit."

I looked up at her reflection in the mirror as she melted into a beautiful, golden-haired witch then my own reflection as I appeared in the tower while I squirmed.

"You have your cow, and I have my freedom. Good luck, Queen Dejanira." Mirror Mirror sneered at me. The mirror shimmered like embers around the edges, as my reflection knelt down. "You could have been a queen, but you wanted to stay a cow. Now you're not even that."

"Get away from me!" I shouted in alarm, but it came out as a series of honks and trumpeted coughs. I looked in the mirror as it shimmered. My own brown eyes looked back from a seal's face. "No!"

"My son deserves a real princess." Queen Dejanira pointed her wand at me. "Go home, sea cow. Stella ardenti reditus."

Red fire surrounded me. Above the roar of the magical flames, I heard Tauran shout, "No! Daisy!"

Then I was flying through the air with Tauran clinging to me.

"I've got you!"

My screams came out as hoarse seal barks before we plummeted into the salty water, choking on the sea, thrashing, trying to swim in the confining cloak, trapping me in a seal's body. I managed to kick my legs together and float on my back. Gasping for air, Tauran tried to help me and swim in the cold water.

"Over th-there, a sh-shoal," he pointed, then he began to sink.

Pushing him up, it took many kicks of my bound legs and waving of my hands to manage to get us to a rocky outcropping. Squirming up onto the shoal, I cried in exhaustion as I pulled at his sleeve with my mouth.

"R-reach up with your h-hand and p-push b-back the hood." His teeth chattered as he weakly struggled to climb out of the waves pounding against us. "Unbutton." His lips were blue as he collapsed.

I reached up and had the weird sensation of pushing my hand out of my mouth. Suddenly my head was free, and I could feel the buttons. Undoing them as quickly as I could, I was shocked by how cold it was as I stripped out of the enchanted cloak and my clothes. Shifting to my minotaur, I threw him over my shoulder and then scrambled away from the waves and spray. There was an abandoned lighthouse. I kicked the door open and carried Tauran inside. He was so cold he wasn't even shivering, so I stripped him and wrapped him in a musty but dry blanket before starting a fire in a little potbelly stove. The room warmed slowly as I wrapped the still dry seal cloak around me sideways, purposely keeping the buttons separated from the buttonholes. Leaving him, I climbed the rickety stairs. I guessed the top of the lighthouse had been torn off in a storm as I stood on the floor around a trapdoor. I looked around, trying to get my bearings. There were only waves and sky in every direction.

I didn't want to live in the sea; I liked living on land.

Baby

<u>**Trigger Warning: Pregnancy Loss**</u>

CHAPTER 1

She was late. She had been for three weeks now. But she wasn't really holding her breath after seven years of dashed hopes. It was only a few weeks back they had decided to stop trying, which is why this came as a shock more than a surprise.

She hadn't taken a test and didn't have the two lines to validate what she already knew. But knew she did.

Despite herself, her heart started to pound, and with a shaky hand, she swept the liner on her eyes. Her lips were compressed, her mouth grim. She had stopped smiling ages back.

But what terrified her were her eyes. Bright and soulful, full of hope.

Taking a deep breath, she looked at the bathroom floor. Hope was a terrifying thing. She didn't want to be hopeful again; she didn't want to hop onto the roller coaster of soaring ecstasy and crash into her soul-crushing reality. So instead, she learned to accept her fate.

But now, she was late. Sooner or later, she would have to bear the consequences.

She resisted the urge to cover her womb with her hand to protect the new life inside her.

Suddenly, the hair on her nape stood up as she felt it, the shadow always lurking behind her.

She had felt its presence before, a dark figure just out of the periphery of her vision. But she didn't know what the shadow wanted with her. Why did it always find her when she had new life growing inside her?

And never left her until she was alone.

Again.

She squeezed her eyes shut at the unfairness of the situation and dug her hands into her scalp, pulling her hair with all her might. "Stop! Please!" she implored the shadow. "Please leave my baby and me alone!"

She collapsed on the bathroom floor, sobbing like a baby.

The tap dripped a staccato as it echoed throughout the empty house.

* * *

"Halloween will be here soon." Della Ramirez, the resident crone at Milcent Bank, shot gimlet eyes at the other employees.

Nisha shrugged and ignored her, but young Felicity Tarrono squealed. "Oh wow, are we dressing up? I have *such* a great idea for a costume!"

Nisha shot a quick smile at her friend and confidant, Saira Sheikh. Six months pregnant with her third child, Saira winked conspiratorially as she stuffed her face with chips.

Never in a million years would Milcent Bank allow employees to dress up in a costume.

But, despite the starchy workwear and the scrappy pay, Nisha enjoyed her job. It gave her a purpose, a reason to drag herself out of bed every morning.

"I can't believe all you care about are costumes!" Della's English became more heavily accented, exposing her Eastern European roots. "Halloween is a terrible time of the year!" She swept her hands across the tiny cubicles where all the tellers, including herself, were crammed together.

The bank was closed, and they were tallying the cash, so thankfully, no customers would witness Della's eccentricities.

"Terrible?" as if on cue, Felicity crooned. "What do you mean? I loved Halloween as a kid. The dressing up, the trick or treat." She dropped her voice and leaned conspiratorially to Saira, who was on her right, though the bank was empty save for the security guard, who was busy with his phone. "It's a great way to meet men."

Saira caressed her protruding belly and grinned, "That's what got me in trouble the first time."

"You met your husband on Halloween?" Felicity asked curiously, and Saira and Nisha shared a smile. Nisha knew about Saira's conservative upbringing in Pakistan, much similar to Nisha's own in India. And now, a world away, these two women were best friends in London.

Della got up with a huff, unhappy with how the conversation had turned. "What I'm trying to say, if you will listen, is that Halloween isn't a time to joke around. It's not all fun and games and slutty dresses and makeout sessions." She gave a pointed look to Felicity, who rolled her eyes.

"No one said my costume was going to be slutty-"

"Ages ago," Della cut in, standing up and ensuring all three women had their rapt attention on her. "Halloween was not a holiday with fun and games. People dressed up as saints..."

"Well, it's fun now." Felicity protested and quietened when Della shot her a quelling look.

"The curtain is going to be lifted! The boundaries will be blurred!" Della raised her arms, encompassing the bank, looking bereft without customers.

Nisha knew which boundaries, but Della stared straight at her. "The boundaries between the living and the dead."

Nisha gulped, uncomfortable under the scrutiny. *Why did Della shoot her a knowing look?*

"Ghouls, goblins, witches, and demons can pass through and mingle with the living. Shadows are moving in our world, hunting for souls to capture!"

"That's enough!" Nisha stood up in indignation. She didn't believe in ghosts and goblins; she refused to acknowledge the presence of the shadow, waiting to collect the soul of the hapless child growing inside her. These stories were beyond foolish, just folklore to con the uneducated and control the desperate.

"You are..." Nisha gulped as the shadow behind her flickered, taunting her and alerting her to its presence. "...taking this too far! You're scaring

Felicity!"

Felicity paused the process of filing her nails and shot Nisha a questioning look.

"You can pretend ignorance, *Neesha*!" Della said, stressing the 'e' sound in her name as she was *wont,* always. "But not everything can be explained away by science. Demons do visit our world and do make their presence felt. I have seen it with my own eyes! My sister-in-law Brenda—I have seen her possessed. She used to stay up at night, looking out of the windows. She looked at us, feral, and I have seen her eat raw meat... "

"Eeew!" Felicity cut in, but Della ignored her and grabbed Nisha's arm, holding her attention.

"I have seen her change as the demon took over her faculties." Della's kohl-rimmed, bloodshot grey eyes bore into Nisha's brown ones.

"H-How is she now?" This was from Saira as she protectively cradled her belly.

"She is fine now, thanks for asking." Della smiled unexpectedly and dropped Nisha's arm after patting it, looking like a benevolent aunt. "But we got her help. We took her to a psychic in Hackney; she pulled the demon out of poor Brenda. She's famous. I can vouch for her."

"I'm going to dress up like Arianna Grande! It will be fab." A long squeal emitted from Felicity, startling them as she browsed her phone.

Della shot daggers towards her fellow colleague for the disturbance and Nisha and Saira exchanged startled looks, shaking their heads.

* * *

"Are you ok?" Saira asked Nisha as they walked to the tube station in the dark and gloomy London evening. The weather had turned quite nippy, and Nisha avoided replying until they slipped into the warmth of the tube station.

"I'm fine!" She gave Saira a bright smile, but her friend looked worried as she readjusted her hijab.

"Is Saurabh going to be home today? Would you like to come to visit for some time? Ahmed and Rubina would love to see you."

Nisha doted on young Ahmed and Rubina. Their mother, her best friend, didn't know that Nisha had also been pregnant at the same time as Saira, but she had miscarried both times when Saira delivered healthy babies. She didn't share her dark secret with anyone.

All Saira knew was that Nisha moved to London after losing her first child in childbirth. But she didn't know about all the longing glances Nisha had shot her as she flourished with the miracle of pregnancy. If Saira found out about it, she would pity her and stop sharing the joys of motherhood with her, and Nisha didn't want that.

"Maybe some other time. Saurabh will be home soon, and I have to get dinner ready."

Saira nodded understandingly and waved as she went her own way.

Nisha boarded the train with her own thoughts. As a Hindu, Halloween seemed like another unnecessary celebration that the British revelled in, but she had to admit, this time was especially difficult for her. Always had been, ever since the first time.

The shadow behind her flickered, its presence getting stronger and much harder to ignore. Mustering up courage in the numbers provided by a train full of indifferent Londoners, she muttered under her breath, "Really? Won't you let me be alone in the crowded tube as well? Don't you have a private conveyance of your own that you can take and then haunt me instead of accompanying me on this harrowing train journey?"

The shadow didn't say anything, but Nisha felt it getting darker. Two elderly ladies shot her a worried glance, and she shook her head before looking out the window. The journey was going to be as uneventful as always.

CHAPTER 2

"There she is! My beautiful wife!"

"Someone's in a good mood." Nisha took off her jacket and scarf and placed it on the coat stand in the entryway.

Her home was a sprawling four-bedroom townhouse in the leafy suburbs of zone 5, away from the hustle and bustle of Central London.

She worked meticulously to keep the house beautiful and spotless; everything always looked perfect. It was pristine but lacked the chaos of being home.

Saurabh came and hugged her, halting her thoughts, then lifted her clean off her feet.

She wanted to laugh. Anyone looking in on her life would call her life blessed, but the more Saurabh showed her love, the more she felt like a failure.

If Saurabh noticed her less-than-enthusiastic greeting, he said nothing. His smile was bright as he announced, "We are going to a party!"

He held her hands, forced her to tango, and she gave him a tight smile.

"What party, Saurabh? Today?"

"Nah, over the weekend. It's a Halloween Party! We will be wearing costumes and everything. My boss, Mr Martinez, invited us all to his new home. He just wants to show off his new place—everyone in the office thinks so, but they are excited to meet you."

Saurabh chattered on, his obsidian eyes twinkling, but Nisha's eyes were fixed on the ceiling.

The black shadow had covered the ceiling, so dark that it swallowed the chandelier whole. It curled around the crown mouldings, beckoning her, taunting her with its increasing size and darkness, as Nisha looked on, helpless.

* * *

The Night of Halloween Party

"I hope this isn't too much," Saurabh stated, wearing an Alladin costume under his jacket and a wine bottle tucked under his arm. He paused and shot Nisha a look, her Princess Jasmine costume was demure, and she meticulously lined her eyes with kohl to simulate the Arabian Nights look.

But she felt a bit silly. Wasn't dressing up only for kids?

"You truly look like a Princess." Saurabh took her hand and placed a kiss on the back of her ungloved palm. They were a short walk from the parking lot to the door, so she hadn't bothered with gloves.

"What do you think?" Saurabh gestured to the grand house, and Nisha shrugged.

"He must be doing very well for himself," she commented, taking in the grandness of the house or, say, mansion.

"Yes, these executives roll in millions of pounds in bonuses."

Nisha said nothing, and Saurabh shot her a look.

"You ok, sweetheart?"

"Uh-huh. I mean, yes." Nisha gulped. She hadn't told Saurabh about her pregnancy yet.

Her mind refused to believe it even though her stomach was gently rounding up.

It was a survival mechanism to cope with her impending loss, and her mind refused to acknowledge that this pregnancy was a big deal.

"Are you still seeing Dr Stevens? Taking her medicines as prescribed?"

"We are going to discuss that here?" Nisha let out an exasperated breath. "On the doorstep of your boss' mansion?"

Saurabh shook his head and gave a good-natured smile.

"No, of course. It's just that you look out of sorts. You know that nothing else matters to me but your happiness."

Nisha gave him a tight smile and squeezed his hand. "I tried the meds, but you know they don't help with the bad dreams."

He squeezed her hand back. "Maybe we should go back for other medication."

Nisha shook her head with a smile. "I'm fine. Let's go in. Let's show them the magic of The Arabian Nights!"

The door was opened by a butler, who led them to a huge parlour.

The party was in full swing with neon lights, some clowns juggling and servers dressed as zombies handing out creepy-looking drinks.

"Care for a bloody mary?" A waiter stopped near them, and they each took a drink, which had an eyeball for an olive.

"Gross! Why do people like this stuff?" Nisha grumbled, but she was laughing. The music was loud, and the noisy atmosphere made her forget her problems.

She lifted the glass for a sip but then remembered she was pregnant and discreetly laid the drink on the side table.

Saurabh chatted with some of his work friends before they traversed the room, hand in hand, talking and chatting with a colourful group of people. Though zombies and witches remained a popular theme, people had gone all out. At least there were no pregnant nuns in sight. But this was an office party, after all, so thankfully, people weren't dressed too wild... or slutty.

Saurabh introduced her to his friends and their wives, and soon the wives started talking about their husbands and their demanding jobs. Then the topic turned to kids, and how they were doing, and before she got stares about her childless status, Nisha wandered off from the group.

The huge hall was tastefully decorated, and there was a nice patio outside, which was enclosed for warmth. There were some tattoo designers, fortune tellers and even acrobats who displayed their acrobatic moves and juggled bottles in the air. Servers circulated with colourful drinks though there was a full-service bar on the side. The whole room was dark, still keeping in line with the Halloween theme. The shadow hadn't made an appearance yet, maybe because of the dark, and Nisha felt grateful as she patted her gently rounded belly.

Only she knew that the skirt was snug around the belly, and she had covered it up with Princess Jasmine-style scarfs.

"You want your fortune told, Princess?" A fortune-teller with a huge turban beckoned her.

"No, thanks." She was terrified of her past, her present and also the future of her baby. She didn't want this stranger to know. The fortune-teller made it as if to move towards her, and Nisha slipped away.

The enclosed patio led to another room, which had a staircase rising up to the higher floor. Those were apparently private rooms, and she had no wish to intrude. She looked at the foyer; maybe there was another room that circled back to the main reception room?

But when she came to the door, all she saw was a black wall. She laid her hand on it, and it came off like goop, circling her hand. She looked at her hand as realisation dawned.

The shadow had found her.

Panicked, she turned around to dart toward the hall where the guests were.

But all she saw was a dark wall of smoke.

The smoke rose up and covered the ceiling, swallowing the crystal chandelier whole.

"No, please stop!" Nisha begged.

She felt the air being sucked out of her lungs as the shadow and smoke curled towards her.

The bright interior turned dark and chilly.

Goosebumps dotted her skin.

It was back, and it was worse than the last time.

"Help! Please, someone!" she screamed, but the dark fog surrounding her was impenetrable.

How wasn't anyone else seeing this? Why did no one come to help her?

Smoke curled towards her belly, and that's when she propelled her leaden feet into action.

The only means of escape was the staircase that went to the upstairs rooms, and not caring for the privacy of her hosts, she ran up, her shoes making no sound on the carpeted stairs.

When she came to the landing, she screamed again, "Help me! Please! Anyone here?"

She ran to the various rooms and threw the doors open, but they were unoccupied.

She turned; the shadow had covered the staircase and was now advancing towards her.

Her heart thudded as tears sprang into her eyes.

She won't let *it* take their baby this time!

She screamed and ran into the corridor, the smoke sweeping up behind her. "No, please!"

She reached a dead end again. It had a door, but she couldn't turn the handle.

She was locked in, and the smoke was rapidly moving towards her.

She closed her eyes, tears rolling down her face.

"Please, God, let this door open!"

Miraculously, she felt the latch turn in her hands, and she sprinted inside the door, inches from the dark smoke.

The door led to an open-air terrace, and she didn't even feel the chill of the moonless night.

She heard the loud music from downstairs and rushed to the parapet, desperate to get help.

"Help!" she ineffectively waved at the guests mingling around the pool.

They didn't hear her over the loud music, going about their business.

"Saurabh! Please call Saurabh!" she screamed at the top of her voice for a full minute, but no one heard her over the din.

That's when she turned around and found herself face-to-face with the shadow.

It was here now, and there was no escape.

With a fresh burst of courage, she climbed up on the parapet.

"Is this what you want? My death? Is this when you will leave me alone?" she yelled in agitation.

The shadow stopped getting closer.

But a tendril curled up (was it shaped like a hand?) and moved close to her womb.

"No! You will not come closer!" she shrieked and looked down. The jump was difficult but not impossible. She spied the shimmering swimming pool below; if she fell in it, she would be safe.

But what about her baby?

She had no way out from this ledge, she thought, looking helplessly as the shadow moved closer. One way or the other, she would lose this baby today.

Baby

Nisha pulled her hair and screamed as two hands grabbed her.

CHAPTER 3

"Nisha! Nisha! Look at me!" She opened her tightly clenched eyes, and Saurabh's concerned face swam into focus.

She managed an unintelligible sound as her eyes darted around for the shadow. It was nowhere to be seen, but she was sure it was lurking nearby, waiting.

Dread crept into her heart. It wouldn't be long now.

"Are you ok? Why are you alone on the terrace? You scared me!" He hugged her tightly, and she bit her lip, valiantly holding back her tears.

"I-uh…" She didn't know what to say to Saurabh. She tried to tell him in the past that when she lost their babies, an evil shadow had followed her. However, he had booked her an appointment with a psychotherapist who took a lot of money and spent lots of time convincing her it was all in her head.

But why did she only see the shadow when she was pregnant?

"Is she ok, Sau-rabh?" It was Mrs Martinez, Saurabh's boss's wife, looking at her with concern.

She gave a weak wave, cringing internally and hoping she hadn't created a scene at the party.

Mrs Martinez came forward, fussed on her like a mother hen and demanded that Saurabh let her rest in one of the bedrooms.

Nisha was overwhelmed by her kindness but shook her head.

"I would rather head home, Mrs Martinez. I'm sorry and hope that's ok?"

"Of course, and call me Nadia." She hugged Nisha and said out of Saurabh's earshot. "Are you truly ok, my dear? Do you want to go with your husband?"

Tears sprang from Nisha's eyes. The woman was offering solace and asylum if she needed one.

"Yes, my husband's very kind. Thanks, Mrs… Nadia."

Miraculously, no one had witnessed Nisha's breakdown besides Nadia and Saurabh. The party was in full swing as they excused themselves.

Saurabh didn't say much as he drove them home.

Nisha, who knew how much he was invested in his job, was at a loss for words herself.

They rode in silence for some time until Saurabh cleared his throat. "We will make an appointment with the therapist soon. I don't think Dr Stevens is working out for us. Let me set up an appointment with Dr Whitehall."

Nisha didn't say anything. She knew she wasn't depressed... she knew why the shadow was following her. It had happened in all her previous pregnancies.

"Nisha?" She turned back to Saurabh, whose mouth was pursed. "You want to talk about it, sweetheart?"

Should she tell him? How the shadow had cornered her from all sides? Forced her to walk up the staircase and climb the parapet of the terrace? How she had screamed and begged, and no one had heard her? How was she certain she was going to die? How relieved had she been that she would die and it be over soon? Were these clear signs of clinical depression and paranoia?

But that made no sense.

And even when she was on the parapet, she hadn't wanted to end her life.

She wanted to live for herself and her baby.

She wanted to fight against this injustice.

Why could other women have children, and she couldn't?

Why was she cursed?

"Nisha, sweetheart, we're home."

They were in the driveway of their home, and Nisha was so lost that she hadn't even realised it.

She managed a smile and followed Saurabh inside.

As they retired to bed, Saurabh sometimes preferred to spend the night in his study, and she didn't mind, but today he cuddled with her.

She let him hold her, wishing she could love him with her whole heart. Wishing she didn't need a child to complete herself.

"Saurabh, you asked me what was wrong."

He kissed her brow. "You don't have to say anything if you don't want to."

"Well, I do." She let out a deep breath. "I'm pregnant."

"What?" Saurabh sat up in bed, his eyes wide. "How long have you known?"

She sat up too. "For a few weeks now."

"And you didn't tell me? My God! Nisha, we have to be extra careful. I want you to stay home. You can quit your job or take a long leave, but please, we…"

She laid a hand on his. "I was afraid this is how you would react. I am fine."

Saurabh swore something he never did in her presence. "But how? I thought we were adopting?"

"Well, I…"

"No, sorry, stupid question." He wrapped Nisha in an embrace again. "If God blesses us this time, we will be most grateful."

"Yes, but it hasn't…"

"No! Don't even talk about the last time. I want you to be happy and not worry about anything."

She sighed. This wasn't the first time they had this conversation.

* * *

She woke to the sun shining on her face. A warm wind blew in from the east, and she got up from her rocking chair to close the curtains so lest the dust come into her bedroom. Her bedroom had old and dated furniture with a distinct lived-in look. Bright, colourful curtains brightened up the room, and the soft cotton embroidered bed sheet adorned the bed.

She wrapped her tie-dyed dupatta around her head and stepped out of their haveli, the roomy, dated seventeenth-century mansion she called home after her wedding.

The roomy bustling halls were devoid of people, and the anklets in her feet rang out as her feet carried her over the threshold of the mansion.

She walked across the giant courtyard, which surprisingly was deserted. The wooden charpoys—the light Indian beds where the men gathered around in the day, were strewn around unoccupied. An earthen pot situated under the hand pump, overflowed with water as the hand pump dripped more water into it.

Someone had left it there, but there was no one to attend to it.

She walked outside the courtyard in the lush green forest surrounding their haveli.

Her footsteps were muffled as they walked over the wet foliage. The sunbeams played peekaboo along the forest floor, shielded by thick leafy branches.

Decisively, her feet turned right, taking her among a small path which may have been frequented by shepherds and their herds of goats. The leaves gave way to a muddy and dusty trail which spewed dirt with her every step.

It was stiflingly hot, and Nisha used her dupatta to wipe the sweat on her brow.

She walked until she came across the well. It was in disrepair. The pail used to pull water lay at the side of the well, with a frayed rope still attached to it.

Her feet carried her towards the well. It was a deep well, and the bottom was dark. So dark that she couldn't make out anything at the bottom. But as she leaned in, she saw it.

A face came out of the well.

She looked in shock, her leaden feet refusing to move as her lips opened in a silent scream. There were other faces in the well as they looked up at her with lifeless eyes.

The vacant glassy eyes stared up at her, and she realised that these were the heads of dolls, their hair matted around their porcelain faces covered in red, sticky blood.

One of the dolls opened its mouth and said in a robotic voice, "Mumma!"

Soon, the other dolls followed suit, repeating the word over and over again.

"No!" She screamed, covering her ears to drown out the cacophony of 'Mumma!' that the lifeless dolls were meting out.

Another sound joined the noise—the loud ringing of bells. The bells reverberated in the well, and she screamed, being sucked into the darkness. She slipped, or was she pushed; she didn't know.

But she fell inside the well with the grotesque doll heads covered with blood.

Sayali D.

Nisha jolted awake, her brow drenched in sweat. She was shivering, and it wasn't cold.

Her heart was racing. This wasn't the first time she had such terrible dreams, but they still left her shaken every single time. She got up from the bed, careful not to disturb Saurabh, and walked to the side table for a glass of water.

After having a sip, she turned around and then she saw it.

The trail of blood she left in her wake.

The dark smear that told her with certainty that she wouldn't be a mother.

CHAPTER 4

Two days later, Nisha found herself on a bus to Hackney. She looked out of the window, Halloween was impending, and the streets were decorated in ghoulish embellishments.

Halloween hadn't been big in India, though Indians weren't less superstitious by any means. On the bus, too, the old and young were dressed to the nines. A pot-bellied man dressed like a fairy winked at her, and she managed a smile back.

Suddenly, the bus erupted in screams as two children, around five, started fighting and crying in unison as the harried mother looked on, trying valiantly to hoard her unruly brood.

Other people on the bus weren't as friendly as the middle-aged fairy man to her right. Harassed from the rigours of their commute, they shot the woman hostile looks as she turned pink from mortification.

Nisha smiled at the little munchkins, dug into her red purse and pulled out a candy bar. She addressed the mother, her pale blond hair sticking in all directions, silently asking for permission to offer the candy.

At her surreptitious nod, she addressed the kids, "Candy?"

The kids pounced on it, and she laughed. Their mother cut the bar in half and let them share, urging them to say thanks, but they were too busy wolfing down the chocolate.

"Thank you. You're a lifesaver!" The mother praised Nisha.

"It was nothing; they must be hungry." She sympathised with the woman.

"Oh yes, it's close to their dinner time, but I thought they could survive a bus ride. How wrong was I!" The woman said, and Nisha laughed.

"This is my stop. Thanks again. You're so good with kids. I'm sure you would be a great mum." The woman grabbed her kids and stepped off the bus with a wave.

Nisha turned to the window again, wishing so badly for the woman's words to come true.

Her stop was at an older section of London, deep in the part of Hackney where gently bred women like her were warned about.

People were milling about the street as she stepped off the bus, pulling her coat together to ward off the late October winds.

The dark pavement was darkened even further by recent rains, but she walked across a few streets and turned left. The street was lined with houses that had clearly seen better days. Garbage and litter lined the streets, and some of the houses were painted with graffiti.

Nisha walked to house number eleven and rapped the brass knocker. The window had a sign proclaiming 'Psychic', which suddenly sprang to life in staticky red colour.

A woman in a housecoat and rollers stuck in her hair opened the door. "The door on the right", she mumbled, her lips not relinquishing the hold on a limp cigarette.

Nisha's nose curled at the cigarette smoke as she stepped inside the house; the interior also reeked of dust and neglect. The right-hand side door opened, and a woman wearing a kaftan, who looked like she was in her sixties, sprung out.

"Come in, come in! Excuse my appearance; I wasn't expecting anyone today!" She chirped, looking happy and exuberant, a turban on her head and her necklace and wrists adorned with beads.

"Or any other day, innit, Phyllis?" The cigarette lady chuckled loudly, and Phyllis harrumphed before shutting the door.

"So, what can I do for you, nice lady?" She bounded to the centre of the table, which, perhaps unsurprisingly, held a dirty-looking crystal ball.

The rest of the room was filled with paraphernalia of herbs, beads, feathers and other knick-knacks. A tiny kitchen on the side housed dirty pans in the sink, and a roll-up bed was laid out in front of the kitchen.

Nisha gingerly occupied a chair at the other end of the round, glass table.

Phyllis held her hand out, and she cautiously placed her own hand in it.

"Oi, I need payment before I say anything. This ain't a charity, innit?" Phyllis said and pointed to the sign next to her. It said, "Consultations 20 pounds, 10 pounds for an extra half hour." A small print below reads:

No Refunds, No Guarantees.

With that ominous start, Nisha pulled out a twenty from her purse and laid it in Phyllis's hand, which she snapped up.

"So, my dear, what brings you to me?"

Nisha gulped. "I-I was recommended to you by a woman in my office. She…"

"Yeah, I meant, my dear, what ails you? I can tell you your future and help you sift through the sands of your past." Phyllis's voice dropped an octave as she launched into theatrics.

Nisha held her hand up as the other covered her womb. She sighed, almost numb with pain. She was still losing blood, and the damned shadow was nowhere to be seen. "I- I lost my baby. Again. This is the…" her voice caught, and she whispered, "seventh time…I- I have to know why…"

Phyllis grabbed her hand. "Was this the seventh time you lost your baby in the womb?" Her voice wasn't at the theatrical falsetto. Instead, genuine concern showed in her eyes.

"No…my…" Nisha gulped. "My first baby, I lost him after childbirth. Since then, I haven't been able to carry full term." The pain that gripped her made it hard to breathe, and she tamped down her nausea. "I- I lost him in India, and now we are here, with supposedly the best medical care in the world, and they can't find anything wrong with me, but still, I keep losing my babies."

"Oh, that's unfortunate." Phyllis nodded sympathetically, then went to a cabinet full of small drawers and rummaged through it, pulling out a few glass vials. She took out a few herbs from another drawer and brought them into the kitchen. There she started grinding them together with a mortar and pestle, adding drops of clear liquid from the vial.

When mixing, Phyllis looked up. "Want to talk about it?"

Nisha readjusted herself in the uncomfortable chair as she recalled the events of seven years past.

It was very close to Halloween when she had gone into labour.

It was customary for the women in the household to give birth at home. A staff of nursemaids and a doctor was available, though, and she was too young to question the decisions of the elders in the family.

She had been newly married and settling into the new home at the haveli. Her home was huge; they lived in a big, joint family. Everyone was excited about the birth of the first child in the house. They treated her like a queen.

Saurabh had also been ecstatic.

"Once I get this new opportunity in London, our life will be perfect, Jaan. I am very close to getting a promotion. I will hear of it soon."

Nisha laughed; she used to laugh often then. "Seems like you are more excited about your job than your child, Mr Singh."

Saurabh had kissed the back of her palm. "That has always been my dream, Nisha. We will go abroad and make a life for ourselves there."

When she went into labour, Saurabh hadn't been allowed in their room. She had writhed in pain for eight hours.

When she finally gained consciousness, she wanted to hold her baby.

However, she only found her mother-in-law in the room, and the house was deathly silent. Shouldn't the house be erupting in celebration? she thought.

"Maaji, where is everyone?"

The older woman looked at her, eyes filled with pain, and left the room without a word. A maid came in then to tend to her and broke into sobs as she recounted the horror they had endured.

Her child was born, a boy, no less, but he hadn't been breathing. They had handed the child to Saurabh. Before she could even see him, hold him or cry over him, Saurabh had taken him away. He hadn't said where, but he was too grief-stricken, and everyone was in hysterics, so he had taken the call.

The only thing she knew was that he had used her saree to wrap her little son's body.

As she recounted the story to a dumb-founded Phyllis, she did it like an automaton. Not even a tear filled her eye. They had moved to London shortly after the loss.

The shadow had followed her after each pregnancy then.

She didn't know why, in her first pregnancy, there had been no shadow.

Nisha didn't tell Phyllis about the shadow, though. She had only told Saurabh the first time the shadow had followed her, but he had taken her straight to a therapist.

Phyllis finally completed whatever concoction she had been preparing. "I have treated many such cases, of course. If I hadn't thought of retiring, I would have been very busy. Mostly it's a thing like your past life or some spirit who wishes you evil. Has anyone in your family died an unnatural death? Anyone who hated you or was especially close to you?"

"No, not that I could think of."

The older woman came to her, holding a bowl with the paste. "Lift up your top, would you, love?"

Nisha dutifully opened her jacket and pulled up her top. The woman smeared the paste on her tummy and then turned off the light.

Sitting in the pitch dark with this ridiculous woman suddenly seemed comical. Nisha Singh, topper of her class, working in a bank in London, had resorted to this, finding strange, kooky women in Hackney and letting them feel up her belly.

Phyllis relieved the darkness by lighting a single candle. Dramatically she raised her hands heavenward.

"O spirit, come forward. Tell me what you want… let me communicate to *Neesha* why you're upset."

Nisha sat up straighter. She was pretty sure that she hadn't told Phyllis her name.

Phyllis made strange gurgling sounds that were part of a foreign chant. Nisha leaned forward in her chair, watching Phyllis' lined face catch the candlelight. She gurgled, shivered and stared at Nisha, a deadly calm in her eyes. They seemed wide; the pupils suddenly turned darker.

A chill crept up Nisha's spine. She felt it then, a tugging in her underbelly. A shadow rose from her belly, extended towards Phyllis, and she felt it touch her. Screaming, Phyllis tumbled back, crashing to the floor.

The candle extinguished, and Nisha stood up, running to the light switch. As soon as it turned on, she rushed to Phyllis lying on the floor, her body contorted in odd angles.

Phyllis opened her eyes as Nisha approached her and scrambled on the floor to get away from her.

"Get out! Take that demon with you!" she screamed.

"Wh-What do you mean?" Nisha asked, shaking now. She had definitely felt something, a power emanating from her midriff, but had she imagined it?

"You- You're cursed. Get out!" Phyllis screamed again.

"Why? Who cursed me?" Nisha was on the verge of crying.

"You should have asked this question when you lost your first baby… don't you think? GET OUT!" Phyllis roared.

Nisha lurched backwards as Phyllis grinned, teeth covered in blood. Her eyes rolled backwards in her head and what she said next turned Nisha's blood cold.

"Will you let a murderer get away? Why would they live when I didn't get to live?"

***

"Nisha, sweetheart, I'm home." Her husband's cheery voice greeted her as she was cooking dinner, lost in thoughts.

Phyllis had finally come to her senses, but she acted as if nothing had happened. Clearly, the woman had some connection with the metaphysical, which maybe she herself was unaware of.

Unfortunately, she had left Nisha with more questions than answers.

She should have asked questions when she lost her first baby. Who in the huge haveli had wished her ill?

Indians believed a lot in the evil eye, and if she spoke to any superstitious Indian, they would have been quick to point out that Nisha was suffering the effects of someone casting her an evil eye.

She, who had been a logical person all her life, couldn't help her mind getting clouded with doubts. She had seen the shadow, hadn't she? Though it had been invisible to everyone around her. Was this the curse or the evil eye following her around?

She recollected the words of Sir Arthur Conan Doyle. *'When you have eliminated all which is impossible, then whatever remains, however improbable, must be the truth.'*

How could she rid herself of the evil eye, then?

It was becoming increasingly apparent that she wouldn't be getting any answers in London.

Saurabh came over to the kitchen, turned her around and gave her a peck on her lips. "How's my gorgeous wife doing today? Are you taking it easy as the doctor asked you to?"

No, I'm contemplating hunting down the person who cursed me and made me unable to carry a baby.

Saurabh didn't know of the dark thoughts running through her mind. He grabbed her hand and pulled her to the living room. "Saurabh, do you want to eat burnt rajma today?" She complained but smiled. She was thankful for her husband. He held her tightly, cuddling her like a baby.

"I don't want you to exert yourself. We could have ordered in today."

"Like we ordered in yesterday." Nisha smiled. "And I don't mind the cooking. It gives me something to do, keeps me occupied."

"You're the most important thing in the world for me, you know that, don't you, my love?" Saurabh kissed her hand.

Nisha was thankful of her husband and felt almost choked with emotion. Her husband was her one support through the turmoil. He had seen her crying in the shower two days back when she had lost her baby again.

Seven miscarriages in seven years.

Her husband was understanding; he didn't want her to go through any trauma. He was more than ready to adopt.

In fact, they had even stopped trying, but she had gotten pregnant again.

"I really have to check the rajma," she said with a smile.

Nisha waited until dinner finished, and her husband was in a good mood when she broached the topic.

"I went to see a psychic in Hackney today."

Her husband paused his daily dose of Netflix and looked at her strangely. "What? Since when do you believe in psychics?"

"She came highly recommended. And you did say I should talk to someone to feel better-"

"I meant a therapist, not a bloody psychic!" Saurabh shook his head. "So, what did she say? How much did you pay her for her hocus pocus? Did she chant garbage and throw things in a bonfire?" He chuckled at his own joke.

"She told me..." Nisha took a deep breath. Saurabh would call her crazy if she told him what Phyllis said about her womb being cursed. "I think I want to visit India."

"What? Why? I can't drop everything right now."

"No, just me. I will go."

"To India? Alone?"

She nodded. It was time.

CHAPTER 5

A week later, Nisha found herself at Saurabh's family home in Sayama, Rajasthan. This had been her own home after marriage until she lost her baby.

She had been married to Saurabh at a young age, and as a newlywed, she always considered this giant mansion as a home. People here loved her, cherished her, and she loved them back.

Until she lost her baby.

After that, people either openly scorned her or avoided even acknowledging her. She was blamed for her own loss, for being the unfortunate mother of a stillborn child. The same people who had shown her such love turned into strangers at best and adversaries at worst.

The biggest change she saw was in her mother-in-law, her beloved *Maaji*, who had promised to look after her like her own mother. But she squarely put the blame for the stillbirth on Nisha's shoulders.

Coincidentally, after the trauma, Saurabh got the opportunity to relocate to London. He had been trying for the move for the longest time, and luckily he got the opportunity soon after. He saw the way his mother treated Nisha, and he convinced her that moving away would be the right thing to do. He said to her that his mother would thaw once they gave her a grandchild.

But here she was, seven years later, still without a baby.

Her mother-in-law had given her a decidedly icy welcome since her dear son hadn't accompanied her.

She stayed in the grand mansion listlessly, mostly in her room, the details of which she had vividly seen in her dream, including the rocking chair and the pattern on the bed sheets. But there was nothing much for her to do because she had servants at her beck and call.

Nisha missed her home in London, which would keep her occupied and her job, which kept her sharp. Her manager had grudgingly approved a month's leave. She knew that coming here was the right thing to do.

But what was she doing here exactly?

She found no solace in India, not in meeting her parents or other family members. Instead, she felt restless, even more so than she felt in

London. Like she was on the cusp of something big, but she didn't know what.

Things at the haveli moved at a glacial pace, the same way they had been run for centuries. It was like looking into the past via a telescope, but it was vibrant and colourful, like looking through a kaleidoscope, maybe?

But Nisha hadn't found what she was looking for. She was convinced that the answers to who cursed her lay in this land, but she couldn't think of anyone who would mean harm to her or her newborn child.

Their family was well-respected, even revered. If there were any political rivals, she hadn't come across any. No one here would think ill of her, not even her mother-in-law, who could barely manage to be cordial towards her. Staying home cooped in her room was driving her crazy, but roaming around alone in the forest by herself was unheard of. However, she knew where she had to go, so she managed one afternoon to slip out of the house without the notice of others in the household.

Quickly, her legs carried her to the dense forest bordering the haveli. Even in the heat of October, the leafy canopy kept the forest floor cool. She remembered the path from her dream; it seemed like she was sleepwalking.

Her legs carried her to the same place she had seen in her dreams. *The well.*

It stood exactly at the same place she had seen it, with the pail lying derelict with the frayed rope in the same way.

With apprehension, she approached the well. It was cool here, and goosebumps rose over her flesh as she soundlessly moved towards it.

Gingerly, Nisha peered inside, half expecting doll heads swimming inside.

But all she saw was the dark bottom, the sloshing sound assuring her that the well was filled with water.

Why had she seen this in her dreams? Her dreams were vivid and often scary, jolting her awake.

But why had she seen this specific well?

Her brow scrunched in concentration. There was another thing from her dream which teased her memory.

And then she heard it. The ringing of bells?

She walked fast in the direction of the sound. The woods were bright and sunny, and she had no idea why this place evoked such bad dreams.

The beaten path took her to the temple.

India was known for its beautiful temples cradled in unsuspecting places. This temple was small, but the Kali Mata statue in it was well-tended. Moreover, the temple boasted some fine engraving, typical of the sculptures in the area. Apparently, she had heard these temple bells in her dream.

But why?

She paid her respects to the deity and walked around the temple. Then, exhausted from her walk and a little bewildered, she sat on the stone steps. The eerie feeling of being watched made her squirm.

She turned her head suddenly to see the small head of a child duck behind a tree. The child squealed and ran off.

Forgetting her worries, she followed laughingly. She was led to a small clearing where around ten children were gathered, playing simple games. The little boy she had followed ran and hid behind the skirt of an older girl who looked around twelve.

"Hello there! Would you like some candy?" She dug into her purse and pulled out a candy bar.

The little boy's face lit up with joy at getting candy, and he pulled it from her hand before rushing away again.

The other kids soon surrounded her, demanding candy, and she laughingly obliged. They ranged from five to around twelve years of age, and soon she was welcomed into their exalted circle as the provider of snacks.

Nisha played with the children and watched their games, finding herself grinning stupidly, forgetting all her worries.

When the kids took a break on the stone steps of the temple, she joined them.

"So, do you live close by?" she asked them.

The older girl answered, "Yes, and we play here every day. This is the temple of Kali Maa. She watches over us."

She took the little boy she had befriended and pulled him onto her lap.

"So, what's your name, little one?" Nisha questioned.

"I don't have a name… I'm still waiting for one." He laughed and ran off.

* * *

The next few days, Nisha found every excuse to slip out unnoticed and hang out with the kids at the Kali Maa temple.

On Halloween, she distributed more candy and eye masks to the kids, and they had a blast in the woods, unnoticed by the adults. Slowly, among these kids, she learned to smile and enjoy the simple joys of life again.

Out of all the kids, she was drawn to the little boy who refused to give his name.

She didn't know where the little boy lived or who his parents were, but she felt a bond towards him, one that she couldn't explain.

Was this the reason she had come to India? To provide this little boy a home?

Did his parents not love him? Why hadn't they given him a name?

And if they didn't care for him, would they mind if she and Saurabh adopted the boy?

She already felt like a mother towards the little child. Her son, if he had survived, would be the same age as this nameless child. Maybe they would be friends, playing in the forest together.

When she arrived home at night, she was exhausted. After dinner and a disapproving mother in-law, she retired to her bedroom.

"I had such fun playing with the little children in the forest!" She told Mala, her old maid, the one she always confided in.

Mala looked at her in shock. "What do you mean, there are no children here!"

"I think they came from the nearby areas then. They gathered to play at the Kali Maa's temple."

Mala clasped her hands together and started praying.

"What's wrong, Mala? Talk to me!"

"That's a cursed place, madam. Did no one tell you? That temple is where they offer sacrifices to Kali Maa, goats, sheep, and even newborn kids! No one goes there, and there are definitely no children there!"

Her womb lurched. That's when she knew. The little urchin that she gave candy to had an impish smile, just like Saurabh's.

That little boy was her son.

CHAPTER 6

"I missed you, darling! It wasn't very nice of you to leave your poor hubby alone." Saurabh and Nisha walked hand in hand through the forest.

He had joined her the day before, and she was glad he was finally here. She had so much to tell him!

Smiling, she gripped his hand and led him into the forest, taking the same path she had taken so many times.

"Oh, as young boys, we swung on the branches of this banyan tree," Saurabh reminisced, and she encouraged him to share more stories of him as a little boy.

"We were very naughty. Did you know that the forest was off-limits for us? There were stories of spirits haunting this very forest. Didn't take us long to escape into it, though. Our antics would have put the spirits to shame," he chuckled.

She let him talk; he seemed really happy to see her.

She waited for a lull in the conversation and said, "Did you know that there's a Kali Maa temple behind this clearing? Why don't we go and pay our respects?"

Saurabh froze in his tracks, looking at her with confusion.

"How did you know about that? No one is supposed to venture this far! Really, Nisha, it was one thing to do as a child, but as an adult, I expect you to be more responsible."

She disengaged her arm and led the way through the clearing, certain that he would follow.

She heard him sigh as he reluctantly followed her.

"Who told you about this place, anyway?" Saurabh asked, and she turned to him, her eyes shimmering with unshed tears.

"My son did! I saw him in the woods, and I played with him. He lives here now."

Saurabh was looking at her, flabbergasted, but she just laughed and stomped on.

"Come on, he likes candy. He's a naughty kid, just like you."

After a long while, she heard Saurabh call out behind her. "Nisha, this isn't funny. Come on, let's go home."

She turned to him and shook her head, leading him into the forest.

"No, let's go down this path. I want to show you something."

Puzzled and worried, Saurabh followed her as they reached the temple.

"See Saurabh, this is the temple. I heard the bells ringing in this temple half a world away! Why is that, do you think?"

Saurabh was looking around the forest with a haunted look on his face. It was around five p.m., and there was sufficient light. But here, in the clearing, everything looked hazy and chilly. She saw goosebumps rising on her husband's arms.

"Nisha, that's enough. What you are saying makes no sense! Come on, let's head back to the house." He moved to hold her hand, but she backed away. She didn't want him to touch her.

In a bright voice, Nisha said, "Do you know what happens here, Saurabh? They offer sacrifices to Kali Maa. Goats, cows, buffaloes. People offer up their most beloved possessions. Sometimes they slay the animals in the temple courtyard. But for younger animals, they just throw them in the well there. The animals struggle and then die."

"Nisha!" Saurabh came to her and shook her shoulders. "Who told you all this?"

She brushed his hands off of her and walked away, throwing him a look over her shoulder. "But it's true, isn't it? A sacrifice of your dearest possession for the greater good. The people here offer their dearest belongings to the Goddess Kali. Even their newborn babies-"

She looked at Saurabh. He had gone quite pale.

"I don't know what you're talking about. But I think this place is having a bad influence on you. Let's go back to the UK. I think you're saner there than here."

"Oh yes, I am definitely saner in the UK, Saurabh. But I am also blind there. But here, I am finally aware."

Saurabh cursed, revealing the agitated state of his mind. "I don't know what's gotten into you. If you have to say something, say it now. Or we can calmly discuss it at home like civilised adults."

Nisha gave a self-deprecating laugh.

"You call yourself civilised? The monster who sacrificed his only son for his ambition?"

Saurabh's jaw was set. "You have gone quite mad! Are you blaming me for the death of our son? How could you?"

"No, I'm blaming you for the *murder* of *my* son! He was breathing, wasn't he? When you wrapped him up and took him to the forest?"

He didn't say anything, so she continued, "It took me a while to connect the dots. You were the one who carried him away. You knew of the temple, and the weird rituals carried out here, didn't you? Weren't you desperate for a chance to go abroad? You thought this would help your chances, didn't you? Following customs you had called barbaric yourself?"

He strode up to her, emanating anger, but she stepped out of his path, deftly pulling her gun out of her purse. She had come prepared.

He looked at the gun and then at her, trying to gauge the extent of her mania.

But this wasn't mania; this was blind-hot rage.

"Did you ask for your opportunity in London before or after you sacrificed him?"

Saurabh looked at the gun and then at her. "I'm not answering anything when you have a gun pointed at my chest." He shook his head angrily. "And you're blaming me for my ambition? You were more than happy when I took you away from this place. You said that the toxic people here were suffocating you. You wanted to live in London too, and you are blaming me for taking you there?"

"I only wanted my baby, you monster. The one you snatched from my womb and offered up to the goddess. You are the demon that cursed my womb. It's your seed that is evil. And that's why it was never allowed to take..."

Saurabh lunged at Nisha. She screamed and fired. That stopped him in his tracks. She pointed the gun at his head. "Confess,"

"Nisha-" she watched him squirm, eyeing her gun. "Please, don't be like that. The baby wouldn't have survived for long. He had been deprived of oxygen after childbirth. I did him a favour. Did you want to spend the rest of your life caring for an invalid?"

Nisha was blinded with rage. "He was my son! How dare you? You didn't even give him a chance!"

"Nisha, I did it all for you!"

"No!" she screamed. "You did it all for you! You were doing yourself a favour!"

He looked morose, his features clouding with regret and, she was glad to see, fear. "It- It's haunted me forever, Nisha. But at that time, I truly thought it was for the greater good. I liberated our son from hurt and a lifetime of pain. And soon after this ritual that you called barbaric, I did get the chance to go to London."

She spits out the bile rising in her throat on the ground. "So, you thought you were playing God? But you are the demon! I hate you from the depths of my soul! And to think I lived for so long with the murderer of my son!"

Laughter rose in a crescendo over the treetops. Children were laughing, revelling in their innocence.

Unaware of the monster lurking in the woods who had taken the life of his own son for a promotion.

Tears flowed from the monster's eyes, but she could never forgive him. She only felt disgusted and rage.

She felt the presence of the shadow before she saw it.

"It's here, Saurabh. It's time."

He turned around and saw it, too. The shadow rose from behind him, creating an impenetrable wall. "Do you see it now? Do you see what you have created?" she taunted him.

Saurabh looked befuddled. "Nisha?" He looked at her in confusion.

"You shouldn't have killed my baby, Saurabh. Now, it's time to pay the price. Vengeance will be mine!"

The shadow swooped in closer to Saurabh. He yelled and tried to run. He managed to get away, but the shadow surrounded him, the only escape being the well.

"Nisha! Nisha! Please save me! I did it all for us!"

She heard a splash. The shadow swooped in after him, and no sound escaped after that. It was over. The murderer had paid the price for his sins.

She sat on the forest floor and wept. Too exhausted to think, she only knew that she had to go on living somehow.

Laughter danced through the trees, mingled with the screams of little children.

Despite her tears, she smiled. "Now you can rest, my little one. And I did give you a name. Your name is Nihar!"

The laughter in the trees rose to a crescendo one final time, then gradually faded away.

About the Authors

Asa Swift

Asa Swift is a police officer in Indianapolis and has been in law enforcement for thirty-four years. He is married to his wife Janet and they have three sons. Ready for something new and having a creative side, he took to writing horror, his favorite genre of books and movies. Born in Hartford, Indiana, despite getting a late start in writing, he improves every day. Swift enjoys fishing, firearms, cooking and his grandchildren, and of course, HORROR! As a means of continue writing, he keeps his grandparents close to his heart and mind for always encouraging him to not give up.

Brandon Ebinger

Brandon Ebinger is a horror/dark fantasy author who lives in upstate New York with his fiancé and two cats. He holds a BA in creative writing. He enjoys horror films,Gothic rock and punk music and video games. He is a huge fan of haunted attractions, and spends October as a haunt actor. Brandon has written four horror/ dark fantasy novels, Ash, Hollow Hills, The Afflicted and Rose. He has also published a handful of short stories within the genre. He has recently finished his most recent novel Broken Night and is at work on a new one.

Phil Hore

Phil likes to point out he was one of the last children born before man walked on the moon. He's worked at Australia's National Dinosaur Museum, the Australian War Memorial, National Film and Sound Archives, the Australian National Botanic Gardens, London's Natural History Museum, the Field Museum in Chicago and The Smithsonian's National Museum of Natural History. Published in newspapers and magazines across the globe, Phil is the paleo-author for the world's longest running dinosaur magazine, The Prehistoric Times. He's also been a comic shop manager, a cinema projectionist, a theatre technician and gutted chickens for a deli. All of these influences seem to make an appearance in his writing, especially the chicken guts bit. His first novel Brotherhood of the Dragon contained another Amun adventure, while 2020 sees the release of his WW1 trench murder mystery, Golgotha.

Draven

Draven is an author who writes paranormal/supernatural which includes vampires and werewolves, and ghosts. Her works include The Immortals Saga vampire series and the Bane Werewolf Colony series. She's working on a revenge crime series of short stories and a science fiction series. She's a graduate of Full Sail University with a Bachelor of Fine Arts degree in Creative Writing for Entertainment. She has experience with script-writing, comic writing, and game writing. When she's not writing, she enjoys reading books, specifically paranormal romance novels and watching anime. She loves to listen to classical music, rock music, and kpop.

M.M.Ward

M.M.Ward - Mama Magie Ward- Farm mom and author who

writes as part of my stroke recovery. My stories are a walk between shadow and light. I write stories about and for those who have been through much. There will be triggers for survivors, things I would wish on anyone, but sadly, these are the trials many face in today's world. Some of will overcome, some will succumb, and I encourage all to seek help. Weep, cope, reach out. You are not alone. There is always the choice... Become Better, not bitter. #MMWard

J. D. Edwards

J. D. Edwards is the award-winning author of The Faerie Chronicles, Killing Time, The Soul Reaper, Dry Bones, and Indomitable. His writing awards include The Charl Ormond Williams Fund, The Ohio Genealogical Society, Notebook Publishing's #IndieApril, and Lulu's Share Your Scare Writing Contest. Since 2012, J. D. Edwards has published over 60 genealogical articles in the United States and Great Britain, winning over a dozen historical writing competitions internationally. Future projects include historical fiction books set in the 18th to 19th centuries and further fantasy series regarding Faerie and Celtic Mythology.

Sayali D.

Sayali (who cannot pronounce her own last name), has been writing from childhood, starting from poems and essays that won her acco- lades to writing murder mysteries for her gang of girls. Embarking on a technical career after college made her appreciate her world of mystery and make-believe even more. She dove into romance as a teen and mostly writes stories about strong, relatable characters who meander their way into love. Her books also contain suspense and mystery, with a lot of plot twists that keep the readers engaged. Sayali is married to her college sweetheart and has a cute kid. She writes when her imagination gets the better of her and her charac- ters demand to be written about. It's the only way she can stay sane, though anyone who has seen her daydream and talk to herself, will disagree. Sayali can be found on FB, Twitter and Instagram, chattering away to all within earshot.

Ashe Woodward

Ashe Woodward is a horror writer from Ontario, Canada. She has been writing spooky stories since she was old enough to type on a Commodore 64. She lives with her husband and their menagerie of pets and poisonous plants.

CHECK OUT OTHER EDITINGLE ANTHOLOGIES

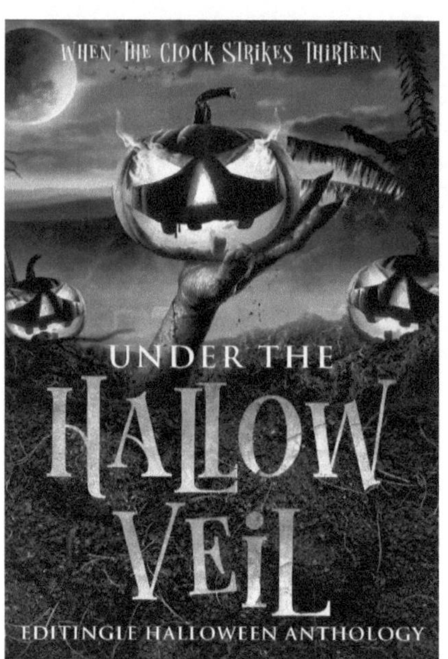

WHEN THE CLOCK STRIKES THIRTEEN
UNDER THE
HALLOW
VEIL
EDITINGLE HALLOWEEN ANTHOLOGY

THE DEAD HAVE RISEN
BEYOND
the
HALLOW
grave
EDITINGLE HALLOWEEN ANTHOLOGY

CURSE OF THE
HALLOW MOON
HALLOWEEN ANTHOLOGY VOL. III
EDITINGLE INDIE HOUSE

Snowflakes
&
Winter Dreams
VOL. I
"And sometimes, winter brings more than
just a white christmas."
EDITINGLE INDIE HOUSE